New Perspectives for Evangelical Theology

Tom Greggs has assembled a group of younger evangelical theologians to compose essays on core theological questions as well as some pressing contemporary concerns. The contributors – with courage, resolution, and some heavy artillery from within the great tradition of the church – break down stereotypes, correct old courses, and build strong, constructive bridges. They are a future generation that is big with promise.

(The Rev. Dr.theol. Paul F.M. Zahl, Rector,
All Saints Episcopal Church, USA)

I warmly commend this book on a progressive evangelical theology. It embodies careful historical research from primary sources and it tackles relevant themes. It provides not packaged, uniform, 'answers', but from a recovery of authentic roots, it stimulates creative thought as we face the future. It is good that doctrine is again viewed as relevant and formative.

(Anthony C. Thiselton, Professor of Christian Theology,
University of Nottingham, UK)

In this exciting edited collection, Tom Greggs challenges us to think afresh about evangelical theology: where it is today, and where it is headed. Bringing together an outstanding group of young theologians to engage critically and constructively with traditional evangelical theology, *New Perspectives for Evangelical Theology* addresses some of the field's major themes, including election, the Holy Spirit, eschatology and sanctification. It examines the Bible and the church, and investigates the interaction of evangelicalism and society, considering politics, sex and the body, and other faiths such as Judaism and Islam. Framed by a foreword from David F. Ford and a postscript from Richard B. Hays, this book is an invaluable collection of new thinking.

Tom Greggs studied Theology at the Universities of Oxford and Cambridge, and is currently a Professor of Theology at the University of Chester, UK.

New Perspectives for Evangelical Theology

Engaging with God, Scripture
and the World

Edited by
Tom Greggs

Routledge
Taylor & Francis Group

LONDON AND NEW YORK

First published 2010
by Routledge
2 Park Square, Milton Park, Abingdon, Oxon OX14 4RN

Simultaneously published in the USA and Canada
by Routledge
270 Madison Ave, New York, NY 10016

Routledge is an imprint of the Taylor & Francis Group, an informa business

Typeset in Times New Roman by Swales & Willis Ltd, Exeter, Devon
Printed and bound in Great Britain by
CPI Antony Rowe, Chippenham, Wiltshire

British Library Cataloguing in Publication Data
New perspectives for evangelical theology : engaging with God, Scripture,
and the world / edited by Tom Greggs.
    p. cm.
    Includes bibliographical references and index.
    1. Evangelicalism. 2. Theology, Doctrinal. I. Greggs, Tom.
    BR1640.N475 2009
    230'.0462—dc22
    2009016669

ISBN10: 0–415–47732–8 (hbk)
ISBN10: 0–415–47733–6 (pbk)
ISBN10: 0–203–86738–6 (ebk)

ISBN13: 978–0–415–47732–1 (hbk)
ISBN13: 978–0–415–47733–8 (pbk)
ISBN13: 978–0–203–86738–9 (ebk)

For Ann and Colette

Contents

Contributors

George Bailey is from England. He has studied theology and philosophy at St John's College, Oxford, and the Partnership for Theological Education in Manchester. He is presently completing a PhD on sanctification at Cambridge University. He is a Methodist minister in Leeds.

Richard S. Briggs is a graduate of Hertford College, Oxford, London Bible College and the University of Nottingham. He is Director of Biblical Studies and Hermeneutics at Cranmer Hall, St John's College, Durham, and is the author of *Reading the Bible Wisely* (SPCK) and *Words in Action* (T&T Clark).

Glenn Chestnutt is a Presbyterian minister in Gourock, Scotland. He holds a PhD in Systematic Theology from the University of Edinburgh, and has also studied at the Universities of Ulster, the Queen's University, Belfast, Princeton Theological Seminary, and in Tübingen.

David F. Ford is Regius Professor of Divinity at the University of Cambridge and the Founding Director of the Cambridge Inter-faith Programme. A world-leading scholar, Ford's most recent book, *Christian Wisdom: Desiring God and Learning in Love*, is published with Cambridge University Press.

Jason Fout is Assistant Professor of Theology at Bexley Hall Episcopal Seminary in Columbus, Ohio. An Episcopal Priest, he is a PhD candidate at the University of Cambridge. Jason previously studied at the University of Illinois at Chicago, Trinity International University, and Seabury-Western Theological Seminary. His pastoral experience includes work on university campuses, hospital chaplaincy, and parish ministry in Chicago and St Joseph, Michigan.

Ben Fulford is a British Anglican theologian, and is currently Tutor in Theology at St John's College, Nottingham. His undergraduate, postgraduate and doctoral studies were all pursued at the University of Cambridge.

Tom Greggs studied theology at the Universities of Oxford (where he took the top first class honours degree in theology) and Cambridge. He is the author of *Barth, Origen, and Universal Salvation: Restoring Paritcularity* (OUP), and numerous articles. A Methodist Local Preacher, Tom is Professor of Theology at the University of Chester.

Richard B. Hays is George Washington Ivey Professor of New Testament at Duke Divinity School. One of the world's leading New Testament scholars, Hays' work focuses on New Testament ethics, the Pauline epistles and early Christian interpretation of the Old Testament.

Paul Dafydd Jones is a British theologian who studied at Oxford University, Harvard Divinity School, and Harvard University. His first book, *The Humanity of Christ: Christology in Karl Barth's Church Dogmatics*, was recently published by T&T Clark. He is currently Assistant Professor of Western Religious Thought in the Department of Religious Studies at the University of Virginia.

Elizabeth Kent is a British Methodist minister, working in the Newcastle area. After degrees in Law at the University of Liverpool, Liz undertook pastoral work at a Liverpool church. She followed this with theological study at the University of Durham, and is presently completing a PhD in theological ethics.

Donald McFadyen spent thirteen years working in the Church Army. He is now the priest-in-charge of two rural Cambridgeshire parishes, Bassingbourn and Whaddon, and the Director of Church Study and Practice at Ridley Hall, Cambridge. Donald studied theology as an undergraduate, postgraduate and doctoral student at the University of Cambridge.

Paul T. Nimmo is a Scottish theologian who has studied in Cambridge, Edinburgh, Princeton, and Tübingen. He is the author of *Being in Action* (T&T Clark), and of a number of articles on subjects in Reformed and evangelical theology. He is presently the Meldrum Lecturer at New College, University of Edinburgh.

Andi Smith is a Methodist minister in Birmingham, and is completing his PhD at the University of Durham. His research offers a theological ethnography of Primitive Methodism across the Durham coalfield (1820–50), in which he argues that the practices of prayer, song and feasting are rightly to be understood as political.

Sarah Snyder is English, but was born and raised in Bermuda. She studied Archaeology and Anthropology at Cambridge University. After a spell working as a television producer for the BBC and as managing editor at Hobson's Publishing, she worked as a journalist and author of educational resources. She has returned to Cambridge to work on a PhD on Muslim–Christian relations.

Simeon Zahl is an Episcopalian American theologian. He is a graduate of Harvard, where he co-founded and directed the Alpha Course. His postgraduate work was pursued at the University of Cambridge, and he is presently Research Assistant at the Faculty of Divinity.

Acknowledgements

This book began its life in conversation – conversation with a whole host of church people, theologians and members of other faith communities; I have always liked talking. However, the book took its form more concretely during a conversation sat on some stairs with a take-away coffee talking to Lesley Riddle (the commissioning editor) at the end of the American Academy of Religion in Washington. Lesley has carried this book through to its publication, with advice, encouragement and enthusiasm, and at every turn I have been immensely grateful for her assistance in guiding a young academic to the publication of his first edited volume.

Following that conversation came many more with friends around the world. A meeting in the lounge of my then house in Cambridge helped to set the task and purpose of the book more clearly, and I must particularly thank from that stage of the project Jeff Bailey, Jeff and Beth Phillips, Greg Seach and Jim Walters. There was also the opportunity to present on the project at the Center for Theological Inquiry in Princeton at its 'The Future of Theology in the Academy, Church and Media' consultation. I was most grateful to the participants at that meeting for their comments and encouragement, and most especially to Will Storrar for inviting and hosting me, and to Stephen Chapman for his support and for the detailed discussions with him. The various reviewers of the proposal also offered insightful and helpful comments, which have certainly made the book much better than it would originally have been. This volume is self-consciously (by all its contributors) a theology which is on its way, and I am grateful for continuing guidance along that way to a host of colleagues and mentors with whom I shared and discussed the vision for this collection. Most particularly, I am grateful to Nick Adams, Mark Edwards, David Fergusson, Douglas Hedley, Mike Higton, George Newlands, Stephen Plant, Janet Soskice, Anthony Thiselton, Susannah Ticciati, John Webster, David Wilkinson and Ralf Wüstenberg. In addition, Peter Ochs has not only discussed many of the ideas behind the book with me, but also read and commented on my own contributions to it; he has been a source of great help and encouragement, as well as someone whose wisdom has always been accompanied with pastoral care and laughter.

David Ford, who has written the foreword of this book, was throughout the planning and writing of much of it, and continues to be, one of my main sources of theological conversation. Having been my *Doktorvater*, he has not simply sent me into the big, wide academic world without keeping a 'parental' eye on my theological development. I remain deeply indebted to him for all of his support and wisdom, not only in this project but in all things. It would be unfair, however, to mention him without at once thinking (with both joy and sadness) of his father-in-law, the late Dan Hardy. Dan was not only a mentor and friend to me, but was also instrumental in forming and shaping this volume: there were long conversations sat in his lounge drinking coffee and eating biscuits, not only about what this project was trying to achieve, but also more generally about what theology needed to be about. Since he has passed into glory, a photograph of him looks down on me from the wall of my study, and I have been glad of the remembered voice at different times when writing and editing this book: 'It's more complex than that, Tom.' Like so many people, I owe so much to Dan, and he is sorely missed.

My most sustained theological interlocutor through the formation of this book has been my friend, Paul Nimmo. Not only did we share a house during the book's early stages, but he has also continued to be my most trusted theological guide (and – quite possibly – my fiercest critic!). Emails, conversations and the odd mid-day rant down the telephone have been graciously received by him, and I continue to be inspired by his passion for the church and for truth.

During the process of this book coming together, I have moved from Cambridge to Chester University. My time at my new institution has been met with excitement at all of the bright new possibilities that there are here. I could not ask for a more supportive, caring or friendly group of colleagues with whom to work. It is wrong of me to single out any individuals, but Robert Evans and Ruth Ackroyd have both shown tremendous support for this project, and have read and commented on my own contributions to it. David Clough has not only done the same, but has also been a constant dialogue partner during (what have come to be known by our colleagues and students as) our 'Barthian lunches'.

Other friends (who do not all share my interest in academic theology) have helped throughout the editing of this book by providing light relief from the intensities of academic life. I would not be who I am without them, and my life would be much less fun, and their part in this book must be acknowledged. My thanks go especially to Chris and Nancy Allen, Alistair and Helen Shepherd, Stephen Jamieson, Mark Perkins, Karen and Alison Williamson, Catherine McMuldroch, Narada Haralambous, Dan and Becks Farr, Sue and Andy James, Fran and George Bailey, Ed and Kirsty Gayton, Rick Gayton, Mel Gayton, and Dominic Traynor.

Many of the concerns that underlie this book arise from real life ecclesial work; it is no accident that a number of the contributors are primarily engaged in church ministry and leadership. In some ways, much of what is contained herein (and certainly the ideas behind it) arise from church life. My own evangelical faith was formed by Elm Hall Drive Methodist Church, Liverpool. They have not only nurtured me (and continue to do so), but have been patient with my preaching, and (since moving back to the city of my youth) have welcomed me back to my first pulpit. I thank God for them.

My faith ultimately, however, has been nurtured by my family, who have lived for many years the sort of theology that I have sought to envision here. Their faith, prayerfulness, care for others, and commitment to God and the world (in all of its messiness) have been an inspiration. My mum and dad never cease to amaze me in their selfless love of and care for others, and in the 'down to earthness' of their trust in Christ. My nan has loved me with such unstinting faithfulness that I could never known how to begin to thank her; she even let me live with her when I first retuned to the north-west, and much of the book was edited in her front room. My sisters, Ann and Colette, have certainly endeavoured to pull me back down to earth. We have shared each other's laughter and sorrow, all surrounded by and confident in Christ's love for us. It is to Ann and Colette that I dedicate this book – in a hope that perhaps it will stop them poking fun at what I do, and make them realize I do actually work on my so-called 'day off'!

Foreword

David F. Ford

For those concerned about the shaping of Christian life and thought in the twenty-first century, this is a very encouraging book. By gathering a group of younger British and American evangelical scholars and theologians in order to think through the main issues facing them and their tradition, the project has done more than analyse and comment upon what has been happening in one of the world's most numerous and lively Christian movements. It has also stimulated fresh engagement with evangelical thinking and opened up critical and constructive ways forward. These are deeply rooted in the Bible and in the evangelical heritage, and in addition they respond creatively to current challenges. The result is a collaboration that is important on several counts.

While reading the chapters of this book it has been fascinating to sense in many of them a mode of doing theology that is both at home in its core tradition and also hospitable and vigorously engaged across its boundaries – what Richard Hays in his Postscript appositely describes as 'centred' without being tightly 'bounded'. This is reflected in there being no single strict definition of 'evangelical' imposed on the book – a number of definitions are discussed and in play, and this suits the varied tradition that is being explored. There is urgency and zeal for the Good News; there is also recognition of diversity, complexity, unresolved problems and some pathologies. It is especially helpful to have perspectives from both sides of the Atlantic. All of this gives a conversational rather than polemical tone to the chapters. Even when quite tough things are said, the atmosphere is of 'speaking the truth in love', in contrast to so many of the bitter and endlessly schismatic enmities that have wounded this (and nearly every other) Christian tradition. The ethos encourages seeking 'wisdom in the Spirit' amidst the complexities of actual Christian living and difficult theological problems.

Perhaps the most inspiring aspect of the book is its re-engagement with the Bible. There is no question but that the Bible is the basic, authoritative text for the evangelicals who write here, but they also see acutely how 'the corruption of the best is the worst'. Several of the authors do detailed interpretation of the Bible, facing its puzzles and intricacies, and this results in some remarkable examples of successfully combining faithfulness to Scripture with constructive teaching for today. We are drawn into 'deep reading', 'reparative reading', charismatic reading, and reading with and beyond Calvin, Luther, Wesley and Barth. Key biblical words such as 'glory', 'grace', 'truth' and 'word' itself are refreshed, and stereotypes of them exploded by renewed attention to their use in Scripture. This at its best performs what evangelicals claim: that the Bible is the unrivalled and unsurpassable source of rich and lively theology.

The approach also draws in key figures from the tradition, such as those mentioned above, as readers of Scripture accountable to Scripture. One of the snares for any Christian tradition is to work out, often through painful wrestling and conflict, its main doctrines, and then to take these as the basis for all future thinking, forgetting their messy origins and throwing away the ladder that they climbed to reach them. Evangelicals should be insured against this by their emphasis on constantly fresh recourse to Scripture, but we know their doctrines too can harden in abstraction from the Bible, and several chapters helpfully try to redress such tendencies.

One fascinating aspect of Christian history is why at a particular time there is an emphasis on certain issues and doctrines and not on others. As regards this, the book does two worthwhile, complementary things. On the one hand, it refuses to go along with fashions, and insists on the continuing importance of matters that were probably of greater concern to previous generations of evangelicals than to ours, such as double predestination, Eucharist, Wesleyan holiness and a pessimistic view of human nature. On the other hand, there is the courage to bring certain items on to the agenda in a positive way, including universal salvation, reading the Bible alongside the Qur'an with Muslims, and sharing with Rabbinic Judaism in a covenantal relationship with God. These are all examples of 'centred' thinking that opens up boundaries in new ways. In theological terms they can appeal to how 'all things' and 'all people' are in relationship with the trinitarian God. That again and again emerges as the horizon of this book, making its boundary-crossing an effort to discern signs of the God who is already on the other side of our fences.

In recent months I have been trying to write a manifesto on the future of Christian theology. Seeking marks of good future theology has resulted in provisionally identifying four key elements in which wisdom and creativity are ideally desired. One is in the retrieval and interpretation of the past; another is in present engagement with both God and the realities of church and world; a third is in constructive and imaginative thinking that allows us to move beyond the dilemmas and oppositions of the past and present; and the fourth is in the quality of communication in many modes and media, to many types of people. The encouragement I felt in studying this book can be summed up as the discovery that in its chapters all four of those criteria are met in various degrees.

I sometimes think that the most radical of all biblical texts for theologians is the Gospel of John. It promises the Holy Spirit – the parakletos, encourager, comforter, strengthener, advocate, helper, the one who speaks alongside us – to believers in order to guide us 'into all the truth' (John 16:12). Right from the start the Gospel itself shows what might be meant by this: its extraordinarily daring Prologue

(1:1–18) has been perhaps the most influential short text in the history of Christian theology. What might it mean to be led into more of that sort of mind-stretching theological truth? This book gives a taste of what we might expect in the twenty-first century from the rising generation of evangelical thinkers.

David F. Ford
Easter, 2009

Chapter 1

Introduction – opening evangelicalism

Towards a post-critical and formative theology[1]

Tom Greggs

This book is a positive engagement with evangelical thought and offers a fresh contribution to contemporary evangelical theology. The topics covered in the book (both individually and collectively) are far from exhaustive. Instead, at some level, the chapters provide an agenda for contemporary evangelical theology. The nature of this agenda is considered in this introductory chapter through a discussion of each of the words of its title. Each essay included in this book is discrete in itself. In different essays, different amounts of emphasis will be placed on each of the themes outlined below. Some chapters will return exegetically to the tradition and engage in reparative reasoning with our history and theology (as perhaps most emphatically in the chapters by Ben Fulford, George Bailey and Simeon Zahl),[2] while others address in an exploratory manner areas and themes often neglected in classical evangelical discourse (as is the case in the chapters by Jason Fout, Sarah Snyder and Glenn Chestnutt). Some chapters are more scholastically and technically framed (as with Paul Jones' and Paul Nimmo's), while others more prophetically critique and offer imperatives to evangelicals (as in those by Elizabeth Kent, Andi Smith and Tom Greggs). A number of the chapters engage with practical Christian living (as in those by Donald MacFadyen and Elizabeth Kent), while still others aim to be directive and programmatic for theology (perhaps most strongly felt in that by Richard Briggs, which begins this book). There are undoubtedly elements of each of these approaches in each of the chapters, but the balances shift between them. However, the overall concern of each of the chapters (regardless of these differing and shifting balances) remains the same – as younger scholars, to articulate a new perspective post-critically on each of the topics tackled for evangelical theology. This involves, therefore, a certain level of programmatic, performative and creative engagement with the tradition, and a sense – in a manner which pervades all of the chapters – of the way in which the Christian life and Christian doctrine interrelate.[3]

Opening

This book forms the beginnings of an active and programmatic approach to evangelical theology. It does not believe or proceed in the belief that the theology contained in this book has 'arrived' or has provided the final word on any given topic herein. There is no sense of locating a static norm for theology on each of the themes and doctrines examined, as if such a norm ever could exist. The book does not provide the reader with a body of text which offers 'the answer'. Instead, this book contains theology which is in process, and the chapters proceed in the belief that theology is always engaging in the exercise of re-articulating and re-describing itself as it seeks better to speak of God to successive present generations.

The active verbal aspect of 'opening' is important, therefore. This book is about an on-going approach to Christian theology. It offers patterns of thinking and ways to raise questions, rather than ever believing it can contain all – if any – of the answers: the topic of each chapter has the potential for many monographs and all contributors would wish for the space to say far more. The theology contained in this chapter is not, therefore, statically 'open' nor 'opened' evangelicalism. Instead, this theology invites the reader to join in the process of 'opening'. The authors model helpful ways of doing evangelical theology, in order to help the reader to think constructively and positively about other concerns or issues not raised in the pages of this book, or else in order to help the reader to take different angles than the perspectives taken here. In Genesis 32:22–32, the patriarch Jacob wrestles with God at Peniel. During this struggle, we are told that Jacob cries out to the one with whom he struggles: 'I will not let you go, unless you bless me' (v.26). And so Jacob is renamed 'Israel' for he has 'striven with God and with humans' (v.28). The chapters in this book build typologically on that image. The authors are striving with God and humanity, with the complexities of living before God in history, and they desire not to let go of the themes, doctrines and issues discussed (in all of this complexity) until God has offered blessing through struggling with him.[4] This striving and wrestling never fully arrives at an end point, nor does it lead to conquest: the one with whom Jacob wrestles still will not tell Jacob his own name; and we need only to look to the history of the people of Israel to see the on-going struggles of a people who take as their name 'the one who strives with God'.[5] In an analogous manner, this volume articulates no final systematizing victory (just as none is present in Genesis 32 since this victory belongs to God), but it demonstrates how to wrestle and strive with God and humanity as theologians in the world in order to receive a blessing from him. As with Jacob, who is blessed with a new name that will be the name of his people, this blessing is not simply ours individually or even collectively; it is, instead, a blessing through which the world might be blessed by God through the life of his people in the world. This book invites the reader to join in this striving and desire to be blessed for the sake of the world; it is for this reason that this book at various points tackles several overtly political or theo-political themes.[6]

Furthermore, in speaking of 'opening' evangelicalism and of the on-going task of engaging actively in the process of theology, this book desires to orientate theological articulation in an eschatological direction. In speaking of 'opening', we are speaking of the idea that theology is not merely a retrospective activity nor singularly an historical discipline,[7] but an ever unfolding and progressive engagement in the present as we move into the future with the tradition of the church. This book believes that, in its various and differing contexts, theology tomorrow (using all the resources of past theology) should be better than theology today. To put it as Karl Barth did, the constructive programme of the theology contained within this book is in essence the belief that we should reflect on last Sunday's sermon to make next Sunday's better.[8] This book wishes to serve theologians, preachers, ministers, pastors and church people by helping them to construct and form better theology for themselves. The chapters in this book do not intend to provide a theoretical system into which thinking Christians may enter, but to orientate readers to think in exciting and new ways about God, Scripture and the world in the contexts and situations in which they find themselves.

The authors engage in constructing theology because they share in a belief that God is not simply the God of the past or simply the God of the present: God also is the God of the future. This is made clear in many places in Scripture. We see it in the burning bush pericope:

> God said to Moses, 'I AM WHO I AM.' He said further, 'Thus you shall say to the Israelites, "I AM has sent me to you."' God also said to Moses, 'Thus you shall say to the Israelites, "The LORD, the God of your ancestors, the God of Abraham, the God of Isaac, and the God of Jacob, has sent me to you":
> This is my name forever, and this my title for all generations.'
> (Exod. 3:14–15)

Hebrew Bible scholars have debated considerably the meaning of the name with which God reveals himself (*ehyer asher ehyer*). It is a name which is difficult to capture in English. However, it does not simply have the static, philosophical sense of 'I am who I am' which is offered in most translations.[9] It also contains an active and dynamic meaning, and can equally well be translated as 'I will be who I will be'; just as it can mean any combination of 'I am', 'I will be' and 'I cause to be'.[10] The God who reveals himself to Moses is not simply the God who is who he is; he is the God who will be who he will be. Moreover, this God who will be who he will be states that this is his name 'forever' and 'for all generations'. The God of Christian theology is the God who is ahead of us – the God of our future.

This futurity of the nature of God is echoed in the New Testament in terms of the return of Christ. This is not only seen in the New Testament's affirmation of 'Jesus Christ, the same yesterday, today and forever' (Heb. 13:8), but it is also echoed in the church's proclamation: 'Christ has died. Christ is risen. Christ will come again'.[11] Christ's return lies ahead of us, and as we move towards his eschatological Kingdom, so we may grow in knowledge and reason. As Paul puts it:

> When I was a child, I spoke like a child, I thought like a child, I reasoned like a child; when I became an adult, I put an end to childish ways. For now we see in

a mirror, dimly, but then we will see face to face. Now I know only in part; then I will know fully, even as I have been fully known.

(1 Cor. 11:11–12)

Temporality and movement towards the future demand such growth.

Part of that eschatological movement is recognizing that we are ever nearer to the future, and that the eschaton is ever closer: in some sense, a belief in the return of Christ determines that the eschaton is sooner tomorrow than it was yesterday. Moreover, God makes his way from his future into our present, allowing the church through the Holy Spirit to anticipate proleptically the coming of his Kingdom as his eschaton impinges on our time. Theology must confront this and recognize that the eschatological nature and direction of the church determines that our speech should desire to be ever better in terms of its correspondence to the reality of God and his salvation. The eschatological determination of the church's speech about God requires theology to remind the church that it must always be *ecclesia semper reformanda*. However, this is not merely an engagement in a retrospective reforming to some pre-determined perfect point in the past,[12] but a prospective ever ongoing reformation in light of the God who is forever ahead of us, and whose Kingdom encroaches from the future.[13] Always reforming does not involve, therefore, any notion of continual purging or stricter levels of exclusivity (as is so often characteristic of evangelical theology), but opening theology to the God who is the God of the future as well as the God of the past. Paul tells us that this God is the One who in the end will be the 'all in all' (1 Cor. 15:28). This book desires, therefore, to be renewed and reformed in opening up its reflections on this God. It engages in articulating a theology which is ever opening up to fresh ideas and new insights into Scripture and theology in the complexly religious and secular world in which Christian theology now speaks.[14] The authors all recognize that we will get things wrong in this complex task – a reality determined by the sinfulness of humanity which is present even (and perhaps especially) as we engage in theology. But the authors wish to engage in this complex articulation of theology in today's world in the belief that the God of Christian theology is the God who is the God of life in all its superabundant diversity and complexity.

There is a need, therefore, to engage in opening ourselves up. The chapters included in this volume thus engage in opening up to the disruptive and complex voice and voices of Christian Scripture, reading the Bible (as the supreme authority of the Christian faith) with fresh eyes for a theology that takes seriously the need to be open to the complexities of a world which has been created and is providentially guided by God.[15] The chapters included herein also continue to be opened and reopened afresh to theology articulated in the reformation tradition and to evangelical theology which is constructed in dialogue with this tradition. In the spirit of reformation, the chapters of this book wish to be engaged in opening up to new ideas. In today's world, this involves being opened up to the ambiguity and complexity of human life, and to the dynamics of existing in a society with many people of other faiths or none.[16] This 'opening' is not an uncritical appropriation of a variety of sources and thought processes, or a subjecting of Christian theology to an external norm.[17] It is, instead, an active, dialogical and (maybe even at times) uncomfortable wrestling for a blessing as evangelicals and Christian theologians who live within the richness of life and thought in the twenty-first century.

Evangelical

The term 'evangelical' has a rainbow-like variety of meanings in the contemporary setting. This book proceeds on the basis of being uncomfortable with unwisely narrow definitions of the meaning of the term, and the theology herein is articulated partly in response to the desire among some evangelicals to narrow the definition of the word in order that it might apply only to them.[18] However, this is not to say that the word is used without any specification, exclusivity or delineated meaning. This book follows the broad definitions given by the likes of Bebbington or Larsen.[19] However, it recognizes that there are considerable disagreements from within evangelicalism as to what the detailed working out of these definitions might be, with broader or more radical interpretations often struggling against narrow and more conservative self-definitions of the movement. Stephen Holmes, in his discussion of British and European evangelicalism, notes the complexity in the historical and contemporary contexts of defining evangelicalism.[20] Helpfully, Holmes states:

> There is no British, still less any European, evangelical theology, if by that is meant an identifiable commonly held and distinctive position; instead, there is an on-going conversation, returning often to central themes, but in different ways, open to other voices, borrowing gratefully sometimes, pausing to denounce stridently at others – or often, different voices within the conversation responding to each of these ways. We are also open, very open, to the influence of culture and society, believing passionately that Jesus Christ is the answer, but often confused and unsure as to what the question might be.[21]

However, it should be noted that this view of evangelicalism does exist in tension with those more conservative members of the tradition who at times seek to narrow the meaning of the word 'evangelical'.[22] The history of evangelicalism in North America has similarly (as with evangelicalisms around the world) witnessed the tension between those who have attempted to restrict the scope of the meaning of 'evangelical' and those who have sought to expand its horizon while remaining committed to its distinctive affirmations, and like evangelicalism in Britain and Europe, evangelicalism in North America has been shaped by a variety of movements, individuals and institutions.[23] Clearly, this book sees itself as a part of the trajectory of evangelical thought that engages (in Holmes' terms) in 'on-going conversation', and in an opening to other voices, culture and society (albeit not uncritically) as it articulates an orthodox protestant theology centred on the Bible, the reconciliation brought about between God and humanity through the cross and resurrection, and the work of the Spirit in conversion and guiding the active, holy life of faith.[24] The book proceeds, therefore, in the belief that evangelicalism should not be a movement that desires to be narrowing and self-limiting, but should be ever opening up while still retaining its distinctive emphases and piety. Less about propositional truths or theological dogmatic statement, evangelicalism is understood by the authors of this book to be in part 'a piety cradled in a theology'.[25] Furthermore, the authors consider dangerous the desire to close evangelicalism down to an ever smaller group of people who represent the true church or the true believers over and against the one holy, catholic and apostolic church.[26]

This book wishes to capture the energy and excitement of evangelicalism on the ground, and to equip today's evangelicalism in a context which includes Fresh Expressions and Emerging Church, so that evangelicals are enabled fully to work in new and creative ways of being church.[27] The book also wishes to capture some of the difficulties and fresh opportunities that young evangelicals have as the children of those who were 'first generation' converts but themselves grew up in the faith,[28] or else that today's evangelicals have living in a contemporary society which is marked by pluralism, relativism and consumerism. This is not to say that the present and past generations of evangelical theologians are engaging and have engaged in a theology which fails to undertake theology as the present book would wish to. The authors of this book owe a debt of academic (and at times personal) gratitude to the likes of John Webster, Oliver O'Donovan, Miroslav Volf, Bruce McCormack, Kevin Vanhoozer, Stan Grenz, Anthony Thistleton, Tom Wright and others. However, this volume includes voices from younger or newer scholars and addresses issues particularly pertinent to the present generation of evangelicals (and especially younger evangelicals) through a series of essays which give fresh perspectives or (from a critical distance) take on fresh themes for consideration from an evangelical point of view. By offering a volume that might serve ministers, ordinands, church leaders and evangelical theologians (and theologians who may understand themselves as outside that particular tradition), alongside the academy more broadly, it is hoped that this book might help contemporary evangelical theologies, and in that serve the church on whose speech it reflects.

Towards

This work is not a textbook in systematic theology. It does not represent any complete or final account of Christian theology. It is, instead, a collection of essays which directs the reader to one possible way of doing theology. It offers some fresh and new voices to traditional themes, and also some comment on themes which are not traditionally considered. The themes themselves do not represent a comprehensive systematization of topics which evangelical theology needs to consider: they are merely areas of interest to theology generally or to the church in the twenty-first century. Nor does any single contribution represent a comprehensive treatment in terms of the sources, issues or evaluation of the themes herein. Moreover, the method is not considered normative for all versions of evangelical theology, but is a demonstration of one way of engagement for theologians who understand themselves to be evangelical and who are open to the broader tradition of the church, to the world and to contemporary life. Thus, this book is only ever an exercise towards an articulation of evangelical theology – an articulation which will never fully be realized. Furthermore, written by early career theologians, the essays included in this volume are self-consciously essays 'on the way', demonstrating patterns of reasoning as we wrestle with Scripture and the evangelical tradition in order to articulate the Christian gospel. Maturity is better than youth for wisdom, but these essays are written by those who cry out for insight, and raise their voices for understanding; who seek it like silver, and search for it as for hidden treasure (Prov. 2:3f.). These essays by younger scholars represent that crying out for and the searching after wisdom; and we invite others to search alongside us.[29]

However, it is hoped that the reader treats the essays with due attention to the humility with which they are presented. A vast horizon of knowledge, wisdom and experience stretches beyond the chapters of this volume, and a further life-time of study, searching and engagement will follow the essays by each of the contributors. These essays merely suggest the trajectory we are on for our individual engagements with each topic. The book does not articulate a single unitary and substantialized partisan manifesto, but is the result of shared concerns and engagements. Much of the thinking behind the individual chapters has been formed through dialogue, conversation and discussion. This has been at times informal, at conferences or during periods of shared collegiality at universities; and contributors have also read and commented on other chapters, and rethought their own thinking in light of the work of others. The versions of chapters here mark the stage of conversation and thinking at which contributors presently find themselves, as they continue to work towards articulating their theology.

Post-critical

The essays in this volume are post-critical. This is not only in the sense that they engage the pre-modern, modern and postmodern,[30] but also in the sense that they take seriously the critiques of evangelicalism. Many of the problems of evangelical theology are all too clearly evident and articulated: from an insider perspective, many evangelical theologians have been humble enough to point to imbalances or flaws in evangelical theology;[31] and from an outsider perspective, there are many who have (wrongly) seen evangelicalism as merely a stage through which to pass on a journey towards a greater level of theological sophistication.[32] The essays within this book are not designed as an apologetic response to these critiques: the book is not 'post' the criticisms of evangelicalism in that sense. Nor do these essays ignore or reject a priori the critiques of evangelicalism. Critique from the wider tradition, from members of the evangelical community and from society at large will not be ignored. However, neither do these essays proceed in any arrogant belief that evangelicalism is an earlier stage through which to pass in a path towards theological maturity: all of the contributors continue to wrestle with evangelical theology or themes in various ways. Ultimately, it will be an openness to the critique of Scripture, which stands over all evangelically orientated theology, that will be considered the supreme yardstick by which to measure the virtue of the theological articulation contained within these pages. This is not to engage in any level of fundamentalist proof-texting but to read Scripture responsibly before God in our world, and to seek its living message for today.

This theme is related to the idea of 'opening' being a marker of the chapters included in this volume: the essays are willing to be open to the critique of evangelical theology and to think afresh evangelical theology from new perspectives and for the contemporary world. This is something that evangelicalism as a movement has always done as it adapts and articulates itself in ever changing cultures and societies. Indeed, it is something that all Christian theologies must do as they speak of the God who will be who he will be. It is a notable feature of Exodus 3 that, alongside giving his name, God promises to be with his people (v.12). This text records a period in the history of the Hebrew people in which they were on the brink of a phenomenal change. According to the Exodus narrative, God is about to bring his people out of captivity in Egypt and the following pages present such monumental events as the Passover, the giving of the law, the parting of the Red Sea, the theophany to Moses and so on. Through all of these changes, God promises to be with his people – through changes in civilizations, societies, cultures, laws and rituals.[33] It is this God whom the Christian church proclaims, and it is that proclamation with which the theology in this book is concerned. Because of this, these essays take seriously the critiques of evangelical theology, and recognize the subject of theology to be the proclamation of the God who is not static, but who is with his people as they adapt to all kinds of changes.[34]

The chapters in this volume take seriously the critique of evangelical theology, and engage in finding a greater level of balance in evangelical theologies where necessary.[35] However, the essays do this constructively. They think within evangelical theology, and engage in reparative reasoning of the tradition, rather than engaging in a critical rejection or third-party description of the tradition. The chapters utilize Scripture, the evangelical tradition and the broader tradition of the church in order to engage in a positive theology which retains its evangelical flavour while still speaking with a fresh voice and to the complexity of late-modern society about the God who is with his people through all the changes of the world. The chapters in this book think beyond the criticism, and ask – if we take this critique seriously – what it is that goes in its place.

The chapters herein each arise, therefore, from a diagnosed problem with the evangelical tradition of which they are a part. However, they do not see as the solution to that problem the complete rejection of that tradition. Rather, they see the healing of the problem as lying within the tradition, and through engagement with the tradition. This will at times mean utilizing voices outside of those normally heard within evangelical conversation, and drawing supremely from the critical voice of the Bible. However, this does not mean either replacing evangelicalism with something entirely alien to its nature,[36] nor does it mean stopping only at the stage of critique and positing nothing positive in its place.

Formative

The chapters in this book desire to be formative for evangelical theology. They are not, properly speaking, pieces of systematic theology (at least not in the sense of a regular dogmatics that covers all topics and deals with the interrelation of doctrines), and they do not represent a finalized thought-through system into which one can enter. They are not simply doctrinal pieces, and at times they tackle themes outside of the normal doctrinal loci. Nor is the word 'constructive' entirely appropriate to the chapters contained here: they engage with the tradition and from within the tradition, taking evangelical theologies, the church and the Bible seriously as the basis for theological articulation. They arise from within a particular trajectory of the church and its tradition, and their fresh creativity is grounded in that tradition.[37] The chapters do not simply construct something else in place of evangelical theology but desire rather to shape that theology.

For these reasons, the term 'formative' is the preferred adjective for the theology found in these chapters.[38] They seek to form evangelical theology through modelling one way in which contemporary evangelical theology can be done. This formative nature of evangelical theology does not exist at variance with the interpretive nature or historical engagement of the theology. If formative theology is to be anything more than creative writing, it must build upon the work of others. It is its basis in scholarship which provides its weight, grounding and orientation in the tradition.[39] However, this engagement with the tradition seeks to shape and form the tradition, rather than simply to describe or repeat it. Formative theology is more than simply conformative theology, as much as it does seek to stand in line with one particular tradition. Nor is formative theology simply reformative theology: although it arises from theology whose historical origins can be found in the Reformation and eighteenth-century Pietism, it does not simply return to a normative point in Christian history but forms the contemporary expression of that historical theology.[40] Formative theology is not simply transformative theology that changes evangelical theology into something alien or different, nor deformative theology which only ever critiques. Formative theology will involve elements of each of these. However, formative theology is not any one of these to the exclusion of any other: it seeks simultaneously to utilize elements of each in the formation of theological speech. These chapters, therefore, form evangelical theology – much as potters might form their clay – at times reshaping, at times returning to the beginning, at times cutting away, at times moulding into an image already pre-established, and at times changing that pre-decided image in order to make something which proves more beautiful. The chapters contained in this volume thus desire to serve the church, and, in so doing, to serve society at large by moulding, shaping and forming theology, which – as theology – is always theology on its way.

Theology

What, then, does this theology look like? The answer to this question must surely come in reading the chapters contained in the book, and one may have a 'feel' for its shape from the discussion that has taken place thus far. However, it may be wise to conclude by simply pointing (telegrammatically, and no more) to a few themes which occur recurrently (if variously) throughout the chapters, and perhaps levels of each of them can be found in all.

This theology will be, first, a theology that takes the God-ness of God seriously. This theme can be found throughout these chapters, but is perhaps most notable in the discussions by Briggs, Nimmo and Fout. This theology also will take the life, death and resurrection of Jesus Christ as being central to any discussion of the Christian faith, and will recognize the challenges of that person to Christian faith and theology (hence the chapter again by Nimmo, and also that of Jones). The continued presence of Christ in the body of his church will be important for this theology, as a theology which is focused on Christ as the one who is for others (hence the work contained here by Fulford and Kent). But this theology will also be a theology which recognizes Jesus as ultimately Lord of all the earth and which will therefore be nervous of drawing lines too sharply around areas where the grace of God can be found (as with the chapters by MacFadyen and Greggs); and this will require a reflection on the manner in which experience and Scripture might relate to one another for theology committed to activism, discipleship and holiness (hence the discussions by Zahl and Bailey). This will in turn determine that this theology must take seriously the world of which God is the creator, and issues and societies within this world (as is most loudly heard in the chapters by Smith, Snyder and Chestnutt).

It is hoped that these themes may be held in mind by readers as they wrestle with the thoughts contained in this book, seeking – as do the authors – some form of blessing from God.

Notes

1 I am hugely indebted in this chapter to David McNutt for his advice on the state of evangelicalism in North America.
2 On reparative reasoning, see N. Adams, 'Reparative Reasoning', *Modern Theology*, 2008, vol. 24.3, 447–57.
3 One should not think, therefore, in this volume of there being 'doctrinal' chapters and 'ethical' chapters, as this division is neither sufficient nor adequate for the attempts at theology contained herein: even the more technically framed and scholastic chapters (such as Jones') contain ethical imperative and material.
4 Notably, David Ford states as the first of his 'Twelve Theses for Christian Theology in the Twenty-first Century': 'God is the One who blesses and loves in wisdom.' D. F. Ford and R. Muers (eds) *The Modern Theologians: An Introduction to Christian Theology since 1918*, 3rd edn, Oxford: Blackwell, 2005, p. 761.
5 The history of Israel that follows is often about getting it wrong, rethinking, and having second chances and, through that, a hope in the future. In some ways this seems the essence of the deuteronomistic account of the history.
6 See the chapters by Smith, Kent, Snyder, Chestnutt and Greggs.

7 Albeit, there will clearly be a need to engage in history, and several of the chapters herein engage creatively with evangelical history as, for example, in the chapters by Zahl, Jones, Fulford and Bailey.

8 K. Barth, *Church Dogmatics* I/1, Edinburgh: T&T Clark, 1975, p. 81. Henceforth, Barth's *Church Dogmatics* will be cited as *CD* and by volume and part.

9 Albeit this also is here: the Septuagint's rendering of the name (*egō eimi ho ōn*) is suggestive of this.

10 On this topic, see H. C. Brichto, *The Names of God*, Oxford: Oxford University Press, 1998, p. 24; B. W. Anderson, *The Living World of the Old Testament*, 4th edn, London: Longman, 1993, pp. 62–3; J. Bright, *A History of Israel*, London: SCM, 1998, pp. 157–8. Bright notes the sense of Yahweh being the One who brings into being. See also L. Boadt, *Reading the Old Testament*, New York: Paulist Press, 1984, pp. 166–7.

11 This is a phrase repeated at the Eucharist. The relation of Christ's resurrection to time and eschatology is something which is discussed in Barth (*CD* I/2, pp. 45–121 cf. IV/1, pp. 313 ff.).

12 Moberly puts this well: 'Theology classically is concerned with constructive questions of what belief and practice *can* and *ought* to be as a living reality in the present rather than simply descriptive, albeit suggestive, accounts of what it has been in the past.' R. W. L. Moberly, *The Old Testament of the Old Testament: Patriarchal Narratives and Mosaic Yahwism*, Minneapolis, MN: Fortress, 1992, p. 152.

13 The Kingdom is so close that it has almost arrived (has 'come near'). This is not to articulate a realized eschatology as classically articulated by the likes of C. H. Dodd, *The Parables of the Kingdom*, London: Collins, 1965. Rather it is in the sense of the Kingdom being imminent. See, for example, C. E. B. Cranfield, *The Gospel According to St. Mark: The Cambridge Greek Testament Commentary*, Cambridge: Cambridge University Press, 1963, pp. 67–8. To compare these views to the variety of interpretations of the Kingdom of God in the New Testament, see M. D. Hooker, *The Gospel According to St Mark: Black's New Testament Commentaries*, London: A&C Black, 1991, pp. 55–8.

14 The phrase 'complexly religious and secular' is borrowed from D. F. Ford, 'Gospel in Context: Among Many Faiths', paper presented at the Fulcrum Conference, Islington, 28 April 2006: 'the world is not simply religious and not simply secular but is complexly both religious and secular, with all sorts of constantly shifting interactions and balances'.

15 Cf. N. Wright, *The Radical Evangelical: Seeking a Place to Stand*, London: SPCK, 1996, p. 11. This aspect of the method in this book is demonstrated implicitly in the various chapters. However, it is also tackled more directly in the chapters by Briggs, Bailey and (more practically) MacFadyen.

16 Hence the chapters by Snyder and Chestnutt.

17 See H. Frei, *Types of Christian Theology*, New Haven, CT: Yale University Press, 1992. The essays in this book are not concerned with versions of Christian theology which fall into types one and two of Frei's schema (pp. 28–32).

18 This is not a new problem. McGrath records Tom Torrance facing this very issue in the early 1930s:

> The history of evangelicalism in the United Kingdom and the United States is frequently dominated by debates over who is in and who is out, not to mention who has the right to draw the somewhat contested boundaries in the first place.
> (A. McGrath, *T. F. Torrance: An Intellectual Biography*, Edinburgh: T&T Clark, 1999, p. 26)

Perhaps even more worrying is the manner in which some evangelicals often talk as if 'evangelical' is simply but constrictively synonymous with 'Christian', with the implication that non-evangelicals are non-Christians. This can be witnessed in some evangelical talk about Roman Catholics, for example. When this syndrome is added to the contesting and narrowing of the term 'evangelical', we see a deeply pernicious tendency at work: there is none saved but for me and thee – and I am not so sure about thee.

19 D. W. Bebbington, *Evangelicalism in Modern Britain: A History from the 1870s to the 1980s*, London: Unwin Hyman, 1989, pp. 2–17; T. Larsen, 'Defining and Locating Evangelicalism', in T. Larsen and D. J. Treier (eds) *The Cambridge Companion to Evangelical Theology*, Cambridge: Cambridge University Press, 2007.

20 S. R. Holmes, 'British (and European) Evangelical Theologies', in Larsen and Treier, *The Cambridge Companion to Evangelical Theology*, pp. 253–6.

21 Ibid., p. 256

22 Ibid., pp. 251–2. Holmes himself hints at this: he notes a concern for contemporary British evangelical theology that both forms of evangelicalism have to recognize the other (p. 253). The spectrum of different evangelicalisms is helpfully recorded in G. Fackre, 'Evangelical, Evangelicalism', in A. Richardson and J. Bowden (eds) *A New Dictionary of Christian Theology*, London: SCM, 1983, pp. 191–2. Rather than point directly to some of the embodiments of these tendencies, this book engages in quiet dialogue with this stream of evangelicalism instead of responding to their unhelpful narrowing of the definition by pushing them out through our own mirrored attempts. At times, it will be overtly clear what is being opposed, but the principal desire of this book is to be constructive rather than simply critical – as below in terms of 'post-critical'.

23 On the history of North American evangelicalism, see M. A. Noll, *The Rise of Evangelicalism: The Age of Edwards, Whitefield, and the Wesleys*, Downers Grove, IL: IVP, 2003; T. George, 'Evangelical Theology in North American Contexts', in Larsen and Treier (eds) *The Cambridge Companion to Evangelical Theology*, pp. 275–92; R. E. Olson, *The Westminster Handbook to Evangelical Theology*, Louisville, KY: Westminster John Knox Press, 2004; R. S. Anderson, 'Evangelical Theology', in D. F. Ford (ed.) *The Modern Theologians: An Introduction to Christian Theology in the twentieth century*, 2nd edn, Oxford: Blackwell, 1997, pp. 480–98; N. O. Hatch, *The Democratization of American Christianity*, New Haven, CT: Yale University Press, 1989; and R. Carwardine, *Transatlantic Revivalism: Popular Evangelicalism in Britain and America, 1790–1865*, Westport, CT: Greenwood Press, 1978.

24 Cf. Larsen, 'Defining and Locating Evangelicalism', p. 1.

25 S. J. Grenz, *Revisioning Evangelical Theology: A Fresh Agenda for the 21st Century*, Downers Grove, IL: IVP, 1993, p. 62, cf. pp. 31ff. and ch. 2.

26 J. Carter, *Faith and Freedom: The Christian Challenge for the World*, London: Duckworth, 2006, ch. 2 (cf. ch. 3). A parallel may be found between the desire to engage in ever narrower definitions of 'evangelical' and the Donatist controversy in the early church: any movement to see one's own small group as the only true church is always unhelpful.

27 Albeit this book does not enter dialogue with these movements as discrete elements within evangelicalism. Rather, the book seeks to offer a theology with which evangelicals (and theologians) of all varieties can engage in dialogue.

28 This reference to 'generations' is not used in the same manner as Bebbington does in his historical presentation (cf. Bebbington, *Evangelicalism in Modern Britain*). Rather, it is used to express the complexity of being brought up as a child in a home governed by evangelical culture – not reaching the moment of crisis and conversion but living one's teenage years etc. as a Christian. Recognizing some of the distinctiveness between evangelical culture and evangelical theology, and seeking at points to disentangle the two (however complex that process may be) may well open evangelicals who have grown up in such cultural settings to different theological articulations: not converting as an adult but being raised in an evangelical culture may provide a greater openness to theologies that find a place for the complexity and ambiguity of human experience.

29 On theology as wisdom, see D. F. Ford, *Christian Wisdom: Desiring God and Learning in Love*, Cambridge: Cambridge University Press, 2007, esp. pp. 1–13. Ford helpfully writes:

> As far as the theologian and any other seeker of such wisdom is concerned, the core activity is crying out for it. The cry goes first to God. It also goes to anyone who might have wisdom or wants to join in seeking it. ... In the Bible, apart from the desire for God there is no desire that is more passionately and loudly encouraged than the cry for wisdom.
>
> (p. 51)

30 Ibid., p. 3.

31 See, for example, from an American context, the likes of Grenz, *Revisioning Evangelical Theology*, and from a British context the likes of Wright, *The Radical Evangelical*.

32 As in Fowler's faith development. Cf. J. Leach, 'The Renewal of Christian Tradition', in M. Forward, S. Plant and S. White (eds) *A Great Commission: Christian Hope and Religious Diversity*, Bern: Peter Lang, 2000. It is also interesting to note evangelical discussions of such themes: see V. Roberts, 'Reframing the UCCF Doctrinal Basis', *Theology*, 1992, vol. 95, 432–6.

33 For an account which recognizes the newness of the Mosaic articulation of faith in comparison to the religion of the patriarchs, see Moberly, *The Old Testament of the Old Testament*.

34 See T. Greggs, 'Why Does the Church Need Academic Theology?', *Epworth Review*, 2006, vol. 33, which states that God is not to be confused with a world view (pp. 31–3).

35 Hence, in this collection, there are essays on ecclesiology and on the sacraments.

36 As broadly defined by Larsen and Bebbington.

37 This approach to theology is analogous to the approach to church history seen in Rowan Williams, *Why Study the Past? The Quest for the Historical Christian Church*, London: Darton, Longman & Todd, 2005, p. 1.

38 For further definition of what is meant by 'formative theology', see T. Greggs, *Barth, Origen, and Universal Salvation: Restoring Particularity*, Oxford: Oxford University Press, 2009, ch. 1.

39 See Greggs, 'Why Does the Church Need Academic Theology?', pp. 28–30.

40 One can see this expressed in the willingness in these essays not to think towards the likes of Calvin, Luther or Wesley, but to think through, with and beyond the likes of Calvin, Luther or Wesley.

Select bibliography

Bebbington, D. W., *Evangelicalism in Modern Britain: A History from the 1870s to the 1980s*, London: Unwin Hyman, 1989.

Grenz, S. J., *Revisioning Evangelical Theology: A Fresh Agenda for the 21st Century*, Downers Grove, IL: IVP, 1993.

Larsen, T. and Treier, D. J. (eds), *The Cambridge Companion to Evangelical Theology*, Cambridge: Cambridge University Press, 2007.

Noll, M. A., *The Rise of Evangelicalism: The Age of Edwards, Whitefield, and the Wesleys*, Downers Grove, IL: IVP, 2003.

Wright, N., *The Radical Evangelical: Seeking a Place to Stand*, London: SPCK, 1996.

Chapter 2

The Bible before us

Evangelical possibilities for taking Scripture seriously

Richard S. Briggs

> Whenever we pick up the Bible, read it, put it down, and say, 'That's just what I thought,' we are probably in trouble.
>
> Ellen Davis[1]

A tale of two evangelical Bibles

'Evangelical' is the best of terms and the worst of terms.

Positively, it connotes a theology and a spirituality centred joyfully around the living and active Word of God, bringing grace and truth in the *evangel*, God's good news for the human race and the whole of creation. When applied to Scripture itself, the term thus offers light and life, and like the law of the Lord (the *torah* of *Yhwh*) in Ps. 19:7–8, it revives the soul and rejoices the heart. An evangelical theology will affirm: 'Your word is a lamp to my feet and a light to my path' (Ps. 119:105).

But as for me, my feet had almost stumbled. ... For negatively, it is spread abroad that evangelical approaches to faith and to Scripture can be naive, literalistic, harsh, given to excessive certainty, and that there is no reasoning either in them or with them. And critics with an ear for the prophets could say, 'Do not trust in these deceptive words: "This is the Scripture of the Lord, the Scripture of the Lord, the Scripture of the Lord."' The implied shock should be worthy of Jeremiah's temple sermon (cf. Jer. 7:4).

In the one evangelical construction of Scripture, God loves the world so much that he gave his only Son, and the music of a hundred psalms plays around the words of Jesus as he invites all who are weary and heavy-laden to come to him for rest. But in the other, Abel's blood cries from the ground and wails down through centuries of sin, death and darkness, from which we and we alone are saved by the skin of our teeth, and by undeserved grace, and – in the sure and certain knowledge that we are right – we offer a hard-edged love in the form of woe to those who step out from the narrow way and choose the easy path to death.

What biblical scholar within touching distance of the orbit of evangelicalism has not been torn between variant versions of these two visions, and has not at some point thought it would be simpler all round to abandon the label 'evangelical' and get on with the task of reading the text in front of us wherever it might lead? Of course, such a withdrawal risks ceding the label to just those evangelicals who thirst for certainty with an unnerving zeal. What happens if instead we try to articulate constructively how an evangelical theology might best attend to Scripture without being dragged down to the 'we and we alone' end of the spectrum?

Scripture and the *evangel*: receiving the Word of God

To be evangelical can involve holding many different convictions, but affirming some kind of central role for the Bible has always been one of them. I shall, with some misgiving, eschew the path of cataloguing all the various ways in which self-confessedly evangelical theologians and biblical scholars have in fact understood the role of Scripture, just as I will also avoid the various discussions about how to define 'evangelical', although it is clear that distinguishing between theological uses of the word and sociological uses of the word could help clear up some confusions.[2] It is obvious, to anyone familiar with this area, that there is vast diversity among evangelical scholars concerning the right way to understand Scripture, both on a broad conceptual level as well as concerning the details of biblical study. A level of further complexity is added by the recognition of the broad ranges of popular and semi-popular ways of handling Scripture which occupy a good many more evangelicals, a level which is arguably not so prominent with some other scholarly approaches. It is easy to criticize other perspectives, as the evidence of both evangelical and other writers demonstrates, but for my part, I shall attempt merely to indicate one or two lines of constructive enquiry which might merit further consideration for evangelicals seeking to understand the nature and role of Scripture at the present time. Not going down the route of sorting out definitions and history comes at a price – generalization, over-simplification, and so forth – but it is a price worth paying if we are ever to arrive at constructive suggestions.

The reason 'evangelical' can be both the best and the worst of terms in the study of Scripture lies in the vast range of self-confessed uses of the term, from the joyfully life-giving through to the deadeningly heavy-handed. I want to simplify this complex spectrum for a moment and explore a crucial conceptual distinction which generates two basically different 'evangelical' ways of looking at the Bible: a distinction pertaining to the perennial question of how one relates the words on the pages of Scripture to the singular Word of God who has been active from before all time. This distinction lies deep in the way most people conceptualize reading the Bible, so deep in fact that my observation is that many evangelicals (and, for that matter, many who reject evangelicalism) do not attend to it too well. We shall approach it by taking seriously Scripture's own testimony regarding the Word of God, since evangelical theology is obviously essentially concerned in some sense with the *evangel*, God's good news. It is worth considering that the real bearer of God's *evangel* is, properly speaking, the Word of God. Scripture's own testimony to this Word is impressive:

- It creates the cosmos as God speaks, 'Let there be', and, day after day, 'it was so' (Gen. 1, e.g. vv. 3, 9, 11).[3]
- It offers practical illumination for one's way through life (Ps. 119:105).
- It never returns empty but accomplishes God's purpose, 'succeeding in the thing for which I sent it' (Isa. 55:11).
- It became flesh (Jn 1:14) – 'The Word became flesh and blood, and moved into the neighbourhood', as the unforgettable paraphrase of *The Message* puts it. This Word is possessed of the glory of the Son. In John's view, it is Jesus who is in some sense the Word of God himself.
- It is characterized as the sword of the Spirit (Eph. 6:17) ... in which capacity, presumably, it is 'living and active, sharper than any two-edged sword ... able to judge the thoughts and intentions of the heart' (Heb. 4:12).
- And it is last seen in Scripture riding out on the second of Revelation's two white horses (Rev. 19:13).

By its very nature this testimony is to a prior reality: the Word of God comes before Scripture,[4] even while it is still entirely fair to insist that it also comes *in and through* Scripture. But there is no inherent reason why it should be limited to Scripture. It is interesting to pause and reflect on how many of the above descriptions are of a book as such: perhaps the Hebrews 4 reference is self-consciously applying the terminology of being 'living and active' to Psalm 95, the text of which is clearly in view at that point, and one could certainly see a reference to written Torah (though possibly not an exclusive reference) in places like Psalm 119. However, overall, the Word of God in Scripture is first God in personal terms, and then derivatively it is the written word. It seems clear, at least in scriptural terms, that the Word of God must be so much more than could ever be contained in the Bible. All this is of course well known, and much of it constitutes one emphasis of the great theologian of the Word of God, Karl Barth.

Perhaps this point is just one example of what I take to be Barth's most profound contribution to the study of Scripture: the repeated insistence that one must always let God's self-revelation set the agenda for one's enquiry. Readers of Barth must oftentimes sense that there are other agendas it would be appropriate to have in play too, but then arguably the question is one of proper ordering, so that whatever other agendas are allowed to the table, the table is set first by God's self-revelation. All other categories are subservient to this one. I have no stake in arguing the finer distinctions of how to balance competing theological claims here, for we must press on to other matters, so I shall take Barth in a somewhat modest sense, noting that the emphasis on God's own agenda through Scripture is to be one profound contribution to all our theological reflection.[5]

One issue this raises, obviously, is how to determine what that agenda is in any given text, and we shall come to that later, but for our present purposes I want to suggest that it is the allied and to some extent antecedent difficulty which is the fundamental point at stake. The antecedent difficulty lies in knowing what sort of framework allows the prospective divine agenda to be heard as near as possible on its own terms. And here, to return to our simplifying disjunction, we come to the fork in the road between those for whom this is an existentially probing question to which we have only fleeting, transitory and always provisional answers, as against those for whom there is a straightforward answer which can be grasped with both hands and affirmed with confidence. Evangelicals have taken both paths, of course, but one might be forgiven for thinking that the noisiest among them seem to belong in the latter group. In such a view the framework is often set by a complex of categories which circle around the notion of truth-telling, whether this be truth about the past (accurate historical writing), truth about the present (the way human beings are and the world is), or truth about the future (the notion that prophecy tells it like it will be). Of course, these frameworks can be used just as often against evangelicalism: given these categories, the Bible may then be found wanting on the basis that things didn't, don't or won't happen that way.

Some suggest that postmodernism, whatever it turns out to be, shows us that the whole debate about factuality and accuracy is flawed, and then we have the compounded spectacle of biblical interpreters arguing over the merits of postmodernism in the belief that if one could only get the notion of truth-telling accurate enough with respect to criteria like facts and logic then the claims of the Bible would be revealed for all to see.[6]

Well, it seems to me that the whole debate is indeed flawed, but not for this reason. It is flawed because the criteria for reading the Bible are best not set by the varying agendas with regard to truth, logic, accuracy and facts. Although all of these agendas will eventually have their place, they will have it within the broader overarching agenda, which is set, as Barth would say so memorably, by God. Barth's questions drive us relentlessly to the point: 'What is there within the Bible? What sort of house is it to which the Bible is the door? What sort of country is spread before our eyes when we throw the Bible open?'[7] In Barth's (uncharacteristically) brief and bracing account, the answer is not history, though there is of course history, as 'one can content himself for a time with this answer and find in it many true and beautiful possibilities'.[8] Nor likewise is it morality, religion or ethics. We may seek practical wisdom or lofty examples, and yet 'large parts of the Bible are almost useless to the school in its moral curriculum because they are lacking in just this wisdom and just these "good examples"'.[9] No, what there is in the Bible is God – the triune Father, Son and Holy Spirit. In Barth's logic, one either decides to accept this and work with the grain of Holy Scripture, or one brings in some other perspective and lets the work of evaluation cut away at the divine revelation.

This is not the place for an analysis of how this basic orientation to Scripture plays out in Barth's work.[10] But it is the place to observe the strange story whereby quite a few evangelicals have taken their stand *against* this argument in the name of truth and factuality as more basic to the evaluation of Scripture than divine self-revelation.[11] In such cases, it is almost as if it could not be conceived that God could do anything other than fit within the schemes which we bring to the text. Such readers puzzle over Alasdair MacIntyre's well-judged epigram, 'facts, like telescopes and wigs for gentlemen, were a seventeenth-century invention'.[12] Even MacIntyre's fuller exposition of the point would probably not convince such puzzled holders of fact-orientated frameworks:

> It is of course and always was harmless, philosophically and otherwise, to use the word 'fact' of what a judgment states. What is and was not harmless, but highly misleading, was to conceive of a realm of facts independent of judgment or of any other form of linguistic expression.[13]

Hans Frei captured something of this notion with respect to biblical interpretation in (perhaps significantly) his reply to the critique of his own position offered by the renowned evangelical Carl Henry. For Frei, it was difficult to understand how one could be so clear about what the Bible was all about historically or factually, but not because it was (if those terms were to be granted) either unhistorical or factually misleading:

> If I am asked to use the language of factuality, then I would say, yes, in those terms, I have to speak of an empty tomb. In those terms I have to speak of a literal resurrection. But I think those terms are not privileged, theory-neutral, trans-cultural, an ingredient ... of reality always and everywhere.[14]

As Frei observed, for many centuries the church did quite well without the language of fact or literalness, so why is it the case that one would have to adopt it today?[15]

What is needed, for those who stick at this point, is some ability to shift perspective, to reorganize perception and to recalibrate judgement around some hitherto unperceived set of criteria. What is also needed, I would say, is some encouragement, from the very Scripture which has propelled us down this road, to think that the God of this Scripture might be interested in such perspective-shifting discourse.

Well, if the Word of God were to become flesh and walk among us, would his speech look anything like such discourse? And if it did, would we have ears to hear it?

Thus, to summarize: (at least) two kinds of use of the word 'evangelical' exist with respect to Scripture. On the one hand, it can be an orientation to the words on the page of Scripture, and that way lie all the familiar pitfalls of the temptation to make such words conform in one way or another to some standard set before them, whether in terms of avoiding error, inconsistency, or whatever some prevailing framework dictates must be avoided. On the other hand, 'evangelical' can be an orientation to the Word of God to whom Scripture testifies, and this way seems to lead a little more easily to a different set of possibilities. In particular it creates a certain hermeneutical space for the endlessly probing and existentially demanding tasks of learning to think in new ways and new categories, all with the wager that if one invests in such strange conceptualities, it will be the God of Abraham, Isaac and Jacob who awaits at the end. Of course, this God stands at the end of the other path too, if only because he stands everywhere, however little appreciated that may be. This argument is not an attempt to annex God to one way of looking at things. On the contrary, it is an attempt to find a way of conceptualizing 'evangelical' theology in the categories which foreclose the least on God's self-revelation in the form in which we do have it in the Bible.

The task of the remainder of this chapter is to try to examine what the implications of this understanding of 'the Word of God' are for biblical scholarship, having arrived at a point in the argument where one can begin to see how the land lies with regard to some of the many varieties of 'evangelical interpretation' of Scripture. A final point at this stage: it is a matter of some frustration that many of the most perceptive accounts of the theological dynamic we have been considering stop short of actually reading any scriptural texts at all, guilty of what Jeffrey Stout once so memorably described as 'endless methodological foreplay'.[16] But what would it profit us to be right about how to read the Bible if we never actually do it? It is in the experience of reading specific scriptural passages and wrestling with their interpretation that our approaches will have the chance to grow in wisdom. And as Dennis Olson points out, there is 'a tendency in some of these discussions to relegate the Bible to the role of a voiceless object for investigation rather than a genuine partner in the conversation'.[17] A way of treating Scripture less like the written form of the Word of God it is hard to imagine.

The way ahead, then, conceives of Scripture as 'before' us in a double sense: it precedes us and thus, in God's economy, the Word of God summons us to interpretive paths which it is not our job to delimit in advance; and it invites us to an attentiveness before what is actually said in Scripture which it is not our job to prejudge in advance. This way lies the chance for a deep evangelical confidence in the Bible we have before us, aware of all its complexity and obscurity, but willing to work long and hard to try to tune in to its various wavelengths. After all, biblical interpretation would only be straightforward if God were straightforward, and the evidence of Scripture, tradition, experience, and – if the philosophers are to be believed – reason, all suggest that this is not (often) the case. On a popular level, evangelicalism often holds out the hope that all you need is to read the Bible and light will dawn, which, in the grace of God, it often does seem to do, but evangelical scholars have long been aware that one cannot offer a proper account of Scripture driven by such popular categories and phenomena. If the biblical witness itself is to be believed, wise interpretation will take time, disciplined imagination, and transformation.[18] All of these categories can best be explored in conjunction with characteristics of Scripture which have perhaps been underplayed in some evangelical reflection.

The strangeness of Scripture and the attentive reader

For much of the modern period, critical introductions to the Bible embodied the conviction that their task was to defamiliarize the biblical text, precisely so as to force upon the reader a rethinking of categories, and to avoid the careless imposition of inappropriate prior frameworks which would distort matters. On the whole, one might note, such a pedagogical move is scarcely any longer necessary in the sense that few readers of the Bible today have much initial momentum which needs any slowing down, although the genre seems to persist regardless. In any case, as a review of such introductory texts can quickly confirm, it was easy for such a presentation to degenerate into the presenting of various 'problems' or conundrums, often concerning questions of authorship, consistency and historical accuracy. Evangelical introductions could then find themselves doing largely the same thing, except with more determinedly 'positive' results.

In retrospect, however, the modern pedagogical device of defamiliarization was perhaps insufficiently robust, and was too easily aimed at the wrong target. Undoubtedly such matters as authorship and consistency within the canon are strange phenomena, but they mask too easily the fundamental strangeness: the God who is at the centre of it all. This is the God whose judgements are, according to Paul, unsearchable and mysterious (Romans 11:33–36); the God known from the book of Job as a wondrous creator in the same story where his ways are inscrutable; the God who, for example, meets Moses on the road and tries to kill him (Exodus 4:24–26).

It is evident that examples like these require a certain attentiveness on the part of the reader of Scripture. This is a virtue which will obviously commend itself to evangelicals, but perhaps oddly the most stirring call to attentiveness in recent hermeneutical literature comes from elsewhere, in the eloquent analysis of John Barton. For him, the key in the reading of (biblical) texts is:

> the desire to be silent in the face of what confronts us, before we turn to consider how we can make it part of our own system. Prayer begins in attention to what is there, and then reflects on that thereness in the light of religious convictions. But attention comes first. To me it seems that biblical criticism is an admirable example of an approach to the reality of texts that similarly begins in contemplation of a given and does not seek to distort that given into something we can make something of.[19]

This rallying cry is issued as a riposte to self-consciously theological interpretation, and there is of course much good sense in it. And let it be acknowledged that the evangelical world is by no means short of those whose first move is to make sure that the text before them fits the theological system which is brought to it, already fully formed and determined that it shall find no troubling new perspective here.

Nevertheless, there is scope for widely divergent practices under the rubric Barton examines, and those who read with theological interests will want to note some important ways in which the rhetoric of Barton's argument does on occasion outstrip its utility. Thus: when does making something of a text cross a line between 'attending to it and its implications' and 'distorting' it? And if attention comes first, what happens second, or to rephrase the point, if biblical criticism 'begins' with attentiveness, does it terminate there also? The wider implications and connotations of biblical language frequently ramify out into all manner of value judgements and even conceptualities of what sort of subjects make up the world of discourse (God, gods, angels, evil, love, forgiveness, faith, hope ... the list is probably very long). In this sense, all significant biblical language is self-involving, and does not conveniently await our disinterested investigation.[20]

Historical criticisms of various sorts have by and large done an excellent job of demonstrating the historical dimensions of the strangeness of the biblical text. One might hope that never again will it be necessary to point out that there was more than one author of Isaiah; that John, for his own purposes, has chronologically relocated various key events (the cleansing of the temple, the timing of the last supper with regard to Passover ...), and so on with regard to many such flashpoints of debates over historical-critical conclusions. In his recent book on evangelical approaches to biblical study, Kenton Sparks offers a lengthy and reasonably secure account of all these 'victories' of the critical approach.[21] But ironically, none of this really touches on the key issues for evangelical readers, which concern the strangeness of what God says and does at various points in the canon.[22] Indeed, if anything, one could argue that some prominent strands of historical criticism operate with a domesticated notion of what might count as divine action, so that, for example, what might look like theological contradiction is 'resolved' by parcelling out the recalcitrant texts to different sources, almost as if theological complexity could somehow be explained away. The key point here is that, yes, attentiveness is essential, but it is not enough unless material content is added to the formal notion of being attentive, for attentiveness always takes place within some framework. The lack of imaginative empathy which characterizes much attentiveness forecloses on the genuinely and irreducibly theological task of attending to the subject matter of the text. So we must move 'up' a level, and seek thicker descriptions of the phenomena we are trying to understand.

The inspiration of Scripture and the implied reader

Strangeness is, in the end, a somewhat preliminary way of characterizing Scripture. Taken as a whole what is really striking is the massive and intricate complexity of Scripture. One occasionally hears the slightly wistful argument that some recent evangelical writing on Scripture and on hermeneutics has muddied the waters of what once seemed so blissfully straightforward – the reading and interpreting of biblical texts. In fact I want to pursue more or less the opposite contention – that certain types of evangelical reflection on Scripture have too often sought to bring a premature clarity to the muddy waters of the biblical text. Two paths to this cautious conclusion may briefly be explored – the notion of 'inspiration' as it pertains to Scripture, but first the notion of Scripture's 'implied reader'.

The notion of an 'implied reader' is a powerful tool for getting at what a text is presumed to be discussing. For Seymour Chatman the concept of the 'implied reader' is 'the audience presupposed by the narrative itself'.[23] There is increasing evidence of sophisticated use of the notion of an 'implied reader' in biblical studies as a way of examining how individual biblical passages presuppose certain types of reader.[24] But I want to ask a slightly more ambitious question in our context: who is the implied reader of the whole canon of Scripture?

One way of answering this question is in terms of *beliefs* that the reader must be supposed to hold in order to make any sense at all of the text and any progress through it (such as belief in God, for instance). Perhaps a more interesting approach is in terms of the *characteristics* of the reader which must be presumed in order to make sense of the idea of reading the whole Bible. On the one hand, such a reader will clearly find much of comfort, inspiration and joy as they make their way through the canon. On the other, we might note that the implied reader of Scripture will have to be someone who is patient, a long-term reader of considerable perseverance, and strikingly tolerant of quite extraordinary diversity in almost every way relevant to the reading of the whole canon. They will not give up upon discovering a variety of names for God, or different styles of literature, or conflicting affirmations regarding what God has or has not done (or will do), or even (to anticipate one obvious rejoinder) that there is a purpose to persevering with the whole project of reading it in the first place, since they will be several chapters into Ecclesiastes before wondering whether they have not found a text which bluntly evaluates the concerns of the whole of the rest of the canon as *hevel* (absurd, meaningless, 'vanity').[25] Might we even say that the implied reader of the whole canon of Scripture is someone who, along with all the positive and life-giving reasons for reading and indeed re-reading, will also be puzzled much of the time, but will nevertheless always persevere, a description perhaps reminiscent of the disciples in the gospels. Markus Bockmuehl puts the matter most helpfully: 'the implied interpreter of the Christian Scripture is a *disciple*', and he even talks of 'the Implied Disciple'.[26]

It is interesting to compare this portrait with one particular kind of evangelical assessment of the appropriate reader of Scripture – someone who wants to affirm that Scripture is in some sense clear, straightforward, accurate as a record of the things that occurred, a ready resource for moral living and decision-making, indeed authoritative in some sense and, in some affirmations, infallible or inerrant. Such a reader will of course be a disciple, but perhaps will have constructed their notion of discipleship rather differently from the 'implied disciple' noted above. Indeed, in a moment of striking self-critique, the impeccably conservative evangelical biblical scholar Craig Blomberg considers the biblical precedent for this second kind of reader and is moved to comment:

> Pharisees were the upstanding 'conservative evangelical pastors' of their day, strongly convinced of the inerrancy of Scripture and its sufficiency for guidance in every area of life, if only it could be properly interpreted.[27]

One could debate how appropriate such a characterization of the Pharisees is or was, but it should give pause for thought if evangelical reading of Scripture were indeed to keep such company.

Any desire for a little too much clarity in matters pertaining to Scripture might also with profit reflect on the *locus classicus* of the great doctrine of biblical inspiration, 2 Timothy 3:16, with its powerful affirmation that: 'All Scripture is inspired (*theopneustos*) and useful for teaching, for reproof, for correction, and for training in righteousness.' In 2 Timothy 3, the Scriptures which are described as *theopneustos* (i.e. God-breathed) are the ones Timothy has known from childhood (v.15) where, presumably, his grandmother and his mother read them to him (cf. 1:5). It seems clear that the form of the Scriptures which would have circulated in this family would have been the Greek translation, the Septuagint, which was at the time the common text of Scripture in circulation, and indeed is the version usually quoted whenever New Testament authors refer to what the Scripture said.[28] The point is that insofar as 2 Timothy 3.16 bears on any doctrine of inspiration, which has usually been presumed to be the case in evangelical discussion, it actually indicates the inspiration of a translation of Scripture. Although this is undeniably good news for those who only read the Bible in translation, it does rather undercut the idea, common in certain circles, that biblical inspiration should somehow properly be said to apply only to the so-called 'original manuscripts', the putative singular originary copies of all biblical texts.[29] From the modern perspective, with its penchant for precision and originality, this can appear to be an ominous retreat into a subjective and complex area, but then, so much the worse for the modern categories.

Built into the very notion of the inspiration of Scripture, therefore, is a certain ambiguity over the precise form of the text which is inspired, but not, crucially, over the theological subject matter to which the canon of texts bears witness. In other words, the real point of the doctrine of inspiration is not tied to a specific form of words on a page (or scroll), or even a specific edition of the text(s), but rather, as Stephen Chapman puts it:

> the claim of inspiration is a public confession by members of the Christian community that they are committed to reading and interpreting Scripture as being entirely meaningful; i.e. that *every part* of the canon, under the right conditions (e.g. careful scrutiny, spiritual discernment, faithful proclamation, communal testing), has the ability to express the will of God.[30]

It is evident that this 'ability' does not always translate into agreement as to what the will of God actually is, in any branch of the Christian church, but such is the way of things when Scripture sets the agenda. We could perhaps call this a functional sort of clarity: enough to live our lives by. Or, to revert to the original image, the waters are muddy, but they are navigable.

The canon of Scripture and the transformed reader

Our discussion of inspiration leads us to move 'up' another level in the attempt to clarify how Scripture stands before the evangelical reader. All the strangenesses of the text are ultimately compounded by recognizing that we are given not just a collection of ancient documents but a canon. The texts that come down to us arrive in certain configurations, which bequeath to us certain figural relationships, which, in turn, are not part of the author's conceptuality, nor the texts themselves severally, but are presented before the reader by dint of the canonical relationships between the canon's constituent texts.

The most profound of these relationships is the canonical structuring of 'old' and 'new', two terms much abused in contemporary biblical scholarship, where it is sometimes averred that one of the things that Scripture models to us is the open-ended trajectory of hermeneutical progress marching inexorably toward the present day:

> 'the new has come' and has relativized the old, suggesting that we, as modern readers, might relativize the position of Christian Scripture by reference to experience just as Paul relativized the Old Testament in the light of his Christian experience of the Spirit.[31]

This relatively common 'suggestion' relies entirely on construing 'new' in terms alien to the interestingly named 'New' Testament, which is not in any sense suggesting that we are in the business of learning how to add new testaments to our canon, of which this just happens to be the first such addition. Such myths of hermeneutical progress would do well to consider how the 'many and various' ways in which God spoke long ago to our ancestors, through the prophets, now find their unity 'in these last days' in Christ, according to the profound structuring of human time and hearing in Hebrews 1:1–2. This passage makes it clear that Jesus is a final word locating us in the 'newness' specific to the new covenant, and not a second word adding a next progressive stage to the first (old) covenant, subsequent to which yet further new words might come.[32]

This kind of slippery appeal to newness as a key hermeneutical category is prominent in our day. Now on the one hand, how the New Testament interprets the Old does tend to undermine a great deal of what passes for wisdom on 'how to interpret the Bible'. In Richard Hays' words: 'Let us not deceive ourselves about this: Paul would flunk our introductory exegesis course.'[33] This is almost certainly worse news for us than it is for Paul. But on the other hand, the reason why Paul's practice looks so alien to readers of Hermeneutics-101 textbooks is not because he is relativizing, contextually careless or theologically open-ended, so much as that he works in categories of intertextuality and typological figuration which are deeply rooted in the canonical structuring of the sacred texts.[34]

The practice of reading Scripture with due attention to its canonical form is of course associated with the work of Brevard Childs and those who have come after him. This is not the place to survey or evaluate Childs' approach,[35] but it is instructive to recognize that ultimately reading Scripture as canon is an attempt to connect the reader to the reality of the God who gives us the canon. In the terms of Mark Elliott's account of Childs' work: the canon helps us to access the realities of God and all God's creation via the way its in-built rule of faith and symbolism presupposes such reality. The canon can, therefore, only be properly received in conjunction with a perception of that reality. Thus: 'The *Sache* or *substantia* of the Bible is *not* so much the subject matter as the reality for human beings who understand themselves with reference to it.'[36]

The allied and fundamental question for those who read the scriptural canon is what it takes to grasp this vision. Speaking hermeneutically, concerns with method and 'how to interpret' will fall short here. As Bockmuehl notes: 'Without facing the inalienably transformative and self-involving demands that these ecclesial writings place on a serious reader, it is impossible to make significant sense of them.'[37] As evangelicals, I submit, we are among those well placed to take up this challenge because we have theological reasons to be willing, at least in principle, to follow wherever the text will lead us. Also, the key issues of transformation and self-involvement are significant elements of evangelical spirituality, with its strong activist and conversion-orientated traditions, and these elements can in turn be profitably shaped by continued reflection upon Scripture itself.

Scripture offers many different images of how such transformation can occur. The prophet Ezekiel and the seer of Revelation both 'ate the scroll' and found that this 'inwardly digested' word was then made manifest in everything they said (cf. Ezek. 2:8–3:3; Rev. 10:8–11). Eugene Peterson takes up this image in his *Eat This Book*: 'There is only one way of reading that is congruent with our Holy Scriptures ... reading that enters our souls as food enters our stomachs, spreads through our blood, and becomes holiness and love and wisdom.'[38] This is reminiscent of the hermeneutically profound imagery of Psalm 1: the reader who meditates on Torah day and night will be like a tree planted by streams of water, yielding their fruit in season. The point is not that this verse of Torah or that command can be suddenly seen to 'apply' to a particular point at issue in the present day, but rather that the reader has been shaped, from the 'inside out' as it were, to be the kind of person who knows what to do in the present situation. The link between the text upon which they meditated and the action they then performed, does not go via some 'principle' or method of application of the text, but by way of the transformed character of the one doing the reading and meditating. Text and action are bound together, we might say, in the transforming of the reader, and the specific text in view for us today is the whole canon of Scripture. Such a text requires a long slow perseverance with regard to reading and living, which is surely what any reader of the Bible we have before us should expect. Although writing only of the Torah, Dennis Olson sums up this point well: 'The truth about God, self, and the world develops over long years of experience, struggle, suffering, and transformation within the context of God's chosen human community.'[39]

The end of evangelical hermeneutics

What is the *telos* (goal, purpose, end) of evangelical reading of Scripture? It is attentiveness to the God mysteriously present in Scripture. It is discipleship illumined by this inspired text in incomparable ways, though of course in the midst of multiple other illuminations. It is transformation before the whole canon received as God's providential ordering of many and various witnesses to his Word, the same 'many and various' voices which we saw brought together (mysteriously) in Christ in Hebrews 1:1–2.

There is extraordinary diversity in evangelical practice and belief today, even in the specific practices of scriptural interpretation. My goal here has been to suggest some potentially fruitful paths for further evangelical reflection on how best to take seriously the Bible which we have before us. It is, appropriately, hard to predict where such reflection might lead, but one may hope that it might contribute to a profound evangelical rejoicing that the life-giving Word of God still moves among us, and remains unconfined in the gracious distribution of eyes to see and ears to hear.

Notes

1   E. F. Davis, 'Teaching the Bible Confessionally in Church', in E. F. Davis and R. B. Hays (eds) *The Art of Reading Scripture*, Grand Rapids, MI: Eerdmans, 2003, p. 16.

2   Witness the brisk clarification offered by W. Brueggemann, *Texts Under Negotiation: The Bible and Postmodern Imagination*, Minneapolis, MN: Fortress Press, 1993, p. 26: 'I use the word "evangelical" in its proper sense as an adjectival form of "gospel." I do not mean to allude to any current popular religious notion of "evangelicals" with a long *e*.'

3   Francis Watson calls this 'the *speech-act model* of divine creativity' in his *Text, Church and World. Biblical Interpretation in Theological Perspective*, Edinburgh: T&T Clark, 1994, pp. 140–2.

4   It is instructive to compare this with ways in which the Qur'an is conceptualized with respect to the Word of God: see the discussion of this point in the chapter in this volume by Sarah Snyder.

5   Barth's views on and handling of Scripture are given excellent treatment in many places, including N. B. MacDonald, *Karl Barth and the Strange New World within the Bible: Barth, Wittgenstein, and the Metadilemmas of the Enlightenment*, Carlisle: Paternoster, 2001; and R. E. Burnett, *Karl Barth's Theological Exegesis: The Hermeneutical Principles of the* Römerbrief *Period*, Tübingen: J. C. B. Mohr (Paul Siebeck), 2001.

6   This argument is presented with admirable clarity by N. Murphy, *Beyond Liberalism and Fundamentalism: How Modern and Postmodern Philosophy set the Theological Agenda*, Valley Forge, PA: Trinity Press International, 1996. However, to my mind she demonstrates *inter alia* the limits of philosophical analysis with respect to the substantive questions of revelation.

7   Karl Barth, 'The Strange New World within the Bible', in his *The Word of God and the Word of Man*, London: Hodder & Stoughton, 1928, p. 28.

8   Ibid., p. 35.

9   Ibid., p. 38.

10   See in particular Burnett, *Theological Exegesis*, and, to anticipate a key point of the argument, the work of those such as Brevard Childs operating under a 'canonical' rubric.

11   Bruce McCormack offers a compelling analysis of (American) evangelical sticking points here in 'The Being of Holy Scripture Is in Becoming: Karl Barth in Conversation with American Evangelical Criticism', in V. Bacote, L. C. Miguélez and D. L. Okholm (eds) *Evangelicals and Scripture: Tradition, Authority and Hermeneutics*, Downers Grove, IL: IVPUS, 2004, pp. 55–75.

12   A. MacIntyre, *Whose Justice? Which Rationality?*, Notre Dame, IN: UNDP, 1988, p. 357.

13 Ibid., pp. 357–8.
14 H. W. Frei, *Theology and Narrative: Selected Essays*, New York: Oxford University Press, 1993, p. 211.
15 I have argued elsewhere that it is *trustworthiness* which comes closest to Frei's concerns about Scripture, and which he thinks has been 'eclipsed' in the modern period by being subsumed under concerns about factuality. See my *The Virtuous Reader: Old Testament Narrative and Interpretive Virtue*, Grand Rapids, MI: Baker Academic, forthcoming, ch. 4.
16 J. Stout, *The Flight from Authority. Religion, Morality, and the Quest for Autonomy*, Notre Dame, IN: University of Notre Dame Press, 1981, p. 147.
17 D. T. Olson, 'Truth and the Torah: Reflections on Rationality and the Pentateuch', in A. G. Padgett and P. R. Keifert (eds) *But is it All True? The Bible and the Question of Truth*, Grand Rapids, MI: Eerdmans, 2006, p. 18.
18 I have elsewhere begun to explore how our hermeneutical thinking might be better shaped by the witness of Scripture itself; cf. my *The Virtuous Reader*.
19 J. Barton, *The Nature of Biblical Criticism*, Louisville, KY: Westminster John Knox Press, 2007, p. 181.
20 A full-scale discussion of these various points is found in R. W. L. Moberly, 'Biblical Criticism and Religious Belief', *Journal of Theological Interpretation*, 2008, vol. 2.1, 71–100. I have argued for the fundamentally self-involving nature of all (significant) biblical language in *Words in Action. Speech Act Theory and Biblical Interpretation. Toward a Hermeneutic of Self-Involvement*, Edinburgh: T&T Clark, 2001, esp. pp. 147–82.
21 K. L. Sparks, *God's Word in Human Words: An Evangelical Appropriation of Critical Biblical Scholarship*, Grand Rapids, MI: Baker Academic, 2008, pp. 73–132.
22 In this sense I find that Sparks' often admirable book falls at the last hurdle, unable to shake the conviction that the 'problems' with which many historical critics occupy themselves are in some sense the central issues.
23 S. Chatman, *Story and Discourse: Narrative Structure in Fiction and Film*, Ithaca, NY: Cornell University Press, 1978, p. 150. Note similarly: 'A text is a device conceived in order to produce its model reader. ... The empirical reader is only an actor who makes conjectures about the kind of model reader postulated by the text.' Umberto Eco, *Interpretation and Overinterpretation*, Cambridge: Cambridge University Press, 1992, p. 64.
24 E.g. M. A. Powell, *Chasing the Eastern Star: Adventures in Biblical Reader-Response Criticism*, Louisville, KY: Westminster John Knox Press, 2001, esp. pp. 75–130 on the resultant distinction between 'expected' and 'unexpected' readings.
25 Cf. the discussion of the term in M. V. Fox, *A Time to Tear Down and a Time to Build Up: A Rereading of Ecclesiastes*, Grand Rapids, MI: Eerdmans, 1999, pp. 27–49.
26 M. Bockmuehl, *Seeing the Word. Refocusing New Testament Study*, Grand Rapids, MI: Baker Academic, 2006, p. 92 (cf. p. 63).
27 C. L. Blomberg, *Jesus and the Gospels*, Leicester: Apollos, 1997, p. 48.
28 An illuminating if somewhat contestable discussion of the 'biblical-theological significance' of the LXX is offered by M. Müller, *The First Bible of the Church: A Plea for the Septuagint*, Sheffield: Sheffield Academic Press, 1996, esp. pp. 124–44.
29 This is a problematic notion in its own way (see e.g. R. T. Beckwith, 'Toward a Theology of the Biblical Text', in D. Lewis and A. McGrath (eds) *Doing Theology for the People of God: Studies in Honour of J. I. Packer*, Leicester: Apollos, 1996, pp. 43–50; and several essays in Bacote *et al.* (eds) *Evangelicals and Scripture*), but since 2 Timothy 3 is not talking about such things we need not linger over this problem.
30 S. B. Chapman, 'Reclaiming Inspiration for the Bible', in C. Bartholomew, S. Hahn, R. Parry, C. Seitz and A. Wolters (eds) *Canon and Biblical Interpretation*, Carlisle:

Paternoster, 2006, p. 188. Differing canons are not really, in practice, a problem for this claim, though space precludes treatment of this issue.

31 C. Rowland and Z. Bennett, '"Action is the Life of All": New Testament Theology and Practical Theology', in C. Rowland and C. Tuckett (eds) *The Nature of New Testament Theology*, Oxford: Blackwell, 2006, p. 195.

32 On this area note further George Bailey's perceptive account of Wesley's discussion of Scripture and experience in this volume.

33 R. B. Hays, *Echoes of Scripture in the Letters of Paul*, New Haven, CT: Yale University Press, 1989, p. 181.

34 Hays, *Echoes of Scripture*, remains a biblical studies landmark for the conceptuality of intertextuality. For thoughtful typological reading see S. D. Walters (ed.) *Go Figure! Figuration in Biblical Interpretation*, Eugene, OR: Pickwick, 2008.

35 A fresh assessment is provided by C. R. Seitz, 'The Canonical Approach and Theological Interpretation', in Bartholomew *et al.* (eds) *Canon and Biblical Interpretation*, pp. 58–110.

36 M. W. Elliott, *The Reality of Biblical Theology*, Bern: Peter Lang, 2007, p. 67.

37 Bockmuehl, *Seeing the Word*, p. 46.

38 E. H. Peterson, *Eat This Book: A Conversation in the Art of Spiritual Reading*, Grand Rapids, MI: Eerdmans, 2006, p. 4.

39 Olson, 'Truth and the Torah', p. 30.

Select bibliography

Bacote, V., Miguélez, L. C. and Okholm, D. L. (eds), *Evangelicals and Scripture: Tradition, Authority and Hermeneutics*, Downers Grove, IL: IVPUS, 2004.

Bartholomew, C., Hahn, S., Parry, R., Seitz, C. and Wolters, A. (eds), *Canon and Biblical Interpretation*, Carlisle: Paternoster, 2006.

Barton, J., *The Nature of Biblical Criticism*, Louisville, KY: Westminster John Knox Press, 2007.

Briggs, R. S., *The Virtuous Reader: Old Testament Narrative and Interpretive Virtue*, Grand Rapids, MI: Baker Academic, 2010.

Davis, E. F. and Hays, R. B. (eds), *The Art of Reading Scripture*, Grand Rapids, MI: Eerdmans, 2003.

Moberly, R. W. L., 'Biblical Criticism and Religious Belief', *Journal of Theological Interpretation*, 2008, vol. 2.1, 71–100.

Sparks, K. L., *God's Word in Human Words: An Evangelical Appropriation of Critical Biblical Scholarship*, Grand Rapids, MI: Baker Academic, 2008.

Chapter 3

Election and evangelical thinking
Challenges to our way of conceiving the doctrine of God

Paul T. Nimmo

> Election/predestination has been one of the most controversial of all Christian doctrines. It has been misunderstood and misapplied, often by being separated from other Christian truths. It has been debated and argued about for centuries. ... We will be well advised to approach this doctrine with considerable humility and to be as free as possible from prejudicial bias.[1]

The doctrine of election has often seemed to be a difficult one for evangelical theology. On the one hand, evangelical theology is fundamentally grounded on and committed to the gospel – the gospel 'of the Kingdom',[2] the gospel 'of God'.[3] This gospel is to be 'proclaimed to all nations'[4] and indeed 'to all creation':[5] it is news 'of great joy for all the people'.[6] On the other hand, the doctrine of election seems to be a rather more ambiguous affair. While there is a positive dimension to the gracious divine elections of Israel and of the church,[7] Scripture also gives grounds for believing that some will ultimately not be elected. When the Son of Man comes in glory, it is said, there will be a separation of people,[8] such that the 'accursed' will depart from his presence into 'eternal fire'.[9]

In what follows in this chapter, two radically different views of election will be considered. The first section will present and assess the doctrine of election in John Calvin, who memorably wrote of election that '[t]he decree is dreadful indeed, I confess.'[10] The second section will present and assess the doctrine of election in Karl Barth, who referred to election by contrast as 'the sum of the Gospel because of all words that can be said or heard it is the best'.[11] The final section will consider recent evangelical responses to the doctrine of election in Calvin and Barth, and offer some tentative suggestions for contemporary thinking about this most aporetic doctrine.

The doctrine of election in John Calvin

Calvin's doctrine of election is one of the most important and also one of the most difficult in the history of the church. At its heart, Calvin writes the following:

we say that God once established by his eternal and unchangeable plan those whom he long before determined once and for all to receive into salvation, and those whom, on the other hand, he would devote to destruction. We assert that, with respect to the elect, this plan was founded upon his freely given mercy, without regard to human worth; but by his just and irreprehensible but incomprehensible judgment he has barred the door of life to those whom he has given over to damnation.[12]

This is the (in)famous doctrine of double predestination: in 'God's eternal decree', 'eternal life is foreordained for some, eternal damnation for others', and – as a corollary – every individual is 'predestined to life or to death'.[13] If a higher cause than this election is sought, Calvin simply answers with Paul that 'God has predestined it so, and that this is "according to the good pleasure of his will" [Eph. 1:5b]'.[14]

For Calvin, the efficient cause of our salvation is 'the mercy of the Heavenly Father and his freely given love toward us'; however 'the material cause is Christ, with his obedience, through which he acquired righteousness for us'.[15] Calvin thus renders Jesus Christ central to his account of election, positing that, 'Christ interposes himself as mediator ... claim[ing] for himself, in common with the Father, the right to choose', and stating that, correspondingly, 'Christ makes himself the Author of election'.[16] This mediatorial office is accorded to Jesus Christ not by virtue of any simple or absolute necessity, but on account of the Father's 'heavenly decree'[17] – 'God's eternal plan'.[18] Calvin therefore concludes in christocentric fashion that Jesus Christ 'is the mirror wherein we must, and without self-deception may, contemplate our own election'.[19]

While this doctrine of election with its double decree is forever associated with Calvin and the Reformed tradition, it should be noted that Calvin was scarcely an innovator at this point. Christians long before Calvin had taught something resembling this doctrine of double predestination, including Augustine,[20] Thomas Aquinas,[21] and Martin Luther.[22] Indeed, if salvation is by grace alone, and if God is in control of grace, then, unless salvation is universal, something like the doctrine of the double decree syllogistically seems to follow. Finally, Calvin does not need to look far in Scripture to find passages which would offer support for this theological position.[23]

From an evangelical perspective, there are a number of admirable and congenial features in this account of the doctrine of election. As can be seen above, the inability of sinful humans in any way to contribute to or to cooperate in their salvation is steadfastly asserted, and the corresponding graciousness of the mercy of God in the face of human sinfulness is starkly portrayed. The doctrine adamantly maintains the *sola gratia* of the Reformation: Calvin asserts that 'our salvation comes about solely from God's mere generosity'[24] and posits that, far from being the cause of election, any human merit or works that may emerge (or even be foreseen to emerge) are the 'result of election'.[25] Moreover, the doctrine also explicitly affirms the Reformation principle of *sola scriptura*, declaring that 'to seek any other knowledge of predestination than what the Word of God discloses is not less insane than if one should purpose to walk in a pathless waste [cf. Job 12:24], or to see in darkness'.[26] Furthermore, as noted above, it renders at its heart the Reformation *solus Christus*, positing the means of election in the person of Jesus Christ the mediator through the eternal decree of God. Given its good evangelical grounding, it is no surprise that the subsequent Reformed tradition broadly adopted Calvin's formulation of the double decree.[27]

As Calvin is readily aware, however, his account of the doctrine of election raises a number of possible theological problems. He attempts already in the *Institutes* to deal with the most common perceived objections.[28] Perhaps the most troubling objection for an evangelical theology, as will be further contended below, is that the will of God by which double predestination is effected remains for Calvin hidden and inscrutable: 'If you ... ask why [God] so willed, you are seeking something greater and higher than God's will, which cannot be found.'[29] Though Calvin attempts to answer the objections as far as he can, then, he recognizes that God's judgement in this connection remains 'just and irreprehensible but incomprehensible',[30] and concludes that the Christian is 'to tremble with Paul at so deep a mystery ... [and] not to be ashamed of this exclamation of his: "Who are you. O man, to argue with God?" [Rom. 9:20 p]'.[31]

The doctrine of election in Karl Barth

Karl Barth, as a Reformed theologian, was particularly attentive to Calvin and the doctrine of election which Calvin and the subsequent Reformed tradition had espoused.[32] In the course of the development of Barth's theology, however, there emerges a profound awareness of the potential danger of considering the doctrine of predestination *in abstracto* – that is, in an arbitrary or speculative manner which does not do justice to the self-revelation of God in Jesus Christ.[33] Barth believes that Calvin himself ultimately does not manage to evade this danger.

Barth approves of the way in which Calvin structurally sets predestination under the rubric of Book III of the *Institutes*, 'The Way We Receive the Grace of Christ', but wonders whether 'some of the decisive insights which dominate his doctrine of predestination derive from the generally acquired conception of the governance of God's omnipotence and will in the world at large'.[34] The charge is that Calvin, along with others in the Reformed tradition, has tried to do justice to the freedom, mystery and righteousness of God in the election of human beings apart from Jesus Christ. In opposition to this perceived abstraction, Barth declares that '[i]f we allow God's self-revelation and the testimony of Scripture to prescribe our concept, then the Subject of election, the electing God, is not at all the absolute World-ruler as such and in general.'[35] The God of election is not a formless or absolute God, but the God who reveals Godself to us in Jesus Christ.

Barth's epistemological focus on Jesus Christ has the effect of refocusing the doctrine of election – from the destiny of individuals to the destiny of Jesus Christ. Barth writes that the direct and proper object of the divine election of grace 'is not individuals generally, but one individual – and only in Him the people called and united by Him, and only in that people individuals in general in their private relationships with God.'[36] This in itself is not contrary to the tradition. After all, the Reformed tradition had always acknowledged with Scripture (Eph. 1:4) that the election of the individual was 'in Christ'. However, Barth pushes this christological centring of the doctrine of election even further. Barth asks:

> Is it the case that ... while Christ is indeed the medium and instrument of the divine activity at the basis of the election, yet the electing God Himself is not Christ but God the Father, or the triune God, in a decision which precedes the being and will and word of Christ, a hidden God, who as such made ... the actual resolve and decree to save such and such men and to bring them to blessedness, and then later made, as it were, the formal or technical decree and resolve to call the elect and to bring them to that end by means of His Son, by means of His Word and Spirit? Is it the case, then, that in the divine election as such we have to do ultimately, not with a divine decision made in Jesus Christ, but with one which is independent of Jesus Christ and only executed by Him?[37]

This is a significant question, particularly for Calvin. If the question is answered affirmatively, as Barth fears that it is by Calvin, then '[t]he thought of the election becomes necessarily the thought of the will and decision of God which are hidden somewhere in the heights or depths behind Jesus Christ and behind God's revelation.'[38]

This, for Barth, is where Calvin and the Reformed tradition, despite their good intentions, went wrong. They rightly made Jesus Christ the mirror in which Christians contemplate their election, but their doctrine did not go beyond understanding Jesus Christ as the functional or instrumental *means* of that election. The actual *decision* to elect remained somehow above or behind Jesus Christ, in that hidden will of God to which both Luther and Calvin referred. And if Jesus Christ is only the object of election in this way, then we cannot know for certain who the electing God is, let alone who the elect might be: the eternal decree to elect remains an absolute decree – a *decretum absolutum* – that is, in the final analysis, inscrutable.

Barth posits instead that Jesus Christ himself takes the place of the *decretum absolutum*.[39] This is the key innovation which Barth introduces, and it is an innovation with massive ontological implications. For Barth, this means there is no God and no *Logos*, and no inscrutable divine will behind Jesus Christ. Jesus Christ is not only the object of election, the one who is elected; for Barth, Jesus Christ is also the subject of election, the one who elects. The self-revelation of God points for Barth to this stunning conclusion: '[i]n the harmony of the triune God He [Jesus Christ] is no less the original Subject of this electing than He is its original object.'[40] Jesus Christ is not only the elect human,[41] but the electing God.[42] Barth explains:

> As we have to do with Jesus Christ, we have to do with the electing God. For election is obviously the first and basic and decisive thing which we have

always to say concerning this revelation, this activity, this presence of God in the world, and therefore concerning the eternal decree and the eternal self-determination of God which bursts through and is manifested at this point. Already this self-determination, as a confirmation of the free love of God, is itself the election or choice of God.[43]

Barth posits a stark challenge to the alternative position: '[i]f Jesus Christ is only elected, and not also and primarily the Elector, what shall we really know at all of a divine electing and our election?'[44]

The consequence of this understanding of the divine revelation is that the doctrine of election is first and last and in all circumstances the sum of the Gospel. For Barth, the substance of the doctrine is Jesus Christ and its form is the covenant of grace: as such, in both its first word and its last word, it declares the 'Yes' of God and not the 'No'.[45]

This is not to say that Barth ignores the clear scriptural 'No' in the face of sin and evil: Barth retains a clear and explicit doctrine of double predestination. The two aspects of predestination are not conceptualized in connection with two separate groups of people, however; rather the negative aspect of reprobation, in parallel with the positive aspect of election, is noetically revealed in and ontically determined by the person of Jesus Christ. Barth writes that while 'God has ascribed to man ... election, salvation and life ... to Himself He has ascribed ... reprobation, perdition and death.'[46] From all eternity, then, God determines Godself to be the one who in Jesus Christ suffers for the sake of humanity and who is cast out and rejected. Here, then, is the miraculous exchange: 'God has ordained that in the place of the one acquitted He Himself should be perishing and abandoned and rejected – the Lamb slain from the foundation of the world'.[47] The eternal and gracious event of the divine self-determination therefore reaches its historical culmination in the cross (and resurrection and ascension) of Jesus Christ.

The replacement of the *decretum absolutum* by the person of Jesus Christ not only has ramifications for our understanding of the doctrine of election; it also has profound significance for our understanding of the doctrine of God. As the substance of this doctrine is now Jesus Christ, so now there is also drawn an explicit ontic connection between what election is and who God is. This means that election not only grounds the meaning and purpose of the divine *work*, but that it also grounds the divine *being* in the act of the divine self-determination. Barth writes in this connection:

> The election of Jesus Christ is the eternal choice and decision of God. ... In no depth of the Godhead shall we encounter any other but Him. There is no such thing as Godhead in itself. Godhead is always the Godhead of the Father, the Son and the Holy Spirit. But the Father is the Father of Jesus Christ and the Holy Spirit is the Spirit of the Father and the Spirit of Jesus Christ.[48]

It is God who has determined to be God in this way – to be for humanity in Jesus Christ – in eternity, in a way that 'precedes absolutely all other being and happening'.[49] Jesus Christ is therefore the second member of the trinity, not just in respect of God *ad extra*, but also in respect of God *ad intra*. There is no mode of existence in God above and beyond and before God's gracious election, because it is in the very act of election that God freely determines the essence of God in eternity to be for humanity in Jesus Christ. This is the fundament of Barth's doctrine of election, and this is why he declares that election is the sum of the Gospel.

Contemporary evangelical challenges on the doctrine of election

It is clear that the doctrine of election found in the later theology of Barth represents a significant doctrinal development over Calvin's doctrine of election. However, developments in theology – as elsewhere – are not necessarily felicitous: Barth's doctrine of election has been rigorously critiqued by an array of theologians, on the grounds both of its internal consistency and of its external conformity to Scripture and to the theological tradition. Despite Barth's reputation in some quarters for being a theological conservative, some of the most vociferous criticism in this connection has come from evangelical theologians. In what follows, three of the most common concerns expressed in relation to Barth's doctrine of election will be briefly considered and evaluated, and in each case Barth's on-going challenge to evangelical Christians will be outlined.

Universalism

The main criticism of Barth's doctrine of election from evangelical quarters has been the universalism that many commentators have taken to be the logical implication of his account.[50] The argument runs thus: if all human beings are elect in Jesus Christ, and if only Jesus Christ is the object of reprobation, then a doctrine of universal reconciliation – *apokatastasis* – appears a logically necessary consequence. Barth is not unaware of this argument; nevertheless, he refuses to affirm *apokatastasis* as a theologoumenon. On the one hand, he declares resolutely the need to 'respect the freedom of the divine grace' and to avoid giving rise to any (universalist) 'historical metaphysics'.[51] On the other hand, Barth denies that we can set any boundaries on the grace of Christ by means of 'an opposing historical metaphysics' which would 'try to attribute any limits ... to the loving-kindness of God'.[52] The result is, for Barth, that while the church will not preach *apokatastasis*, nor will it 'preach a powerless grace of Jesus Christ or a wickedness of men which is too powerful for it'.[53]

The two main problems that evangelicals find with this argument are as follows. First, it is often contended that Barth's unwillingness to rule out *apokatastasis* runs contrary to the witness of Scripture. Donald Macleod posits, for example, that 'Barth's doctrine on this issue lies unconformably across the biblical strata',[54] while Michael S. Horton suggests in this connection that Barth is simply speculating: 'what other conclusion can there be when the New Testament texts confirm in even darker lines the prophetic anticipation of a final separation of humanity into "saved" and "damned"?'[55] The trouble for such views is that there are passages in Scripture which seem to have a less dualistic eschatology in view.[56] This is not to settle the case, which would require much careful exegetical work, but merely to observe that Scripture is not simply univocal in this matter, and that the scriptural tension deserves to be respected and investigated, and not denigrated or ignored.

Second, it is often contended that Barth's rejection of *apokatastasis* is simply incoherent, for even Barth himself confesses that 'theological consistency might seem to lead our thoughts and utterances most clearly in this direction [*apokatastasis*]'.[57] Oliver D. Crisp writes rather critically of this position: 'to quote Schopenhauer's dictum, an argument is not like a cab. You cannot pay off an argument when you have gone as far as you want.'[58] Whether one considers Barth to be incoherent at this point, however, depends upon the extent to which one recognizes Barth's caveat that 'we must not arrogate to ourselves that which can be given and received only as a free gift'.[59] Alternatively expressed, in the words of Tom Greggs: '[i]f we are to "charge" Barth with universalism, it cannot be a universalism that has been articulated previously.'[60] Any 'universalism' with which Barth can be associated must be a highly particular universalism, one which continues to allow God to be the subject of salvation in Jesus Christ and not one which is founded on an abstract, degraced and ahistorical principle.

While the argument over Barth's stance on universalism will not be settled by such brief remarks, it is clear that Barth's doctrine of election sets a challenge for evangelicals in this connection. Barth contends that 'there is no theological justification for setting any limits on our side to the friendliness of God toward man which appeared in Jesus Christ'.[61] The challenge is to ensure that evangelical Christians, in all their ministries of preaching and teaching and witness, never seek to limit the grace of God that confronts humanity in Jesus Christ. It is not the task of human beings to divide people into Christians and non-Christians temporally, or into elect and reprobate eternally. Rather, we are to attest the Gospel as the Good News of Jesus Christ to and for all, in the hope that it might work its gracious outcome in all places and in all hearts, and in an appropriate agnostic humility about where this might be happening.[62]

Ontology

Another common criticism of Barth from evangelical quarters – particularly in recent literature – concerns the doctrine of God which arises out of Barth's doctrine of election. If we follow Barth's argument to its conclusion (or, perhaps better, its source), it seems that the doctrine of election, the eternal decree in which God determines God's Being in eternity, in an important sense precedes the doctrine of the trinity. Barth writes:

in Himself, in the primal and basic decision in which He wills to be and actually is God, in the mystery of what takes place from and to all eternity within

Himself, within His triune being, God is none other than the One who in His Son or Word elects Himself, and in and with Himself elects His people. In so far as God not only is love, but loves, in the act of love which determines His whole being God elects.[63]

If the incarnation of Jesus Christ is thus constitutive of the being of God in eternity, then, it must be the case that, for Barth, in a formulation made famous by Bruce McCormack, the act of election logically precedes the triunity of God.[64]

Evangelical critics have raised the question of the subject of this act of self-determination: who is the God who is determining Godself to be God in this way? The concern is twofold. First, Barth's view seems to make the action of a subject prior to the existence of the subject itself. Paul Helm posits on the contrary that '[t]he act of electing must be the action of someone; it cannot be an act of no-one that, upon its occurrence, constitutes the agent as a someone'.[65] Second, and consequently, Barth's view seems – against his explicit intention – to assume an unknown and hidden subject *behind* the act of election. Edwin Chr. van Driel, for example, therefore asks, 'what subject precedes the divine choice?'[66] The fear is that Barth is setting up a (modalist or Sabellian) God behind the trinity who makes the decision to be trinitarian.

How might one briefly respond on behalf of Barth to these two concerns?

In respect of the first concern, one might note initially that it betrays a very substantialist mode of thinking, wherein substances are complete and definable in themselves above any historical action or relation. The corollary to this is that in order for there to be an action, there must be a subject. This might be intuitively satisfying (and perhaps even true) for contingent beings such as human agents; but to assume that it holds for God without further analysis is nothing less than anthropomorphic speculation without biblical foundation. The Christian tradition has traditionally held that God is *actus purus* – pure act, and Barth adds to this simply the qualification '*et singularis*' (and singular/unique), in order to indicate that 'God is ... the One who is event, act and life in His own way, as distinct from everything that He is not Himself'.[67] Barth further posits that '[s]eeking and finding God in His revelation, we cannot escape the action of God for a God who is not active.'[68] God is always in action: God's actions correspond perfectly to God's essence and *vice versa*. This is in no instance more true than in the act in which God determines God's own being in eternity to be for humanity in Jesus Christ. McCormack comments here that 'while it is true that there is no act (or decision) without a subject, the identity of that subject may not be distinguished from the identity of God as constituted *in* the event in which God chooses to be God "for us"'.[69]

In respect of the second concern, one might note again the underlying substantialist view of God. In this connection, the corresponding assumption is well, if unwittingly, expressed by Sung Wook Chung, who writes that '[m]ost evangelical theologians believe that the God of the Bible is a self-contained Being who has his own unique substance and nature'.[70] It is precisely this conception of the 'God of the Bible' that Barth wishes to challenge, and he wishes to challenge it precisely because he does not believe that it represents the 'God of the Bible' at all. Barth writes:

> When we have to do with Jesus Christ we do have to do with an 'economy' but not with the kind of economy in which His true and proper being remains behind an improper being, a being 'as if.' We have to do with an economy in which God is truly Himself and Himself acts and intervenes in the world.[71]

For Barth, then, God is truly Godself in Jesus Christ: there is no self-contained God over and above this decision. As to the identity of the 'decision-Maker', however, we can perhaps gain an initial approach to the solution by recognizing that, for Barth, God is one subject in three modes of being. According to Barth, then, in this eternal decision of election 'God posits Himself as the Father, is posited by Himself as the Son and confirms Himself as the Holy Ghost'.[72] There is therefore only the one subject in God: positing in a first mode as Father, being posited in a second mode as Son, and confirming the decision in a third mode as Spirit. In this sense, then, the Father might be considered to be – strictly speaking – the primary 'subject' of election; however, precisely as the one subject in Father, Son, and Spirit, there is no 'hidden' Father here. Barth declares that:

> He is the same as the Son, i.e., as the self-posited God (the eternally begotten of the Father as the dogma has it) as is the Father as the self-positing God (the Father who eternally begets). ... The Son is therefore the One who ... shows and affirms and activates and reveals Himself – shows Himself to be the One He is – not another, a second God, but the Son of God, the one God in His mode of being as the Son.[73]

In this way, it can be seen that, for Barth, the Son is finally the same subject as the Father and thus that the Son can also be accounted the 'subject' of the eternal divine act of election. God is one person in these three modes of being.

While the argument over Barth's view of the divine being will not be settled by such brief remarks, it is clear that Barth's doctrine of election sets another challenge for evangelicals at this point. Barth demands that we abandon metaphysical pre-suppositions when we encounter the revelation of Jesus Christ and that we allow God to tell us who God is. We must follow Barth's practice, in John Colwell's words, of 'humble reflection (*nachdenkend*), a commitment to take the event of God's Word seriously as the event of His self-definition'.[74] And this means, according to Barth's doctrine of election, that we must be prepared to take on board the possibility – which is at no point discounted by Scripture – that there is no Son or Word of God who is not Jesus Christ, that there is no difference in content between the immanent trinity and the economic trinity, and that it is in the decision to be for us in Jesus Christ that God determines God's own being.

Freedom

A third (and subsequent) criticism of Barth from evangelical quarters is connected with the freedom of God which arises out of Barth's doctrine of election. Paul

Molnar contends in this connection that 'the order between election and triunity cannot be logically reversed without in fact making creation, reconciliation and redemption necessary to God'.[75] Edwin van Driel concurs, arguing that, for Barth, 'since creation is logically implied by election and incarnation, creation is constitutive of divine being'.[76] In other words, if we somehow posit the decision to become incarnate as integral to the essence of God in eternity, then we render God in some way dependent on creation.

We are left wondering, however, whether this view of Molnar and van Driel does justice to the freedom of God as Barth himself describes it, or whether they are actually retreating to the kind of abstracted notion of absolute divine freedom which Barth shuns. Barth writes:

> God must not only be unconditioned but, in the absoluteness in which He sets up this fellowship, He can and will also be conditioned. He who can and does do this is the God of Holy Scripture, the triune God known to us in His revelation. This ability, proved and manifested to us in His action, constitutes His freedom.[77]

The freedom of God is not a form without content: rather, it is a very particular freedom which, without ceasing to be freedom, allows itself to be conditioned and determined from outwith. It is a freedom chosen freely, elected even, and exercised freely. And therefore, as Kevin Hector argues, 'to suggest that God cannot use God's freedom to bind Godself ... would be to make God a servant of God's freedom and thus "God" a predicate of "freedom" rather than vice-versa'.[78] Instead, the freedom of God is not naked and sovereign without further specification. God is not faceless or tyrannical; nor is God capricious or random. As Barth writes, 'His rule is determined and limited: self-determined and self-limited, but determined and limited none the less'.[79]

In an eternal yet free decision, then, God determines Godself to be bound to humanity. Barth explains in respect of the event of the atonement, the historical culmination of that determination, that:

> If we can speak of a necessity of any kind here, it can only be the necessity of the decision which God did in fact make and execute, the necessity of the fact that the being of God, the omnipotence of His free love, has this concrete determination.[80]

The eternal decision of election, then, in which God determines God's being to be for humanity in Jesus Christ, is a decision taken in the absence of external compulsion and condition: God remains free! Barth declares that 'in so far as this act of love is an election, it is at the same time and as such the act of His freedom'.[81] However, Barth posits that, precisely on the basis of the *freedom* in which God eternally determines God's own being in election, there arises – *a posteriori* – a certain and very particular *necessity* in respect of what will transpire in the history of Jesus

Christ. Within the covenant of grace which this history constitutes, the ontological distinction between Jesus Christ and the rest of humanity is at no point abrogated, and what is 'essential' to God takes place in Jesus Christ alone and not in us. In this way, the freedom of God in respect of the creation is preserved at every step.[82]

The argument over whether or not Barth's view of the doctrine of election compromises the freedom of God will no doubt continue. Yet, whatever its final outcome, if such there is to be, it is clear that Barth's theology at this point bequeaths the evangelical tradition a particular challenge in this dimension also. The challenge is to understand the freedom of God as it is revealed to us in Jesus Christ and not elsewhere. It is not the task of evangelical theologians to import Enlightenment or other anthropological ideas of freedom into the divine life, but to allow the witness of Scripture to speak for itself as to the form and content of the freedom of God. This freedom is therefore to be sought precisely within God's loving decision to enter into a covenant of grace with us in Jesus Christ and in the necessity to which God is therewith freely compelled.

Conclusion

It was posited at the beginning of the chapter that the doctrine of election is to be approached with humility and lack of prejudice. To acknowledge at the end of the chapter that the doctrine remains a source of both controversy and mystery is not so much to admit defeat; it is perhaps rather to recognize that, at certain points in the theological endeavour, a line might have to be drawn beyond which one must ultimately fall silent before the majesty of the triune God of grace. The glass remains dark this side of the days to come. At the same time, it must continually and ever anew be asserted that if evangelical theologians and evangelical Christians are to learn about the God whom they worship, it must be God who reveals such knowledge to us. As Barth noted, in words that Calvin would approve: '[God] shows Himself to be more great and rich and sovereign than we had ever imagined. And our ideas of His nature must be guided by this, and not *vice versa*.'[83] In allowing human thought to be taken captive over and again by the glory of God revealed in Jesus Christ, it may be that our theology has ever new places to go in its explorations of Christian doctrine.

Notes

1 J. L. Garrett, *Systematic Theology: Biblical, Historical, Evangelical*, 2 vols, Grand Rapids, MI: Eerdmans, 1995, vol. II, p. 433.
2 Cf. Mt. 4:23, 9:35, 24:14; Luke 4:43, 8:1, 16:16; and Acts 8:12.
3 Cf. Mk 1:14; Rom. 1:1, 15:16; 1 Thess. 2:2, 2:8, 2:9; 1 Tim. 1:11; and 1 Pet. 4:17.
4 Mk 13:10.
5 Mk 16:15.
6 Lk. 2:10. It is news 'of God's grace' (Acts 20:24), news of 'the power of God for salvation to everyone who has faith' (Rom. 1:16; cf. Eph. 1:13).
7 The election of Israel in Scripture is rooted in the Abrahamic covenant (Gen. 12:2) and in the Mosaic Exodus (Exod. 3:10). The election of the church would seem to apply both

to the church as a whole (cf. 'You are a chosen race, a royal priesthood, a holy nation' [1 Pet. 2:9]) and to the church considered as individuals (cf. 'You did not choose me but I chose you' [Jn 15:16]).

8 Mt. 25:32.

9 Mt. 25:41.

10 J. Calvin, *Institutes of the Christian Religion*, Louisville, KY: WJKP, 2006, II.xxiii.7 – '*Decretum quidem horribile, fateor.*'

11 K. Barth, *Church Dogmatics*, 4 vols in 13 parts, eds G. W. Bromiley and T. F. Torrance, Edinburgh: T&T Clark, 1956–75 [hereafter: *CD*], II/2, p. 3.

12 Calvin, *Institutes*, III.xxi.7.

13 Ibid., III.xxi.5. Calvin later implies a certain symmetry to the two outcomes of foreordination, insisting that 'election itself could not stand except as set over against reprobation' (III.xxiii.1, cf. III.xxiv.12). However, a certain tension in this symmetry later becomes evident: while the cause of *election* is always unequivocally attested to be the divine 'good pleasure' (III.xxi.1), Calvin later argues that one should 'contemplate the evident cause of *condemnation* in the corrupt nature of humanity – which is closer to us – rather than seek a hidden and utterly incomprehensible cause in God's predestination' (III.xxiii.8). If Calvin's intention to avoid ascribing sin or caprice to God is clear, the result is less than convincing.

14 Ibid., III.xxii.2.

15 Ibid., III.xiv.17.

16 Ibid., III.xxii.7.

17 Ibid., II.xii.1.

18 Ibid., II.xii.4. It is significant that Calvin renders the decree to elect prior to the decree to appoint Jesus Christ as Mediator.

19 Ibid., III.xxiv.5.

20 Augustine, 'The Enchiridion on Faith, Hope, and Charity', 26 (100), in *On Christian Belief*, New York: New City Press, 2005, p. 331.

21 T. Aquinas, *Summa Theologiae*, New York: Benzinger, 1947, 1a.23.3 and 1a.23.5 ad 3.

22 M. Luther, 'On the Bondage of the Will', in P. S. Watson, *Luther and Erasmus: Free Will and Salvation*, Louisville, KY: WJKP, 2006, pp. 200, 206–7.

23 Gospel texts such as Mt. 3.11–12 and 25.31–46 point clearly to such a soteriological dualism, albeit without linking directly to the theme of election.

24 Calvin, *Institutes*, III.xxi.1.

25 Ibid., III.xxii.2. Calvin later explicitly affirms that election does not depend on faith, for 'it is false to say that election takes effect only after we have embraced the gospel, and takes its validity from this' (III.xxiv.3).

26 Ibid., III.xxi.2.

27 One might mention the *French Confession* (1559), xii; the *Scots Confession* (1560), viii; the *Belgic Confession* (1561/1619), xvi; and the *Second Helvetic Confession* (1566), 10, all found in A. C. Cochrane (ed.) *Reformed Confessions of the 16th Century*, Philadelphia, PA: Westminster Press, 1966, which attest a clear soteriological dualism. The explicit double decree is found in the *Irish Confessions* (1615), 12; the *Canons of Dort* (1619) I.vi; and the *Westminster Confession* (1647), III.iii, found in P. Schaff (ed.) *The Creeds of Christendom*, vol. 3, Grand Rapids, MI: Baker Books, 1998. These understandings of election are resolutely christocentric throughout in terms of the mediatorship of Christ in time and the eternality of the decree by which Christ was appointed to that office.

28 The objections Calvin considers (and attempts to refute) in respect of his doctrine of election are: that it renders God a tyrannical figure (*Institutes*, III.xxiii.2–5); that it removes guilt and responsibility from human beings (III.xxiii.6–9); that it involves a divine partiality (III.xxiii.10–11); that it destroys any motivation towards for good action (III.xxiii.12); and that it renders all exhortation to good action meaningless (III.xiii.13).

29 Ibid., III.xxiii.2.
30 Ibid., III.xxiii.7.
31 Ibid., III.xxiv.17.
32 Indeed, in his early work, as McDonald notes, Barth's understanding of predestination is 'emphatically individual, unconditional and double in accordance with the strictest Reformed orthodoxy', in S. McDonald, 'Barth's Other Election', *International Journal of Systematic Theology*, 2007, vol. 9.2, 137.
33 *CD* II/2, p. 59.
34 Ibid., p. 46. Barth makes a similar criticism of the later Reformed tradition, noting that '[i]nto the doctrine of predestination there was now brought as a ruling concept that of the general, absolutely free divine disposing' (p. 46) – 'the error of supposing that God is irresistibly efficacious power *in abstracto*, naked freedom and sovereignty as it were' (p. 45).
35 Ibid., p. 49.
36 Ibid., p. 43. Again, Barth states that '[i]f we listen to what Scripture says concerning man, then at the point where our attention and thoughts are allowed to rest there is revealed an elect man, *the* elect man, and united in Him and represented by Him an elect people' (p. 58). Clear priority is thus afforded by Barth to the election of Christ as being over and encompassing the election of the church.
37 Ibid., p. 64.
38 Ibid.
39 Ibid., p. 75.
40 Ibid., p. 105. In his accompanying argumentation, Barth draws heavily on Jn 1:1–2.
41 Ibid., p. 116.
42 Ibid., p. 103.
43 Ibid., p. 54.
44 Ibid., p. 105.
45 Ibid., p. 13. For Barth, indeed, the problem for theology came when the book of life came to be spoken of as if it contained a death column (p. 16). He reproaches Calvin's doctrine in particular on this count:

> All the dubious features of Calvin's doctrine result from the basic failing that in the last analysis he separates God and Jesus Christ. ... Thus with all his forceful and impressive acknowledgment of the divine election of grace, ultimately he still passes by the grace of God as it has appeared in Jesus Christ.
>
> (p. 110)

46 Ibid., p. 163.
47 Ibid., p. 167. Crisp has argued that 'to suggest God incarnate is the subject of a divine decree that has two aspects, reprobation and election, is to suggest something simply inconceivable given other orthodox theological commitments'; in O. Crisp, 'Karl Barth and Jonathan Edwards on Reprobation (and Hell)', in D. Gibson and D. Strange (eds) *Engaging with Barth: Contemporary Evangelical Critiques*, Nottingham: Apollos (IVP), 2008, p. 307. This seems an unnecessary conclusion, however, and rests on the imposition of a univocal reading of the terms 'election' and 'reprobation' as used by Barth in respect of Jesus Christ and of (the rest of) humanity; not even Calvin's teaching would pass this test of univocality.
48 *CD* II/2, p. 115.
49 Ibid., pp. 99–100.
50 There is an extensive literature on the subject of Barth and universalism. For two articles which cover much of the necessary ground, see O. D. Crisp, 'The *Letter* and the *Spirit* of Barth's Doctrine of Universalism', *Evangelical Quarterly*, 2007, vol. 79.1, 53–67, and T. Greggs, ' "Jesus is Victor": Passing the Impasse of Barth on Universalism', *Scottish Journal of Theology*, 2007, vol. 60.2 , 196–212.

51 *CD* II/2, p. 417. Barth writes: 'we must not arrogate to ourselves that which can be given and received only as a free gift' (*CD* IV/3, p. 477).
52 *CD* II/2, p. 418.
53 Ibid., p. 477.
54 D. Macleod, '"Church" Dogmatics: Karl Barth as Ecclesial Theologian', in Gibson and Strange (eds) *Engaging with Barth*, p. 339.
55 M. S. Horton, 'A Stony Jar: The Legacy of Karl Barth for Evangelical Theology', in Gibson and Strange (eds) *Engaging with Barth*, p. 366.
56 Cf. Ezek. 33:11; Rom. 8:38–9 and 11:32; 2 Cor. 5:19; Phil. 2:10–11; and 1 Tim. 1:4.
57 *CD* IV/3, p. 477.
58 Crisp, 'The *Letter* and the *Spirit*', p. 64.
59 *CD* IV/3, p. 477.
60 Tom Greggs, ' "Jesus is Victor" ', p. 212.
61 Karl Barth, 'The Humanity of God', in *God, Grace and Gospel*, Edinburgh: Oliver & Boyd, 1959, pp. 49–50.
62 Cf. Tom Greggs, ch. 11 this volume, pp. 153–67.
63 *CD* II/2, p. 76. Or again: '[i]t is in the decision in favour of this movement [towards humanity], in God's self-determination and the resultant determination of man ... that God is who He is' (p. 52).
64 B. McCormack, 'Grace and Being', in J. Webster (ed.) *The Cambridge Companion to Karl Barth*, Cambridge: Cambridge University Press, 2000, pp. 101–4. This reading of Barth is not unanimously accepted: see G. Hunsinger, 'Election and the Trinity: Twenty-five Theses on the Theology of Karl Barth', *Modern Theology*, 2008, vol. 24.2, 179–98.
65 P. Helm, 'Karl Barth and the Visibility of God' in Gibson and Strange (eds) *Engaging with Barth*, p. 284.
66 E. Chr. van Driel, 'Karl Barth on the Eternal Existence of Jesus Christ', *Scottish Journal of Theology*, 2007, vol. 60.1, 54. This, for van Driel, is not a temporal problem, but 'a logical and ontological one' (p. 56).
67 *CD* II/1, p. 264.
68 Ibid., p. 263.
69 B. McCormack, 'Seek God Where He May Be Found: A Response to Edwin Chr. van Driel', *Scottish Journal of Theology*, 2007, vol. 60.1, 67.
70 S. W. Chung, 'A Bold Innovator: Barth on God and Election', in S. W. Chung (ed.) *Karl Barth and Evangelical Theology: Convergences and Divergences*, Milton Keynes: Paternoster and Grand Rapids, MI: Baker, 2006, p. 64. Chung denies Barth's contention that God's being is always a being in act on the grounds that it 'is a pattern of thought that the Bible does not endorse explicitly or implicitly' ('A Bold Innovator', p. 64), without pausing either to examine Barth's copious supporting quotations from Scripture and the tradition (*CD* II/1, p. 263) or to 'endorse' his own position from Scripture.
71 *CD* IV/1, p. 198.
72 *CD* III/2, p. 220.
73 *CD* IV/1, p. 209.
74 J. Colwell, *Actuality and Provisionality: Election and Eternity in the Theology of Karl Barth*, Edinburgh: Rutherford House, 1989, p. 203.
75 P. D. Molnar, *Divine Freedom and the Doctrine of the Immanent Trinity*, London: T&T Clark, 2002, p. 63.
76 Van Driel, 'Karl Barth on the Eternal Existence of Jesus Christ', p. 54.
77 *CD* II/1, p. 303.
78 K. W. Hector, 'God's Triunity and Self-Determination: A Conversation with Karl Barth, Bruce McCormack and Paul Molnar', *International Journal of Systematic Theology*, 2005, vol. 7.3, 256.
79 *CD* II/2, p. 50.

80 *CD* IV/1, p. 213. Barth writes that '[i]t takes place in the freedom of God, but in the inner *necessity* of the *freedom* of God and not in the play of a sovereign *liberum arbitrium*. There is no possibility of something quite different happening' (p. 195), emphasis added. There is thus no contradiction between necessity and freedom at this point, for Barth. What is clear is that the historical events of the life and death of Jesus Christ follow by necessity from the eternal free decision of God to elect to be for humanity. That this decision is said to be free rests upon the recognition that the decision is one of grace. Whether God could have decided differently is entirely a matter of speculation, and is thus unworthy of theological attention; given the divine ontology which Barth advances, furthermore, it does not need to involve any reassertion of a 'hiddenness' of God, *pace* Helm, 'Karl Barth and the Visibility of God', pp. 287, 290.

81 *CD* II/2, p. 76.

82 McCormack, 'Seek God where he may be found', p. 70.

83 *CD* IV/1, p. 186.

Select bibliography

Barth, K., *Church Dogmatics* II/2, Edinburgh: T&T Clark, 1957.

Calvin, J., *Institutes of the Christian Religion*, Louisville, KY: WJKP, 2006.

Muller, R. A., *Christ and the Decree*, Durham, NC: Labyrinth, 1986.

McCormack, B. L., *Orthodox and Modern*, Grand Rapids, MI: Baker, 2008.

Chapter 4

The atonement

God's love in action

Paul Dafydd Jones

Is there an evangelical view of the atonement? The best short answer to the question: no, of course there is not. From a historical angle, the diverse character of evangelical life undermines most summary statements. While one might plausibly propose a set of 'family resemblances', no static essence awaits definite description here. There is only a disorganized cluster of lives, ideas and commitments, scattered across various times and places; a movement that has taken various forms in the past and will undergo countless transformations in the future. From a dogmatic angle, that which guides evangelical thinking militates against a settled position. Scripture does not enshrine as authoritative a single view of Christ's reconciling life and death. It offers instead a disarray of motifs, metaphors and concepts – a discursive jumble, the coherence of which is less a matter of logical consistency, more a consequence of the event to which reference is made. Indeed, since Scripture points away from itself in diverse ways, the provisional standing of all claims about atonement seems undeniable. Dogmatic closure is neither desirable nor possible: *a posteriori* statements do not and cannot encompass the *a priori* 'actuality' of atonement.[1]

So let us begin differently. How could the reconciling life and death of Jesus Christ be conceptualized in an evangelical (or, more broadly, an *evangelisch*) context? What new theological perspectives, in particular, does this event provoke? To answer these questions, this chapter begins with an interpretation of John Calvin. It considers Calvin's presentation of God's jealous love for God's people, Christ's vicarious obedience, and the Spirit's application of God's grace. My second section pursues a more constructive agenda. Drawing inspiration from various quarters, I sketch an outlook that foregrounds God's startling love for humankind, identifies Christ as one whose history proves ontologically determinative of God's second way of being and of humanity as such, and construes Christ's death as the event in which God and humanity condemn, defeat and renounce sin. Finally, after some summary comments, I affirm the need for 'ethicized' reflection on the atonement.

Calvin on the atonement

Although Calvin is often portrayed as a theologian obsessed with the bare fact of divine sovereignty, a keen sense of God's *love* supplies the starting point for his view of atonement. For sure, the Christian often struggles to apprehend this love. Although he or she wants desperately to enjoy the benefits of Christ's reconciling life and death, ingratitude and disobedience are the order of the day: Paul's memorable description of the 'divided self' in Romans 7 tells a familiar story. Yet the struggle to live Christianly is enabled by a piety grounded in, and responsive to, God's 'pure liberality'.[2] God's solicitude for creation, God's covenant with Israel, the Law and Prophets, and, most dramatically, the missions of the Son and Spirit – these actions, not our mediocrity and faithlessness, define a life both justified and sanctified. As such, while none can shuck off the 'ruin and destruction of our nature' and all contend with a deep-set drift towards rebellion, a scripturally invigorated faith is always moving away from despair and towards a delighted reception of God's generosity.[3] God's people approach God not as a judge but as a loving Father – a name that 'suggests only the idea of pure kindness'.[4]

The atonement makes possible this approach to God. Calvin's understanding of it can be described in three steps, the first of which identifies the incarnation as the realization of God's primordial commitment to relate graciously to his people. 'Christ', Calvin writes, 'was promised from the beginning ... to restore the fallen world and to succor lost men'; he alone forms 'the material cause ... of eternal election'.[5] Doubtless, theologians must proceed cautiously at this point. Exegesis must be the dominant mode of reflection; debates about divine decrees, as later occurred between supralapsarians and infralapsarians, risks replacing attention to the biblical witness with freewheeling speculation. Yet, because Calvin wants to present God's love for humanity as *jealous* – that is, fiercely committed to bringing God's people into a meaningful covenantal relationship – claims about God's primordial promise, God's decree and God's eternal plan play an important role in theological writing. They identify the 'why' behind the incarnation. Although humanity willfully embraces sin (and God foreknew as much), in no way does God concede this condition to us. God has always made the decision to incarnate and to save his people; God's enactment of this decision, in the person of Jesus Christ, defines the economy of salvation.

Who, then, is Jesus Christ? On the one hand, he is the only-begotten Son. He is a 'real hypostasis, or subsistence, in the essence of God'; he is therefore uniquely able to 'magnify the fervour of the love of God towards us'.[6] The assumption of human nature, importantly, does not denude the Son of divine attributes. Beyond insisting that the concrete person of Christ possesses the attributes proper to deity, Calvin gestures towards what is later called the *extra calvinisticum*. The Son is not confined by the humanity he assumes; while incarnate, he continues to govern, order and pervade all of creation.[7] Still, Christ truly is Emmanuel, 'God with us'. His life, death and resurrection ensure the covenantal relationship for which we yearn, but fail constantly to effect. On the other hand, and granted that the *hypostasis* definitive of Christ's person is the divine Son, Christ is wholly human, possessing the characteristics associable with human being. Just as Christ's '[d]ivinity retains all that is peculiar to itself', so 'his humanity holds separately whatever belongs to it'.[8] And what 'belongs' to humanity? Calvin tackles the issue boldly.

Christ neither possesses only the formal attributes of human being nor exists in a prelapsarian condition. Rather, he embraces the misery and wickedness of *fallen* humanity. So, while talk of the Son taking on 'sinful flesh' might be a stretch, to state simply that Christ shares our 'common infirmities' would be saying too little. Christ involves himself in the strife, ambiguity and intransigent disobedience that characterize fallen life and, ultimately, undergoes God's judgment against it. The reason for his so living is soteriological. Although God alone pardons sin, it is 'necessary that the disobedience committed by man against God should be expiated ... in human nature'.[9] Through Christ, in fact, humanity helps bring about the salvation that God intends. Covenantal disobedience is not disregarded; the guilty party takes responsibility for its waywardness and is refashioned as an obedient servant.

Thus the second step of Calvin's understanding of atonement – an account of Christ's obedience, rendered to God the Father. One might say that this obedience is at once comprehensive, difficult and vicarious – three qualities that highlight Calvin's attention to the details of the scriptural witness and his emphasis on Christ's humanity. The *comprehensiveness* of Christ's obedience is evidenced throughout the commentaries and given concise statement in the *Institutes*. In the latter text, Calvin asks: 'How has Christ abolished sin, banished the separation between us and God, and acquired righteousness to render God favorable and kindly towards us?' He answers: 'he has achieved this for us by the whole course of his obedience ... the basis of the pardon that frees us from the curse of the law [is] the whole life of Christ.'[10] The purpose of salvation (making humanity obedient to God) and the means of salvation (a human life thoroughly obedient to God), then, are coextensive. It is not just Christ's death that brings salvation; also important is his 'ministry', for it discloses what God demands of his covenant partners. The *difficulty* of Christ's obedience becomes evident at key moments in the *Institutes*, especially when Calvin considers Gethsemane and the *descensus ad infernos*. Constitutive of Christ's atoning history is his voluntarily embracing an end more horrifying than that which other humans undergo. In pursuit of our salvation, he must lead himself to the place in which the world's sins are loaded upon him; he must take on the 'role of a guilty man and an evildoer' and stand condemned before the Father.[11] Indeed, Christ's willingness to become the 'man of sorrows ... wounded for our transgressions' (Is. 53.3 and 5 [KJV]) *enables* God to convey his fury towards sin. Precisely because Christ, discerning what was needful to effect salvation, 'placed himself in our room, and thus became a sinner', God's anger is outworked against the right object.[12] It follows, also, that Christ's atoning death cannot be considered an intradivine transaction, with the Father and Son contending with sin by way of divine fiat. Although the divine Son brings God's saving love to humankind, the concrete person of Jesus Christ makes atonement. Divinely *and* humanly he bears the brunt of God's wrath; he lays down his life in order that God's people might be reckoned righteous. As Calvin puts it, 'when Christ is hanged upon the cross, *he makes himself* subject to the curse'.[13] Indeed, for this reason Christ's obedience must be deemed *vicarious*. God's love passes through the horror of Calvary – a 'conclusion' to Christ's life that he intends, seeks and, in a significant way, effects.

Is there a particular model of atonement operative here? Does Calvin transpose Anselm's 'feudal' outlook into a legal context, updating *Cur Deus Homo* to make it comprehensible for his time? These are not really the right questions. Although Calvin obviously uses juridical rhetoric, his best writing juxtaposes terms from different 'language games' to describe the atonement. In a crucial section of the *Institutes*, for instance, Calvin mixes the motifs of satisfaction, sacrifice, punishment and warfare: Christ took 'Adam's place in obeying the Father, to present our flesh as the price of satisfaction to God's righteous judgement and, in the same flesh, to pay the penalty that we had deserved ... he vanquished death and sin together that the victory and triumph might be ours'.[14] Later, he even risks an Abelardian flourish: 'Will ... man not then be even more moved by all these things which so vividly portray the greatness of the calamity from which he has been rescued?'[15] The reason for such diversity of expression is that Calvin has no interest in discrete 'models' of atonement. He prefers a *mimetic* style of writing. A commitment to the principle of *sola scriptura* spurs him to recall the way in which biblical authors 'mix metaphors' when describing the atonement; his goal in so doing is to re-accustom readers to the figurative pluralism of the text that governs Christian life and thought. And, to reiterate a point made earlier, whatever the apparent incongruity of the language games employed, Calvin's description of the atonement does not chance upon coherence. As with the Bible, dogmatic cogency is secured by way of the event to which Calvin refers – Christ's reconciling life and death. This concrete occurrence, accessed by way of Scripture and made vital by the Spirit's witness, engenders, dynamizes and makes coherent a dogmatic perspective that utilizes multiple conceptual schemes.

Yet dispensing with textbookish talk about 'models' of atonement only makes more urgent some difficult questions. To wit: Why is Christ's *death* necessary? Why is this expiation and propitiation (*hilasterion* encompasses both meanings) required?[16] Two longer quotations – one from the first edition of the *Institutes*, the other from Calvin's commentary on Isaiah – prove useful at this juncture.

> Jesus Christ ... put on our flesh, to enter a covenant with us and to join us (far separated from God by our sins) closely to him. He also by the merit of his death paid our debts to God's justice, and appeased his wrath. He redeemed us from the curse and judgment that bound us, and in his body the punishment of sin, so as to absolve us from it. Descending to earth, he brought with him all the rich heavenly blessings and with a lavish hand showered them upon us.[17]

> *The chastisement of our peace* [Is. 53:5] ... I take to denote simply reconciliation. Christ was the price of 'our chastisement,' that is, of the chastisement that was due to us. Thus the wrath of God, which had been justly kindled against us, was appeased; and through the Mediator we have obtained 'peace,' by which we are reconciled.[18]

Notice, first of all, that sin is met by God's just punishment. Juridical phraseology accentuates the point: God's relationship with humankind is inclusive of human responsibilities that, if left unfulfilled, deserve reproof. This does not mean that God is an inflexible ethical rigorist, nor that God is 'quick to anger'. At issue is the consistency of the divine identity and the consistent way in which God deals with humankind. God punishes because a covenantal relationship requires that human action be taken seriously. Were God to accede to a relationship with a pervasively flawed people, God would not only appear to impugn his sovereign regard for humankind but, far worse, would 'settle' for humanity being less than what it should be – a humanity tormented by its failures, made miserable by the propagation of wickedness, and incapable of genuine service. Nevertheless, in an act of long-suffering patience, God forestalls his full punishment of sin until the moment at which Christ is nailed to the cross. Only then does God punish without inhibition. Calvary, one might say, provides God with the occasion to be true to God's own self; Christ's obedience-unto-death enables God, finally, to articulate an identity both perfectly loving and perfectly just. On the one hand, Christ makes himself a target for God's attack on sin. He disposes himself as one willing to bear the full force of God's just wrath. God's wrath then strikes home, in part because Christ offers himself as a vicarious substitute, with the punishment owed to us transferred to him, in part because Christ willingly *pays* for sin, rendering himself a propitiatory offering. (For this reason, incidentally, Calvin often counterpoises descriptions of priestly intercession and juridical condemnation: the former paradigm underscores Christ's 'giving himself up', the latter accentuates Christ's 'passivity' in face of God's wrath.)[19] On the other hand, since Christ concludes his earthly life in this way, the peace that defines God's life now gains uninhibited articulation – a perfect counterpoint to God's unchecked outburst of wrath. In light of Christ's expiatory and propitiatory death, God relates to us as a loving Father. God does not see our sin; God sees only Christ's perfect obedience, exercised on our behalf. We are both covered by, and clothed in, Christ's righteousness.

This brings us to the third aspect of Calvin's understanding of atonement – the action of the Spirit in conferring the *beneficii Christi*. The 1536 *Institutes* again proves useful. Commenting on the third section of the Apostles' Creed, Calvin writes:

> We are persuaded that there is for us no other guide and leader to the Father than the Holy Spirit, just as there is no other way than Christ ... the Holy Spirit, while dwelling in us ... illumines us with his light, in order that we may learn and plainly recognize what an enormous wealth of divine goodness we possess in Christ. He kindles our hearts with the fire of love, both toward God and toward neighbor, and day by day He boils away and burns up the vices of our inordinate desire, so that if there are in us any good works they are the fruits and powers of his grace.[20]

The key claim: the Spirit *applies* the salvation that Christ effects. On one level, this application has noetic dimensions. In delivering the existentially vital and justifying knowledge that 'God is our merciful Father, because of reconciliation effected through Christ', the Spirit enables the believer to apprehend her incorporation into Christ and consciously to enjoy the benefits Christ wins.[21] Indeed, only as the Spirit works in the Christian's mind and heart, superintending the reading of Scripture and ecclesial life, does she recognize herself to be justified and set on the path to sanctification. On another level, the action of the Spirit ramifies practically. Graced by Christ's Spirit, the Christian is emboldened to suffer mortification, to delight in a joyous vivification, and to express God's love for humanity with saintly works inside and outside the church. Christ's atoning work prompts worship of God and service to all humankind.

While various assessments could be offered at this point, I want initially to draw attention to the breadth of Calvin's vision, since this helps to chart the critical and constructive course ahead. By 'breadth' I mean that, for Calvin, Christ's vicarious death forms but one moment in a far-reaching theological statement. The part cannot be detached from the whole; as an 'episode' in the scriptural story that Calvin (re)tells, the passion must be understood in light of God's primordial commitment to God's people, God's patient forbearance of sin, God's self-giving, and God's activity in and for the church. Now, can atonement be described in terms of substitution? Yes. Christ does indeed stand in our stead. Christ bears God's condemnation and offers obedience on our behalf. Has talk about Christ's vicariousness been put in service of oppressive modes of behavior, as numerous scholars have argued? Again, yes. There is mounting evidence to show that some of Calvin's most cherished terms – 'substitution', 'sacrifice', 'self-denial', 'obedience', for example – have been enlisted to justify the oppression of women, persons of African descent, and others.[22] Calvin himself bears some responsibility for this: he draws a fairly crude connection between Christ's voluntary suffering and the demeanor required of beleaguered Christians.[23] At the same time, Calvin can and should be read against himself. The meaning of words like 'sacrifice', 'self-denial' and 'obedience' becomes available, at least in principle, only as one reckons with Christ's enactment of an identity that *cannot* be deemed paradigmatic, given Christ's singular role in the narrative of salvation. 'Substitution', one might even say, refers to an action constitutive of Christ's '*un*substitutionable identity' since he – *and he alone* – enables God to articulate fully God's just and loving character.[24] While a substitutionary death may be the pivot around which Calvin's soteriology turns, substitution need not define discipleship as such.

While I feel optimistic about recasting Calvin's attitude towards discipleship, I am less confident about repairing other aspects of his work. Of especial concern is an ontological deficit in his theology; an undue reticence about the divine being as such. That is to say: granted the insistence *that* God loves, Calvin is reluctant to articulate an ontology of the divine being, the descriptive weight of which tallies with its doctrinal importance. And precisely because Calvin's treatment of the divine life lacks ontological density, questions threaten. Most troublingly: is God's economic activity consonant with God's eternal identity? This question arises, in part, because of Calvin's antipathy towards speculation. Also unhelpful is his (admittedly complex) construal of 'accommodation', since it retards the development of a theological metaphysics that, being tethered to God's economic activity, avoids unwarranted abstraction. At any rate, the fact that the question arises at all is significant: it indicates that the eternal identity of Calvin's God has become altogether too inscrutable. Claims about 'substitution' are therefore easily disconnected from Calvin's broader theological scheme. And as a gap opens up between descriptions of the economy and claims about God as such, the questions multiply. Is God, for all eternity, truly *pro nobis*? Granted that God acts beneficently on our behalf, do God's actions tell the whole story about who God is and what God has in store for us – or are there other, rather more sinister, avenues for thought?

The ontological shortcomings of Calvin's perspective become further apparent when one considers imputation. Does Calvin posit a thoroughgoing renewal of God's people, or does his soteriology, at a crucial moment, seem curiously restrained? Certainly, Christ's righteousness is genuinely communicated. United by the Spirit to the Son and thenceforth to the Father, we are participated in by God – a transformative action that enables and empowers our (non-deifying) participation in God.[25] Sinners are 'cleansed by the secret watering of the Spirit'; when baptized, the Christian is 'imbued with a new and spiritual nature'.[26] There is also no doubt that Calvin views God's people as 'on the way' towards saintliness: the pronouncement of pardon cannot be separated from the process of regeneration. However, a construal of imputation as 'reckoning', as opposed to re-creation, impedes Calvin from stating plainly that humanity is *determined*, essentially, by Christ's perfect obedience. While we are indeed *simul iustus et peccator*, the asymmetrical relationship between the terms is not a matter of *iustus* being what we *are*, deep down, with *peccator* referencing that from which we have been liberated. Rather, *iustus* is a status lent to us. It is not constitutive of human being as such; God's declarative pardon does not ramify ontologically in the here and now. So, even as Christ's righteousness is imputed and his benefits applied, what we should be can appear akin to an eschatological promissory note – not an 'extrinsic' gift that, by way of a dialectic supported by God's present desire to have the best covenant partner *at this very moment*, has been imparted and become intrinsic to our being. Can one dispel the suspicion, then, that God's people not only 'hide' but perhaps also *cower* 'under the precious purity of our first-born brother', given that our essential selves remain, at present, blighted by disobedience and ingratitude?[27] Can the Christian experience true assurance while aware that God's grace is not now complemented by a gratitude and obedience that God has made basic to human being – that is, a gratitude and an obedience that, even in our least faithful moments (for they are legion), proves impossible to overturn? Does Calvin grasp, with sufficient vigor, that God's 'work of reconciliation ... is a work which is *finished*, and which we must conceive to be finished, *before the gospel is preached*'?[28]

Towards a constructive account of atonement

To begin thinking constructively about atonement, Barth's famous description of God – the 'one who loves in freedom' – provides a useful point of departure. What does this expression mean? Not that God dispenses love arbitrarily or whimsically! At issue is God's decision to exist as one who seeks, creates and delights in fellowship with humankind. For sure, God is neither obliged to create nor to act beneficently. The sole condition of God's action is God's own good pleasure. Yet theological accounts of sovereignty fail unless they make direct and constant reference to God's love for humanity. Exodus 3:14 ('I AM WHO I AM') is more than an exhibition of power. The one revealed here – that is, the one who reveals himself – is none other than the God who has guided Israel from the very first and who draws humankind towards a future defined by companionship, justice and peace. Indeed, how would Christians know of God's sovereignty were it not for God's loving approach? God's sovereign freedom and God's love are inseparable in Scripture and in Christian experience; theological writing must pay tribute to this elemental fact of faith.

With an eye towards overcoming the ontological shortfall in Calvin's account of the divine being and therefore providing a robust foundation for particular claims about atonement, one might characterize God's love as elective, jealous and exuberant. God's love is *elective* because it has as its principal preoccupation the flourishing of humankind. Election, on this reckoning, has nothing to do with a pre-temporal apportionment of grace. It is part of the doctrine of God. Specifically, it is a first-order statement about the identity that God has assigned Godself. Just as a description of God's triunity regulates and shapes theological discourse, so too a description of God's elective decision to be *pro nobis*: it is basic to the 'grammar' of Christian reflection. God's love is *jealous* because at every moment God demands a grateful and obedient response to God's sovereign love. There is no range of options available here; God's demand is unequivocal. As God relates to us passionately and intensely, God seeks from us an analogous passion and intensity. And when such a response is not forthcoming – that is, when humanity falls into ingratitude and disobedience – God is not quietly dismayed. God attempts constantly to bring us back into line, with various strategies employed to achieve this end (chastisement, charm, subterfuge; whatever it takes, really). God's love is *exuberant*, finally, because it expresses itself in startling and extravagant actions. The gift of a created order of astonishing complexity and beauty, the guiding light of Scripture, prophets and saints, political movements of uplifting liberative energy: all this, and more, reveals God's desire to be 'with us' in an intimate and provocative way.

The quite radical extent of this exuberance is revealed when God gives Godself to us in the incarnation. Exchanging the time and space of the divine life for the time and space of a fallen world, God applies God's elective decision to be *pro nobis* in a profound way, enacting a decree 'that He Himself in person, in the person of His eternal Son, should give Himself to the son of man, the lost son of man, indeed that He Himself in the person of the eternal Son should *be* the lost Son of Man'.[29] God's realization of this decree means that humanity has no choice about its relationship with God. God has engaged and endured the sinful reality of human life; indeed, God has imposed Godself upon us in a way that would be inconceivable, were it not for the actuality of the Word become flesh. God is 'with us', whether we like it or not.

Yet more needs to be said. Specifically, the claim that God is 'with us' has as its dogmatic partner the claim that we are 'with God' in a surprising way. The incarnation is not merely an event of divine self-presentation. It is also an event in which God freely binds God's own life to the human that the Son assumes. Beyond a mere acclamation of God's self-sufficient independence, 'despite' God's taking on flesh – as per Calvinistic avowals of the *extra calvinisticum* and recent defenses of the *logos asarkos* – it is possible, and important, to say that God's love for humanity is such that God wills that the incarnation prove constitutive of the eternal identity of the Son. Why this step beyond Calvin? Why think that God's jealousy and exuberance lead to God's *self*-election, as Son, as Jesus Christ? Well, if one reads the Gospels as narratival expansions of Exodus 3:14, one must not shrink from understanding the ontological significance of the incarnation. Granted that the Word is 'in the beginning with God', this 'beginning' is always moving towards the event of incarnation. God, to borrow from Eberhard Jüngel, is a 'being in becoming'.[30] And it is part of God's communication to us that God reveals God's own self as a being in becoming: one who, as Son, assigns himself an identity that moves towards, and then embraces eternally, the concrete person of Jesus Christ.[31]

To say that the *logos asarkos* is always becoming and being the *logos ensarkos* indicates, most pertinently, the depth of God's commitment to us. By way of God's Christic self-qualification, God grants to humankind a unique ontological validity from the very first. On one level, even as God makes Christ's concrete existence and history constitutive of God's second way of being, God does not overwhelm this human or his history. God preserves and embraces Christ's creatureliness in eternity, just as God preserves and embraces the flesh that the Son assumes in time. As such, in his eternal session at the right hand of the Father, Christ, while definitely *vere deus*, is never other than that human whose life passes from Nazareth, to Golgotha, to a (mysterious) resurrected state. On another level, since the human identifiable as Jesus of Nazareth is always-already a part of the divine life, humankind as such is always-already given a share in the permanence and security that defines that same life. Since we are 'in Christ', we are always 'with God'.

The atoning value of Christ's life can now be considered directly. Taking as a cue the first two volumes of *Church Dogmatics* IV, one can present Christ's atoning work as sanctifying and justifying humankind.

To connect *sanctification* and atonement is not merely an instance of christocentric thinking that reorders dogmatic conventions. It is an attempt to 'ontologize' theological anthropology in ways that retain continuity with Calvin, while overcoming his overly restrictive understanding of imputation. It means, specifically, that Christ's history, beyond being ontologically determinative for God's second way of being, is ontologically determinative for humankind as such – and that this determination is itself part and parcel of God's atoning action. Because of Christ's perfect relationship with God, humanity is always-already conformed to God's will. Because the covenant has been fulfilled, we are – right now – faithful servants.

One can even say that because Christ, not Adam, defines us, wrongdoing is inessential to humankind. We may not do what we ought, but our failures are not symptomatic of who we really are. What is most real about human existence is obedience to God and, complementary to this obedience, many of the qualities that Christ consistently embodies: unmitigated gratitude for the gifts God gives, confidence in God's love for humankind, an intolerance for blind convention and, last but not least, fierce resistance to oppressive economic, social and cultural structures. It is not enough to say that God beholds the faithful favorably because we have had Christ's righteousness imputed to us. One must also say that humankind, in an ontologically significant way, has been situated 'in Christ' and, by dint of this inclusion, has been given a Christic disposition. That human beings fail to enact this disposition is of course undeniable. The conviction that human beings genuinely have this disposition, however, provides the starting point for theological anthropology.

This ontologically charged view of sanctification, moreover, allows two claims to be put in dialectical tension. On the one hand, sanctification depends on an event – more precisely, a person – that happens *extra nos*. There are therefore no grounds for self-aggrandizement.[32] We cannot save ourselves; we have been saved by way of an utterly particular, divinely initiated, action. On the other hand, the ontological impact of Christ's history allows for a more expansive exposition than that proffered by many Reformed theologians, for what happens 'extrinsically' proves ontologically determinative of human being. Just as no part of God's life is unconnected with the concrete history of the incarnate Son, so no part of the human remains untouched by that same history. We are *re-created*, in a basic sense, by Christ. Indeed, beyond an obvious convergence between talk about human rights and the Christian doctrine of sanctification (for the claim that human beings are made *imago Christi* converges nicely with the conviction that all people, no matter their contingent qualities, have indefeasible worth), our participation in sanctification affords us the opportunity to cast off debilitating forms of essentialism. The sanctified human is constantly 'opened up' to new possibilities; she has, now, the chance to *become* as well as be. A confident avowal of human dignity, then, tendered from a robustly theological perspective, can be complemented by an uninhibited celebration of human diversity.[33] This celebration does not expose Christianity's accommodation to 'secular' norms; rather, it pays tribute to the continuing vitality of Christ's sanctifying life, made real by the work of the Spirit.

The impossibility of self-aggrandizement and, more positively, the possibilities inherent to a soteriology that goes beyond talk of assurance is nicely illustrated by John 8:1–11, where a woman charged with adultery is set before Jesus. On the face of it, the 'case' is a malevolent ruse: Jesus' enemies hope that he will demonstrate legal laxity and thereby incriminate himself. Rather more sinisterly, there is here a menacing exertion of patriarchal power. The woman's supposedly dubious background has little interest for those who indict her. Finding their authority and prestige threatened, a group of men have seized on an unknown woman, intending to exploit her for their own purposes. If she is stoned, so what? Israel will be rid of another 'loose woman'; Jesus will have approved the litigants' interpretation of the law, thereby rendering himself superfluous. And if Jesus counsels against stoning, he will be exposed as an upstart devoid of religious sagacity, shown to have more sympathy for social outcasts than respect for God's covenant legislation. Yet Jesus refuses to take the bait. He starts to draw in the sand. When pressed, he simply asks which of the accusers has the requisite moral purity to begin stoning. At this point, a kind of collective exorcism occurs. Violence is no longer a possibility. Whereas Jesus' enemies had earlier embraced the role of a lynch mob, now they are dispersed. Indeed, since the men cannot deny Jesus' challenge, they are suddenly confronted by their own wrongdoing. They understand, at the very least, that all human beings are blighted by sinfulness; they become aware that an (alleged) violation of heterosexual mores hardly compares with a political strategy that tolerates the execution of adulterers. And after this exposé of patriarchal abuse, there is Jesus' empowering conferral of forgiveness upon the woman herself ('Neither do I condemn you. Go your way, and from now on do not sin again'). Showing no interest in the charges leveled, Jesus simply indicates that the woman exists, now, in a context in which no one *could* condemn her. God's pardon is as absolute as it is complete; heedless of a reciprocity governed by the logic of *do ut des*, it appears shocking, transgressive, almost incomprehensible. Furthermore, Christ's command to the woman – that she not 'sin again' – is meant sincerely. She has been transposed into a new condition; she now inhabits a 'place of love which is infinitely capacious' and lavishly invigorative.[34] All that remains is for her to become the person that she is: one who is liberated to enjoy and honor God's validation of her being.

With reference to the *justifying* dimensions of atonement, three particular points require elucidation. The first pertains to Christ's vicarious articulation of divine love; the second, to the passion as a direct confrontation between incarnate love and human sinfulness; the third, to the cross as an event whereby God and humanity overcome sin.

Matthew's account of Jesus' baptism provides a starting point for understanding Christ's vicarious existence, itself expressive of God's love for humankind.

> Then Jesus came from Galilee to John at the Jordan, to be baptized by him. John would have prevented him, saying, 'I need to be baptized by you, and do you come to me?' But Jesus answered him, 'Let it be so now; for it is proper for us in this way to fulfill all righteousness.' Then he consented. And when Jesus had been baptized, just as he came up from the water, suddenly the heavens were opened to him and he saw the Spirit of God descending like a dove and alighting on him. And a voice from heaven said, 'This is my Son, the Beloved, with whom I am well pleased.' (Matt. 3:13–17)

More than a public disclosure of Christ's identity as the only-begotten Son, this passage intimates that Christ's identity, from the first, is bound up with his intention to live on behalf of others. It announces Christ's decision to live as the Word become *flesh*: one who takes upon himself responsibility for human sin and who identifies with the plight and misery of his fellows. Certainly, Christ's decision is difficult to comprehend. John poses the obvious question: ought not their roles be reversed? Yet Jesus insists that he be baptized. Contesting the supposition that there could be a ranking of charismatic leaders, Jesus' 'consent' provides a striking indication of what righteousness means for him: living in unreserved solidarity with those who confess their sins, even to the point at which he shares their confession.

This radically vicarious posture raises a difficult question: did the Son assume a 'fallen' human nature?[35] Scholars who answer this question negatively suppose sinlessness and a fallen nature to be incompatible. An affirmation of Christ's moral purity ought to regulate discussions of his human nature; fallenness is coextensive with sinful, moral *im*purity; Christ's humanity must therefore be adjudged unfallen. Those who answer positively take a different line. The assumption of a fallen nature does not render Christ sinful as such; rather, it emphasizes Christ's unreserved solidarity with humanity in its corrupted state. Only as Christ contends with the concrete reality of human existence does his life and death have an impact upon us: his soteriological 'value' requires that there be as extensive a correlation as possible between the humanity to be saved and the humanity that is assumed. Why suppose, though, that these options are mutually exclusive? One can affirm Christ's sinlessness *and* construe his humanity as maximally coessential with ours, the outer limits of this affirmation allowing the claim that Christ comes to have a 'fallen nature'.

On one level, dogmatic treatments of sinlessness ought to avoid abstraction. It may be tempting to say that in Christ, one finds a perfect demonstration of the categorical imperative, a heroic coincidence of justice and care, even a supremely moving instantiation of religious genius. But none of this assists with the task of christological and soteriological description; instead, one is kept at a distance from what ought to inform dogmatic reflection on this issue, *viz.*, the scriptural texts that narrate Christ's history of obedience to God the Father. The dogmatic function of the term 'sinless', at least when governed by the New Testament texts, is simply to summarize Christ's enactment of an 'unsubstitutionable identity'. It is because Christ lives and acts as the person that God intends him to be – one who 'learned obedience' (Heb. 5:8) and realized this obedience in a unique way – that he is deemed sinless. Was Christ unable to sin (*non posse peccare*)? Was Christ able not to sin (*posse non peccare*)? These are not the right questions. More important is the fact that, through a series of coherent and integrated decisions, Christ enacts his identity perfectly, living out a particular life that was (and is) wholly 'for God'. On another level, Christ's sinlessness entails his being the 'human for others' in an unrepeatable way, taking full responsibility for sin. The fact that Christ commits to living as one maximally coessential with his sinful fellows does not entail his being corrupted in the sense that he intends or practices wrongdoing. At issue is the way in which Christ takes up the cross. Beyond sharing our 'common infirmities', Christ discerns the necessity for a radical solution to humanity's degeneracy. He recognizes that he must 'become sin'; that he – *and he alone* – must dispose himself as the one in whom God confronts, condemns and overcomes disobedience. He then enacts this unique identity (although not without temptation and excruciating existential distress).[36] Christ draws into himself the full weight of wrongdoing; his 'becoming' is such that he dies as the one who is elected *and* rejected by God. A fallen state 'happens' when Christ's perfect mediatorial work is concluded; his enactment of sinlessness culminates in his becoming sin for us.

This leads to my second claim – the cross as a direct confrontation between incarnate love and sinfulness. Why *confrontation*? While Jesus' life always entails conflict and misunderstanding, in the passion narratives the juxtaposition of divine love and human sinfulness becomes ever more vivid, albeit in unexpected ways. On one level, the resistance offered by those previously arrayed against Jesus (the state, his family, his peers and, in a complex way, his disciples) is intensified by the actions of religious and political authorities. Jesus is no longer a 'nuisance'; he is a marked man. On another level, Jesus himself raises the stakes. He aggravates a possibly defusable crisis, revealing that, alongside those who would have him killed, he himself intends a terrible end to his life. Think of it: he needles and provokes his enemies; he combines evasion and threatening prophecy (Matt. 26:63–4; also Lk. 22:70); he lists towards 'blasphemy' (Mk 14:61–62); he offers sullen silences in face of imperial questioning (Matt. 27:14); he even engages in mocking, philosophical dispute (Jn 18:38). Such 'variations' in the Gospel narratives do not bespeak evangelical creativity in the face of a shortage of historical information. The texts rather suggest that Jesus effects his own death, using diverse strategies to realize an end accordant with his self-assigned identity as savior. Finally, it seems that God *qua* Father propels Christ to his death. Whereas Jesus' earlier life was providentially protected in various ways – recall the angel's warnings about Herod's murderous designs and Jesus' eluding a murderous crowd – God does nothing when Jesus needs help the most. What providential action there is recalls a tragedy of Shakespearean proportions: a series of highly contingent events are coordinated in such a way to ensure the worst ending possible. Judas's treachery, Peter's weakness, the surprising malice of the religious authorities, Pilate's amateurish politicking – taken individually, these events would not necessarily lead to crucifixion; collectively, they manifest God's authorial hand. So it is that Christ's death forms a macabre finale to his life. His identity as the one obedient to God and committed to his fellows converges with his own efforts to bring about his own crucifixion; the wickedness of his enemies is unleashed as they seize on God's providential permission, and put Jesus to death.[37]

But why must atonement involve *this* end? Why is Christ's death intended by his opponents, himself, and by God the Father? Again, a word like 'substitution' seems unavoidable if one wishes to do justice to Christ's own agency. Christ's life ends on Calvary because (in part) of his enactment of a vicarious identity; it ends, shockingly and tragically, because (in part) he wills this extremity of self-giving. James Denney puts it nicely: there is 'a deliberate and conscious descent, ever deeper and deeper, into the dark valley where at the last hour the last reality of sin was to be met and borne. ... Our Lord's Passion *is* His sublimest action – an action so potent that all his other actions are sublated in it, and we know everything when we know that He *died* for our sins.'[38] However, it is crucial to define 'substitution' very carefully. On one level, theological language must be ruled by the narratives that recount Christ's unique history; on another level, theological language must, so far as is possible, be distinguished from discourses of domination and put in service of human liberation. I want therefore to parse the word 'substitution' with three additional terms – condemnation, defeat and purgation.

Granted the juridical connotations of condemnation, the dogmatic meaning of the word pertains to the Father forsaking Christ on the cross, rejecting him as the sin that he has become. The fact that Christ lives as the 'human for others', as already suggested, involves his adopting an intensely vicarious posture from the first. So Barth: 'faced by the sins of all others', Christ 'did not let these sins be theirs, did not regard, bewail, or judge them from a distance with a tacit or open accusation, but ... *caused them to be His own sins*'.[39] Yet baptism is not exhaustive of Christ's identity; it is only the opening act of his salvation history. As this history runs its course, Christ's identification with sinners becomes ever more intense, ever more complete. On Calvary, Christ's vicarious self-disposing reaches full term: at this point he *becomes and is* the sin that God condemns, having drawn into his person the full force of human corruption. (As Luther says, commenting on Galatians 3:13, Christ 'was accursed and of all sinners the greatest'.)[40] Coincident with this vicarious conclusion to Christ's earthly life, the Father and the Spirit withdraw entirely, thereby providing a temporal reiteration of God's eternal rejection of all that opposes God. As our sin is concentrated in Christ's person – genuinely so, for there is nothing fictional about Christ's vicariousness; his purposeful absorption of sin is as real as it is total – God shows that sinfulness will *not* be tolerated. Christ is unequivocally forsaken. His solidarity with us provides God with the opportunity to *re*-reject, in the context of human history, what God has rejected for all eternity – *viz.*, everything that opposes God's love. Indeed, during the time of the passion, God no longer holds Jesus' enemies at bay. Sinful humanity is free to do its worst and, unsurprisingly, lives up to expectations; God's providential governance of history therefore coincides with the atrocity of an imperial execution. Is this a *punishment* of sin, then? Not in the sense of retribution: it is not as if God lashes out, punitively, to denounce lawlessness. At issue is condemnation understood as *rejection*, articulated in order that sin might be exposed, confounded and cancelled. When the Father 'permits' the passion, it becomes clear what 'the world, as run by human beings, taken to its logical conclusion' means: murder, futility and the vanquishing of hope.[41] God turns away, refusing to shelter Christ from the consequences of sin, and this turning away coincides with the manifestation of pure nihility. And in the moment in which sin rushes into the vacated space, it is exposed as self-annihilative. It buckles under its own weight; the most it can offer is pointless murder. Sin in fact shows itself to be backward looking, incapable of futurity. Only as God 'returns' to the scene and raises Christ from the dead does human life again move forward.

It is not only that sin attacks and assaults Christ on the cross. Precisely because the Son is the *logos ensarkos*, Christ's crucifixion becomes an event that happens, eternally, in the life of God; it forms a key moment in the history that God wills should be constitutive of Godself *qua* Son. Does this legitimize talk of divine suffering? Only in a limited sense: Christ's death is not his whole history, even granted that it forms a pivotal moment of this history. Rather more important is the fact that, as sinful humanity presumes to attack the divine Son, it receives the most decisive invalidation imaginable. In the same moment that Christ appears most lost, consigned to 'suffer the wrath of God in His own body and the fire of His love in His own soul', sin is decisively defeated.[42] Having been brought into direct conflict with God's love, having been drawn into the time and space of the divine being, it has no chance of success: God's love exerts itself jealously, 'burning up' everything that works against God's purposes and reasserting control over God's relationship with humankind. Everything that Christ has drawn to himself, the whole compass of evil, then, is overcome; nihility is crushed by God, *in* God, in the moment in which it overextends itself. So at the moment in which Christ cries, 'Father, into your hands I commend my spirit' (Lk. 23:46), sin really *is* 'finished' (Jn 19:30). It has no place; it has no future. Luther, again:

> Not only my sins and thine, but the sins of the whole world, past, present, or to come, take hold upon Him, go about to condemn Him, and do indeed condemn Him. But because in the self-same person, who is the highest, greatest, and the only sinner, there is also an invincible and everlasting righteousness; therefore these two do encounter together, the highest, the greatest, and the only sin, and the highest, greatest, and the only righteousness ... in this combat, sin must needs be vanquished and killed, and righteousness must overcome, live and reign.[43]

It follows, moreover, that all instances of human wrongdoing now lack for ontological worth. Since sin has no place in God's life, it cannot really dominate in the creaturely realm. Even as it attempts, inexplicably (and ludicrously, were it not for the victims), to sustain itself, it cannot truly take hold of human being.

The final dimension of Christ's justifying and atoning work involves humanity being purged of sin and liberated, in principle, from any inclination to sin. At this point my statement connects again with Calvin. As suggested earlier, a distinction of Calvin's christology is its careful treatment of Christ's obedience to God. In continuity with Maximus Confessor, Anselm of Canterbury and others, Calvin in fact grants Christ *qua* human a share in God's atoning work. It is only because Christ submits to God's condemnation and offers himself as a substitute on our behalf that God and God's people are brought into right relationship. Alan Spence makes the point nicely: while 'God is complete and sufficient in himself, he has freely chosen to use the agency of his creation, that which is other than himself, to accomplish his purpose, to bring glory to his name'.[44] Indeed, since Christ divinely *and* humanly embraces the cross, so humanity, by extension, is involved in its liberation from sin. Because Christ decides to live for God and his fellows, he rejects sin on our behalf; because of his action we are propelled towards a state of covenantal compliance, with a sinful 'whence' outbid by a redemptive 'whither'. None need mimic Christ's passion. He alone cries out from the depths of abandonment. He alone dies in face of the radical nihility of wrongdoing. But, given God's primordial election of all humankind in Christ, all participate in his decision to purge humanity of sin, being shaped by 'the absolute active death of self-will *into* the holy will of God'.[45] As justified and sanctified people, we have rejected sin, even granted that we are still harried by the impulses of the flesh; we are therefore free, now, to live in gratitude, obedience and peace.

Concluding comments

Although my constructive statement may appear to have moved far from the *Institutes* and the commentaries, there do remain multiple points of continuity between the previous section and the thoughts of my famed predecessor. Like Calvin, I believe that claims about atonement ought to be nested in a broad theological scheme. It is a mistake to treat any doctrinal locus in isolation from others; reflection on atonement, in particular, degrades terribly when isolated from talk about God's love, the incarnation, and theological anthropology. I also believe, with Calvin, that finely grained thinking about atonement is preferable to pronouncements about 'models' or theories. The best expositions of atonement elucidate a *ratio* governed by Christ's concrete history; they have little in common with tidy conceptual schemes. Finally, like Calvin, I would foreground an approach to atonement that holds a place for the word 'substitution'. This does not mean a dismissal of concerns about the way that Christian language has functioned in the past. If certain construals of atonement have facilitated wrongdoing, there is a *prima facie* reason to consider doctrinal revision. Nevertheless, I am reluctant to ditch substitution. To hurry past Christ's self-substituting activity does violence to the shape of the gospel narratives. It risks making Christ a victim of tragic circumstances, thereby diverting attention from the fact that, because of Christ's purposeful, atoning obedience, tragedy cannot now have the last word.

At the same time, there are differences here. On one level, I want to commend a more ontologically daring perspective that, marginalizing the *logos asarkos* motif and the so-called *extra calvinisticum*, commits its energies to thinking imaginatively about God's decision to live as a 'being in becoming', even to the point at which God is transformed by the incarnation. This perspective also considers human beings in Christic, not Adamic, terms. We may not live as we ought, but what we are is a cause for delight; in light of the atonement, we – that is, *every one of us* – are loved by God, saved by God, and impelled towards a better future. On another level, and complementary to such ontological innovation, I want to explore how the gospel narratives might newly fund theological reflection. This turn to narrative, facilitated in part by the work of Hans Frei, spurs a christological and soteriological perspective that draws attention to the interplay of divine and human intention and action in the gospels. It provides, I hope, a clearer sense of the person that Christ is and the atonement for which he dies.

One last question: what kind of *ethics* might this constructive statement yield? A passage from one of P. T. Forsyth's small masterpieces, *The Cruciality of the Cross*, suggests the beginnings of an answer.

> Life must be ethicised, all say; faith must do it, most say. But what is to ethicise faith, and especially Christian faith? The cross, must we not say? ... Have we anything else for it but the cross and its cruciality (however newly read) as the re-creative centre of our moral world – the cross which is the central act of God's holiness, and the centre of the central moral personality, Christ?[46]

With these words Forsyth hoped to mediate between Ritschlian moralism and a staurological approach to atonement. Today, a different kind of mediation is needed. Faith must indeed be 'ethicized': this is something that liberationists from the 'first' and the 'developing' worlds, along with many philosophers, have emphasized. Yet if such 'ethicization' is to have lasting impact on Christian thought and life, it must make sense of – and perhaps must begin with – Christ's atoning life and death. What might happen, should the insights of liberationist thought be coordinated with the doctrinal achievements of the Protestant tradition? Maybe an ethics of the atonement is the next step for an evangelical theology invigorated by God's love, fascinated by actuality of Christ's unique history, and liberated into the time and space of the resurrection.

Notes

1 See here C. E. Gunton, *The Actuality of the Atonement: A Study of Metaphor, Rationality and the Christian Tradition*, London: T&T Clark, 1988.
2 J. Calvin, *Commentary on the Gospel According to John*, vol. XVII of *Calvin's Commentaries*, Grand Rapids, MI: Baker Academic, 2005, p. 51. Subsequent references to Calvin's commentaries will note the title and refer parenthetically to the relevant Baker volume.
3 J. Calvin, *Institutes of the Christian Religion* (2 vols), Louisville, KY: WJKP, 2006, II.3.2.
4 J. Calvin, 'Catechism of the Church of Geneva', in *Calvin's Tracts*, vol. 2, Eugene, OR: Wipf & Stock, 2002, p. 75.
5 *Institutes* II.12.4 and *Commentaries on the Epistle of Paul to the Ephesians* (vol. XXI), p. 201.
6 Calvin, *Commentary on John*, pp. 45 and 124.
7 See esp. *Institutes* II.13.4.
8 Calvin, *Commentary on John*, p. 46. As is well known, Calvin's emphasis on the distinction of the two natures becomes a distinguishing feature of Reformed thought.
9 Calvin, 'Catechism', p. 44.
10 *Institutes* II.16.5. Calvin's programmatic account of the *munus triplex* (*Institutes* II.15.15.) reinforces his emphasis on Christ's comprehensive obedience. For an important reading of Calvin in light of the threefold office, see S. Edmondson, *Calvin's Christology*, Cambridge: Cambridge University Press, 2004.
11 *Institutes* II.16.5.
12 Calvin, *Commentaries on the Epistle to the Galatians* (vol. XXI), p. 92.
13 *Institutes* II.16.6. My emphasis.

14 Ibid., II.12.3.
15 Ibid., II.16.2.
16 See Calvin, *Commentary on Romans*, p. 142.
17 J. Calvin, *Institutes of the Christian Religion*, 1536 edn, Grand Rapids, MI: Eerdmans, 1986, p. 18. The quotation has been shorn of interpolated scriptural references.
18 J. Calvin, *Commentary on the Book of the Prophet Isaiah*, vol. IV (vol. VIII), p. 116.
19 See here H. Blocher, 'The Atonement in John Calvin's Theology', in Charles E. Hill and F. A. James III (eds) *The Glory of the Atonement: Biblical, Historical and Practical Perspectives*, Downers Grove, IL: IVP, 2004, pp. 279–303.
20 Calvin, *1536 Institutes*, p. 57. Again, interpolated scriptural references have been removed.
21 *Institutes* III.2.2. 'Knowledge' has a complex meaning for Calvin, somewhat at odds with modern epistemological conventions. Beyond mere intellectual 'comprehension', it involves an affective assurance of God's fatherly care. See *Institutes* III.2.14–19 and III.2.33–37.
22 Some important texts: J. C. Brown and R. Parker, 'For God so Loved the World?', in J. C. Brown and C. R. Bohn (eds), *Christianity, Patriarchy, and Abuse: A Feminist Critique*, New York: Pilgrim Press, 1989, pp. 1–30; D. Williams, *Sisters in the Wilderness: The Challenge of Womanist God-Talk*, Maryknoll, NY: Orbis Books, 1993; J. M. Terrell, *Power in the Blood? The Cross in the African American Experience*, Eugene, OR: Wipf & Stock, 2005.
23 See N. J. Duff, 'Atonement and the Christian Life', *Interpretation*, 1999, vol. 53.1, 24.
24 I borrow this phrase from Frei; see H. W. Frei, *The Identity of Jesus Christ: The Hermeneutical Bases of Dogmatic Theology*, Philadelphia, PA: Fortress Press, 1997.
25 For more on this issue, see J. T. Billings, *Calvin, Participation, and the Gift: The Activity of Believers in Union with Christ*, Oxford: Oxford University Press, 2007. This important study shows plainly that much recent criticism of Calvin misses the mark. Participation *is* a part of Calvin's outlook; loose talk about 'nominalism' has diverted attention from the way he understands the believer's transformation by (and 'in') God. My concern is that Calvin's understanding of participation does not go far enough. Not only is it not partnered with an expansive ontology of the divine life, but the eschatological 'deferral' of the human's full participation in God discloses a deeper problem – the fact that our location 'in Christ' does not determine who we are essentially, *now*.
26 *Institutes* III.1.1 and IV.15.6.
27 Ibid., III.11.23.
28 J. Denney, *The Death of Christ*, revised edn, London: Hodder & Stoughton, 1911, p. 103.
29 K. Barth, *Church Dogmatics*, 13 vols, Edinburgh: T&T Clark, 1956–75; *CD* II/2, p. 157.
30 E. Jüngel, *God's Being Is in Becoming: The Trinitarian Being of God in the Theology of Karl Barth*, trans. John Webster, Edinburgh: T&T Clark, 2001.
31 For more on this issue, see Paul Nimmo, ch. 3 in this volume.
32 This theme is developed further by Zahl in ch. 6 of this volume.
33 Limits ought not to be imposed, artificially, on this celebration of diversity. It can and should include, for example, an unequivocal delight in racial difference, cultural variety, and the open-ended possibilities of human sexuality.
34 D. Ford, *Self and Salvation: Being Transformed*, Cambridge: Cambridge University Press, 1999, p. 119.
35 See, recently, K. Kapic, 'The Son's Assumption of a Human Nature: A Call for Clarity', *International Journal of Systematic Theology*, 2001, vol. 3.2, 154–66; O. Crisp, 'Did Christ Have a *Fallen* Human Nature?', *International Journal of Systematic Theology*, 2004, vol. 6.3, 270–88; I. J. Davidson, 'Pondering the Sinlessness of Jesus Christ: Moral Christologies and the Witness of Scripture', *International Journal of Systematic Theology*, 2008, vol. 10.4, 372–98; and I. A. McFarland, 'Fallen and Unfallen? Christ's

Human Nature and the Ontology of Sinlessness', *International Journal of Systematic Theology*, 2008, vol. 10.4, 399–415. My own perspective has much in common with Davidson's.

36 So P. T. Forsyth, *The Person and Place of Jesus Christ*, London: Independent Press, 1909, p. 7:

> The sinlessness of Jesus was not that natural, sweet, poised, remote, and æsthetic type. It was not the harmonious development of that principle of Sonship through the quietly deepening experiences of life – just as His nightly communion cannot have been simply a blessed and oblivious respite from the task of each day, but its offering, outspreading, and disentangling before the Father who prescribed it. Gethsemane was not the first agony. Each great season was a crisis, and sometimes a stormy crisis, in which the next step became clear.

37 Much of this paragraph is indebted to Frei's *Identity of Jesus Christ*.
38 Denney, *The Death of Christ*, p. 311.
39 Barth, *CD* IV/4, p. 59, emphasis added.
40 M. Luther, *Commentary on Galatians*, Grand Rapids, MI: Kregel Classics, 1979, pp. 172 and 165.
41 E. Jüngel, *Justification: The Heart of the Christian Faith*, London: T&T Clark, 2001, p. 67.
42 Barth, *CD* IV/1, p. 95.
43 Luther, *Galatians*, pp. 169–70.
44 A. Spence, *The Promise of Peace: A Unified Theory of Atonement*, London: T&T Clark, 2006, p. 49.
45 P. T. Forsyth, *The Cruciality of the Cross*, p. 92.
46 Ibid., pp. 65–6.

Select bibliography

Barth, K., *Church Dogmatics*, 13 vols, Edinburgh: T&T Clark, 1956–75.
Calvin, J., *Institutes of the Christian Religion*, 2 vols, Louisville, KY: WJKP, 2006.
Forsyth, P. T., *The Person and Place of Jesus Christ*, London: Independent Press, 1909.
Frei, H. W., *The Identity of Jesus Christ: The Hermeneutical Bases of Dogmatic Theology*, Philadelphia, PA: Fortress Press, 1997.
Luther, M., *Commentary on Galatians*, Grand Rapids, MI: Kregel Classics, 1979.
Terrell, J. M., *Power in the Blood? The Cross in the African American Experience*, Eugene, OR: Wipf & Stock, 2005.

Chapter 5

Entire sanctification and theological method

A Wesleyan dynamic for discovering good news in every context

George Bailey

> Like obedient children, do not be conformed to the desires that you formerly had in ignorance. Instead, as he who called you is holy, be holy yourselves in all your conduct; for it is written, 'You shall be holy, for I am holy.'
>
> (1 Pet. 1: 14–16)

There are many verses in the New Testament which could be selected to begin a discussion of the nature and implications of sanctification for Christian discipleship and theological expression. This passage from 1 Peter serves the purpose well because through the use of the term 'holy' it illustrates the central dynamics of the doctrine of sanctification. It also opens the way to commenting on some strengths and problems with John Wesley's account of it, and the ways in which a Wesleyan form of a theology of sanctification can be of use for exploring and developing contextual methodologies within evangelical theology.

The first letter of Peter is addressed to 'exiles' and 'aliens' (1:1, 2:11) who are suffering at the hands of the society to which they have previously belonged, and within which they have now been marginalized by the call to become followers of Christ (1:6, 4:12, 14, 5:9). This establishes the context for the pastoral concern of the letter to provide assurance and encouragement in the difficult present times by reference to the scriptural narrative spanning creation (1:20), God's faithfulness to Israel (1:10–12), the sending, suffering, death and resurrection of Jesus Christ (1:19–20), God's faithfulness to the community (1:12, 21), and the promise of the final revelation of Jesus Christ in the future (1:13).[1] The application of this narrative to the situation of the readers of the letter results in the imperative to 'be holy'; to live in a way that separates them from the surrounding culture, and to cease to 'be conformed to the desires that [they] formerly had in ignorance'. There is a stark contrast drawn between the culture and norms of the surrounding society, and that of the new community: 'who have been chosen and destined by God the Father and sanctified by the Spirit to be obedient to Jesus Christ and to be sprinkled with his blood' (1:2a). This sharp division between the unholy old and holy new way of living has often been characteristic of evangelical theology and ethics, and in spite of developments of the last fifty years, continues to be so.[2] When the process and aim of sanctification is more fully explored, the distinction between a person engaged with being sanctified and a person who is not is less easy to maintain and the problems with it become increasingly clear. I heed the caution of John Webster that a doctrinal account of holiness should be based purely on the exegesis of Scripture and the traditional doctrinal formulations of the church, viewing the host culture 'not as Athens, but as Babylon'.[3] However, there are problems with pursuing this in an overly binary way. The first problem is theoretical: holiness implies a relationship with culture. To be set apart as holy is not to be set apart in isolation from culture, but to be set apart in relation to culture, and for the purpose of the transformation of culture. This leads to the second problem, which is practical: to seek doctrinal formulations of holiness and sanctification with one's back turned on the culture in which the Christian community exists and participates makes the evangelical transformation of that culture impossible. Communication is necessary to evangelism, and communication entails a reciprocal relationship. Furthermore, the denial of the cultural context in which doctrine is formulated contributes to the paralysis of the church when it is called upon to respond practically to problems which have hitherto not been addressed in doctrinal formulations. With these objections to a methodology which deliberately ignores the culture within which sanctification is experienced, I suggest that a more complex relationship between doctrine and context pertains in theological thinking. A Wesleyan account of holiness and sanctification provides resources based on Scripture and the traditional doctrinal formulations of the church which allow for, and encourage, this more complex methodology. I will return to these questions of doctrine and context after discussing the central features of sanctification theology, and then the Wesleyan account of these.

To seek holiness demands a consideration of the 'host culture' because holiness is relational. To be sanctified is to be *made* holy, which implies a transformation from one state of affairs to another. Holiness is represented and defined by the nature of God, and it is the will of God that humans are transformed in a way that conforms them to this holiness: 'as he who called you is holy, be holy yourselves'. God is holy because he is wholly other, transcendent from the world, separate as Creator from all else that has been created. However, God's holiness is not simply an attribute of God, or in any way describable distinct from the experience of God; it is the way in which God is present to humans when he reveals himself to them. The content of such revelation is primarily of God's otherness and separateness now made discernible. The theophanies to the patriarchs (e.g. Gen. 28:10–17) and prophets (e.g. Isa. 6:1–8) are experiences of God and thus of holiness. God is holy in relation to the world and this is the basic content of God's self-revelation to humans. As divine holiness is relational, so too is the human holiness to which we are conformed. While human holiness is a state of affairs that pertains for an individual and is realized by a change in the way they are ('be holy'), this change is necessarily related to the relation between individuals and the world external to them; hence 'desires' and 'conduct' are the relational concepts by which holiness is defined in 1 Peter 1:14–16. This relational description of the holiness of God and humans is, though, incomplete and begs the question of how divine and human holiness are connected. Dan Hardy follows his description of holiness as relation with a warning against the tendency to stop there and limit holiness to a 'dyadic' relation when in fact the 'relational propriety of the holiness of God' entails a 'triadic' relation involving the relations of the holiness of God, the relations of the holiness of humans, and the relationality between them: 'one set of relations related to other relations by a stable relation.'[4] Intrinsic to God's holiness is the impulse and means to make humans holy.

In giving the law, the prophets, and sending Jesus Christ, God says 'You shall be holy, for I am holy' (cf. Lev. 11:44, 19:2), and the relation between divine and human processes by which this becomes the case is the central dynamic of a theology of sanctification. The origins of British evangelicalism are bound up with the eighteenth-century controversies over this set of relations at the heart of a theology of sanctification. These controversies include the nature of humanity, the atonement and its effects on humanity, the relation between faith and works, the respective roles of Christ and the Holy Spirit in Christian life and piety, and the possibilities for Christian discipleship in this life, combined with the eschatological vision for the individual, community and all creation. Why do we need to be sanctified? How are we sanctified? What does sanctification entail? John Wesley's theological work, discernible through his relatively few specifically theological writings (including his published extracts of others' work) and many pastoral and polemical writings (sermons,[5] tracts, journals and letters) displays a detailed negotiation of these questions. Furthermore, 'entire sanctification' and the desire for the utmost holiness are intentionally at the heart of his theology and his practical engagement with the life of the societies he contributed to founding and maintaining: 'This doctrine [full sanctification] is the grand depositum which God has lodged with the people called Methodists; and for the sake of propagating this chiefly He appeared to have raised us up.'[6]

Wesley's sanctification theology, and some Wesleyan interpretations

While it is clear that a Wesleyan theology has at its centre the doctrine of sanctification, there remain forensic questions as to what Wesley himself understood to be the content and process of sanctification towards entire sanctification. Wesley's varied use of 1 Peter 1:15–16 illustrates some of the problems Wesley had to address with his doctrinal account of sanctification, and the resolutions he came to. The tension between the realization of sanctification along with justification and the striving towards sanctification as the *telos* of the process of salvation is already apparent in the text of 1 Peter. The 'exiles' to whom the letter is addressed are both already 'sanctified by the Spirit to be obedient to Jesus Christ' (1:2) and exhorted with verbs in the imperative to act 'like obedient children' and to 'be holy' (1:14, 16). When Wesley uses the phrases and terms of 1 Peter 1:14–16 it is sometimes to express the current realization of holiness in the life of believers, a sign of the new birth,[7] but at other times to urge Christians to strive towards holiness as a synonym for entire sanctification, the goal of Christian living.[8] These tensions between the promise and realization of salvation, the gift and the demand of the gospel, pushed Wesley to the careful forging of a *via media* between a number of theological complications: imputed and imparted righteousness, the total fallen-ness of humanity into original sin and the hope for universal salvation, the effects of sin on the believer and the possibility of entire sanctification.

Wesley's decisions as to the ordering of the essential aspects of the development of Christian living towards entire sanctification were made gradually throughout his life, and in response to pastoral situations or critical polemics, rather than as the result of reflective systematization. As such, he presents a 'way of salvation' which points us towards the recovery of the image of God in human holiness, rather than a systematized *ordo salutis* in the style of the Reformed tradition. In presenting Wesley's soteriology in this looser manner, which is fully described and justified by Randy Maddox,[9] I am hoping to release the underlying theological structure of his work from the problems of transitions between each 'stage', and the nature of the final stage, perfection, which dominated the eighteenth-century reception of Wesley's theology, and much nineteenth-century development of it within the Holiness tradition. His 1765 sermon, 'The Scripture Way of Salvation', gives an outline of this *via salutis*. The whole of salvation is a therapeutic growth from a sinful nature towards restoration of the image of God in which humanity was created. This way begins with God's prevenient grace, awakening the soul to the need for salvation from sin, and provoking the repentance which leads to justifying faith.[10] Justification is forgiveness and pardon for sins, made possible by the atonement of Christ. Justification is accompanied, simultaneously, by the commencement of sanctification – the new birth. Wesley stresses this distinction, insisting that justification is the ground of our changed relationship with God, but not alone the means by which we are made righteous (in opposition to some Reformed accounts of purely imputed righteousness). He explains the difference between justification and sanctification as that between a 'relative' and a 'real' change. In justification there is a relative change in the inauguration of a new relationship between God and his pardoned child, and in the new birth there is a real change in the heart and will of the believer beginning the process of sanctification.[11] Wesley identifies the work of Christ in the atonement particularly with justification, affecting the relative change, and the work of the Spirit in the believer with sanctification, affecting the real change.[12] Sanctification is thus the work of God in the life of believers following justification, a process by which a believer is changed in order to become entirely sanctified, or perfect.

For Wesley, it was the end point of this process which caused most problems theologically. He insisted that perfection was realizable in this life, wrought by the action of the Holy Spirit in the life of the believer. He claimed this to be a sinless perfection, but only with a careful definition of sin which included only 'the voluntary transgression of a known law'.[13] Wesley was also careful to explain that he did not insist on the possibility of reaching this perfection because of a scriptural principle, but because of the experience testified to by members of the Methodist Societies.[14] He conceded that Scripture could be used to present valid arguments both for and against the instantaneous nature of entire sanctification.[15] Bearing this in mind, and as there are no longer the same volume and intensity of testimonies to experiences of entire sanctification, it is reasonable to operate within a Wesleyan theology of sanctification without insisting upon the instantaneous actualization of entire sanctification. Wesley himself, and some current advocates of a holiness tradition, might argue that the reason a community finds itself lacking in such testimonies is due to the lack of expectation of such experiences.[16] However, it could also be attributed to twentieth century changes in attitudes to sin and the subconscious self, which reasonably cast suspicion upon claims to sinlessness and complete purity of intention.

By the early to mid-twentieth century, many Wesleyan theologians were taking an approach similar to the latter perspective. R. Newton Flew's reservations about Wesley's doctrine in his expansive study of the *Idea of Perfection* throughout Christian history serve as an exemplar of this.[17] He critiques Wesley's attitude to sin as offering only an inadequate account of moral evil, and attributes this to his dependence on an Augustinian model (as Newton Flew perceives it) of sin as substance. Thus, Wesley can posit an over-optimistic instantaneous end to the effects of sin, of which one can be assured by reference to this particular point of experience. Most telling of Newton Flew's criticisms is that the result of these problems is an 'intramundane asceticism', whereby the one assured of sanctification merely endures secular life, allowing a barrier to exist between one's work and worship. Newton Flew argues that a more adequate account of sin as the thorough corruption of faculties that are essentially good would lead to a more careful attitude to the possibility of rescue from sin and to the assurance of this only ever being in, and for, the present moment, neither resting solely on a previous experience nor able to underpin future sanctification. This negative attitude to Wesley has been countered more recently by detailed forensic study of Wesley's texts and particularly the development of his doctrine over time. Randy L. Maddox's work represents the most accomplished synthesis of this approach. He finds within Wesley's texts precisely the corrections offered by Newton Flew, though only amidst a multiplicity of views over time on most key issues. Maddox applies the interpretative key of 'responsible grace' to Wesley's internal inconsistencies and developments in response to particular situations; in all aspects of the Christian life God's grace is given freely but also graciously dependent upon human response. He hopes that demonstrating the way that, from this perspective, Wesley's whole theological work over his lifetime maintains coherence can contribute 'to the broader contemporary discussion about the possibility of consistency in situation-related theological activity'.[18] My ambition goes further, hoping that the central doctrinal positions to be discerned as underlying Wesley's sanctification-focused soteriology can also offer a doctrinal basis and even a necessity for situation-related, or as it is described above, contextual, theological activity. This alternative view of Wesley's sanctification is the opposite of the 'intramundane asceticism' offered by Newton Flew; it is something akin to the fully relational way of holiness, and a way towards resolution of the tensions between holiness and cultural context apparent in 1 Peter.

Doctrinal foundations of Wesleyan entire sanctification

Wesley's insistence upon the possibility of entire sanctification reflects a reluctance to limit the work of God's grace and its effects on human life. Wesley offered a thorough 'optimism of grace'[19] by which all things and all people are redeemable and perfectible. This very basic impulse can be seen to permeate all of Wesley's doctrinal positions and to be the essence of the most significant of his theological polemics, those against eighteenth-century Calvinism. Herbert B. McGonigle outlines Wesley's opposition to Calvinism on philosophical, theological, biblical and pastoral grounds, but perceives as running throughout and behind all of these his doctrine of prevenient grace, or as Wesley often calls it, 'preventing grace';[20] grace which works ahead of, and in preparation for, our responsive acceptance and cooperation. While this is primarily developed around the question of initial conversion (as in the outline above derived from the sermon 'The Scripture Way of Salvation') and the state of humanity prior to salvation, it also underpins Wesley's whole sanctification-led anthropology, soteriology and indeed eschatology.

Wesley's theological anthropology is distinctive because he tended to base it neither on the situation of humanity before the fall, nor on the situation subsequent to the fall, but on the situation of humanity as it is in the process of being transformed by God. Borrowing Maddox's phrase, it is based on 'a third state, the gracious and gradual restoration of humanity to God-likeness'.[21] Wesley does include the original perfection of humanity prior to the fall and the state of fallen humanity in his theology, but only insofar as they are related to his primary concern of explaining, proclaiming and promoting the theology of sanctification. He was only drawn into an extensive consideration of his own anthropology when he perceived this soteriology to be threatened. Hence, his most extended reflections on anthropology were in reaction to Dr John Taylor's *The Scripture Doctrine of Original Sin: Proposed to Free and Candid Examination* (1740) that threatened Wesley's soteriology by arguing against the doctrine of original sin. Wesley prefaced his defence of original sin with an appeal to soteriology, using Plato's phrase, *therapeia psyches* to describe the whole of Christian philosophy, as based on the Christian revelation which 'speaks of nothing else but the great "Physician" of our souls'.[22] The primary reason to uphold the doctrine of original sin is the need to preserve the explanation for the *therapeia psyches*, the essence of his soteriology. He is concerned to ensure that salvation both avoids moralism and thoroughly relies upon grace, and so his anthropology develops into what resembles a combination of the Reformed emphasis on 'entire deprivation'[23] and the Greek patristic emphasis on *therapeia psyches*; by our fallen nature, humanity is totally deprived of the image of God, but by the grace of God it can be restored to us. Wesley's explanations of the original state of humanity, as represented by Adam, and the process and consequences of the fall from that state are informed by this need to establish an anthropology of current humanity that holds nature (that which we find ourselves to be as long as we are without any specific change wrought by God) and grace (that which God intends us to be, and the means by which this can be realized) in a carefully balanced tension. He charts a middle way between, at one extreme, an excessive optimism about nature, and at the other an excessive pessimism about grace. He rejects any excessive optimism of nature because it implies a complementary 'redundancy of grace',[24] and excessive pessimism about grace because it limits the power of God to be able to effect real change in human lives and character.[25] Steering away from these two extremes, Wesley instead holds together a thorough *pessimism of nature* with a thorough *optimism of grace*.[26]

His pessimism of nature is founded upon the effects of the fall which entail that all humans are corrupted by 'inbeing sin'. The fact that Wesley increasingly preferred this term to 'original sin'[27] illustrates his progression through discomfort with the notion that all are born guilty with the accompanying attitude to all flesh that 'it deserveth God's wrath and damnation',[28] towards an account of inbeing sin which maintains the individual responsibility for its effects on their lives. Such individual responsibility entails that everyone has some power to resist the effects of inbeing sin. However, rather than completely dispensing with the notion that original sin results in universal guilt, he instead tempered it with an equal and opposite grace that is always active preveniently. The power to resist sin is supplied, even prior to reception of justifying faith, 'from the first dawning of grace in the soul'.[29] This power is evident in 'all that is wrought in the soul by what is frequently termed "natural conscience", but more properly, "preventing grace"'.[30] This gracious anthropology is most clear with respect to Wesley's mature position on infants, which he expressed in a letter of 1776: because of both universal condemnation and universal justification: 'no infant ever was or ever will be "sent to hell for the guilt of Adam's sin," seeing it is cancelled by the righteousness of Christ as soon as they are sent into the world'.[31] Thus, although Wesley does on some occasions give time to the consideration of the process and consequences of the fall, of more importance for understanding his mature anthropology is his account of prevenient grace. It is the universality of prevenient grace that throws the focus of his anthropology onto the 'third state' of humanity in process of sanctification.

Some of Wesley's later sermons in particular develop the implications of prevenient grace as the presence of the Holy Spirit operative throughout the process of sanctification, for individuals and for the world. In his sermon 'On Working Our Own Salvation' Wesley establishes that not only is specifically prevenient grace operative prior to the new birth of the individual, but also that the nature of all grace is prevenient. He allows that 'heathens' have access to prevenient grace through conscience such that, though they do not know God's law, they are able to act in accordance with it:[32] 'There is no man that is in a state of mere nature; there is no man, unless he has quenched the Spirit that is wholly void of the grace of God. ... Everyone has some measure of that light, some faint glimmering ray, which sooner or later, more or less, enlightens every man that cometh into the world.'[33]

Prevenient grace, acting as 'natural conscience' is at work in all people, and this is no less than the presence of the Spirit of God. Wesley divides the action of the Son and the Spirit in salvation such that the Sprit works preveniently to move people towards a knowledge of the work of the Son in justifying faith, but conversely, this work of the Spirit is also founded upon the offer of grace to all people through the sacrifice and intercession of the Son. The heathens to whom Wesley's anthropology is so generous do not, though, know of the Son of God who has given himself to be 'a propitiation for the sins of the world',[34] nor of the Spirit of God who is renewing people in that image of God wherein they were created. However, it is the work of the Spirit, as yet unknown, that preveniently prepares people for salvation. This passage from the sermon 'On the Fall of Man' explains how the Spirit is constantly at work preparing and effecting our sanctification through the transformation of our relation to contextual experience, and merits full quotation as it is central to the contextual methodology I pursue:

> For God hath also, through the intercession of his Son, 'given us his Holy Spirit,' to 'renew' us both 'in knowledge,' in his natural image, 'opening the eyes of our understanding, and enlightening' us with all such knowledge as is requisite to our pleasing God; and also in his moral image, namely, 'righteousness and true holiness.' And supposing this is done, we know that 'all things will work together for our good.' We know by happy experience that all natural evils change their nature and turn to good; that sorrow, sickness, pain, will all prove medicines to heal our spiritual sickness. They will all be 'to our profit'; will all tend to our unspeakable advantage, making us more largely 'partakers of his holiness' while we remain on earth, adding so many stars to that crown which is reserved for us in heaven.[35]

In this passage, Wesley addresses the problem of the clash between the striving of the faithful community for holiness and the 'natural evils' that beset us. His proposal is not an ascetic escape from the bodily secular world, but the transformation of its relation to the Christian person. This transformation is wrought both by a change in the holiness of the individual and community, and also by a change in their knowledge and understanding. The way that we perceive the context within which we seek to exercise righteousness and true holiness is transformed by the renewal of the Holy Spirit: we experience 'natural evils' as 'medicines to heal our spiritual sickness'. Expressing this within the narrative discord of holiness versus culture in 1 Peter 1:14–16 explored at the outset, both the internal conflict between obedience to unholy desires and obedience to holy conduct, and the external conflict between the community and its persecutors, are resolved not by a cessation of relations but by their transformation. This transformation results in the struggle and striving of the conflict itself becoming redemptive and sanctifying, and it is produced by an end to ignorance (which was causing 'the desires that you formerly had in ignorance') and consequently by an 'opening of the eyes of the understanding'. The outworking of this method of relating sanctification, Scripture and cultural context can be seen later in the letter when the issues of slavery (2:18–15) and marital relations (3:1–7) are brought to bear on the question of what being 'holy in all conduct' entails. The practices of the host culture for the Christian community are neither fully opposed nor endorsed, but rather engaged with in order to allow the believers involved in them to pursue holiness. That is not to say that the positions taken are neutral; they are transformative in the way they relate the overarching narrative of the text, primarily the work of Christ, to the cultural practices, and through this dialogue are laid the foundations for the development of a challenge to slavery and the subjugation of women by later readers of the text. These later readers were communities with a different relation to their context and whose understanding had been transformed both by this new situation and the continuing work of the Spirit in successive generations of Christian communities.

This opening of the eyes of our understanding corresponds to the reliance of Wesley's theological epistemology on the concept of the awakening of the 'spiritual senses'.[36] The centrality of this concept is apparent from Wesley's theological treatise 'An Earnest Appeal to Men of Reason and Religion'. He begins this with a description of the 'fundamental principles'[37] of his doctrine which consist primarily of a definition of faith based on the spiritual senses. Citing Hebrews 11:1, the main scriptural source of this concept, Wesley describes faith as 'the demonstrative evidence of things unseen, the supernatural evidence of the invisible, not perceivable by eyes of flesh, or by any natural senses or faculties ... the spiritual sensation of every soul that is born of God'.[38] This is the epistemological complement of the *via media* between nature and grace: natural faculties are unable to perceive spiritual things, nor furnish ideas and thence understanding of spiritual realities. Human reason is unable to understand divine things, so unable to be sanctified by its own work:

> This cannot be till the Almighty come in to your succour, and give you that faith you have hitherto despised ... [then] your enlightened reason shall explore even 'the deep things of God', God himself 'revealing them to you by his Spirit'.[39]

This epistemology is based on a Lockean account of reason and the processes of the faculties of the mind, not easily transferable to current accounts of knowledge with more prominent narrative and communal features. However, the fact that Wesley relates the awakening of a spiritual sense to faith cements the important place of new insight and understanding in the process of sanctification. Faith is the gift of God whereby humans are enabled to participate in salvation, and this 'salvation by faith is ... the love of God by the knowledge of God, or the recovery of the image of God by a true spiritual acquaintance with him'.[40]

This raises one final point regarding the Wesleyan doctrine described thus far: the place and limits of experience as an authority is crucial to the construction of a contextual methodology. The primary experience for the spiritual senses to apprehend is a perception of God and divine things. However, the above account of the relation between prevenient grace and engagement in a 'natural' context entails that the very struggle of this engagement is transformative. Hence, drawing on the relation in Wesley's epistemology between salvation and understanding, the Spirit at work in every person and situation produces 'spiritual acquaintance' with God through such experiences. All experience is potentially spiritual when seen with the eyes and understanding of faith. Experience is a source of authority for Wesley – we have already noted how the experience of entire sanctification among the Methodist Societies influenced his scriptural interpretation. Indeed, Wesley admits that if there were no such testimonies of perfection, he would consider himself to have misinterpreted the Scriptures.[41] Despite this theoretical admission of an occasion when Wesley would allow the authority of experience to correct what seems to be the plain interpretation of Scripture, the role for experience as an authority is fairly limited. Scott J. Jones offers an important corrective to some earlier analyses which over-emphasized Wesley's view of experience.[42] Referring not even to perfection, but to justification and regeneration, Wesley makes clear that 'experience is not sufficient to prove a doctrine which is not founded on Scripture',[43] and that the role of experience is to confirm scriptural doctrine.[44] It is at this point that a divergence with the Wesleyan method I am constructing and the attitude of Wesley is most apparent.

Wesley had an optimistic attitude to the Scriptures and the expectation of accurate interpretation, provided that the reader employs reason which has been, and is being, enlightened by the Spirit.[45] He reads Scripture in order to discover the nature of salvation,[46] which entails holiness, and the means to attain it, but also as a means of grace by which the Spirit works to give the faith necessary to salvation and sanctification.[47] In contrast to this optimistic expectation of finding the way towards holy living made clear, the reading of 1 Peter above finds tension within the narratives of the text, and between them and those narratives arising from the context in which Scripture is being read. This is an analysis that offers less optimism than Wesley presumes when interpreting the text in isolation. Applying the dynamic of Wesley's prevenient grace to the reading not only of Scripture but also of context and experience provides a way to engage contextually within a scriptural and theological methodology. This proposal relies on approaching the contextual reading of Scripture, and the complementary scriptural reading of context, only from the perspective of a reader in the process of sanctification.[48] Couching this within a Wesleyan doctrinal framework retains the primacy of Scripture in the process because of the expectation that Scripture is a means of grace for sanctification. Scripture as sanctifying text shapes and informs the reader's response both to itself and to the reader's context. When read with eyes of faith, Scripture enlightens the reason in order to produce a spiritual and rational interpretation of both text and context.

Conclusions

A Wesleyan dynamic for entire sanctification models and impels an evangelical contextual methodology, and provides the motivation, the doctrine and the tools with which to pursue it. I have identified the outline of these, pointed to some of the work that has been undertaken to describe better Wesley's attitude to them and to develop them for new contexts, and I suggest that these are fruitful areas for further study. First, a Wesleyan dynamic provides the impetus for submitting Scripture and theology to dialogue and interrogation by the context of the reader, for by engaging in this way the Christian community is drawn further into the process of sanctification. Second, it provides the doctrinal basis for this contextual reading through the notion of universal prevenient grace. The justifying work of Christ is for all people, whose response to this grace is encouraged and prepared by the work of the Spirit in all situations and lives. To engage in Christian theology and the interpretation of Scripture in dialogue with secular thought and practice, and in a multi-faith context, is not to abandon the authority of Scripture, but to allow the Spirit's work to become apparent, drawing all to experience the confirmation of Scripture and to live within the drama of the narrative of Scripture.[49] Third, this Wesleyan dynamic provides the tools necessary for a contextual reading. Practically, this refers to the theological methodology of balancing the primary authority of Scripture with that of human experience, and, though not explored here, also that of the various theological expressions throughout Christian tradition. This practical methodology is complemented by the spiritual resources provided by a Wesleyan theological epistemology; central to a fitting theological expression and interpretation of Scripture is the sanctification of the individuals involved. The spiritual senses are awakened, the eyes of faith opened, and the Spirit enlightens our reason as we apply ourselves to the task of fully engaging in our context and seeking the way to holiness within it. Through this set of motivations, doctrines and tools, the Wesleyan doctrine of entire sanctification should not be forgotten, ignored or lost amidst the controversies over the sinless perfection of individuals, but can be utilized for the discovery of good news in every situation and context. At the heart of our pursuit of holiness is to love God and to love our neighbour – and so we are fully immersed in our context in order to work with our neighbour to discern the prevenient grace of the Spirit in all our lives, challenging and encouraging all people towards discovering the knowledge and love of God for themselves.

I will end by noting briefly that the complexities of the relationship between the Christian pursuit of holiness and the particular cultural context for that pursuit are to an extent mirrored by the relationships between recent evangelical theological work and the post-liberal theological context. This Wesleyan dynamic can provide an evangelical methodology which bears some relation to contextual methodologies which do not arise from evangelical roots. Most theology which pays a deliberate and constructive attention to context, since George Lindbeck's coining of the phrase, can be characterized as 'cultural-linguistic'.[50] It aims either to describe the cultural-linguistic patterns of Christian practice (while accepting that this description is not neutral),[51] or more self-consciously to shape them with a particular aim in view.[52] A Wesleyan doctrinal and methodological approach can produce an attention to contextuality, with either of these emphases, but only does so by asserting the priority of the experience of sanctification. This experience of sanctification is primarily that of the individual Christian reflecting on practice, but it is also informed by the experience of the universal prevenient work of the Holy Spirit. The process and the content of theological formulation in relation to cultural context is provoked and guided by the Holy Spirit, and then results in new ways of participating in the on-going and future work of the Spirit. This pneumatological embrace around theological work is what allows a Wesleyan sanctification perspective to provide connections between, on the one hand, an evangelical focus upon the spiritual experience of conversion and sanctification and, on the other, the many valuable insights of contextual methodologies arising from other theological perspectives. The potential that these connections offer must be explored more fully in the future.

Notes

1 This account is assisted by Joel B. Green's helpful narrative reading of 1 and 2 Peter. He argues that the theology of the text is more adequately elucidated for the context of current readers when read within this overarching story as it is being related to the situation of the addressees, rather than by extracting propositional doctrinal statements from the epistle; J. B. Green, 'Narrating the Gospel in 1 and 2 Peter', *Interpretation*, 2006, vol. 60.3, 262–77.

2 In this volume, this issue is addressed specifically with regards to eschatology by Tom Greggs in his chapter, 'Beyond the Binary'. I also note the conclusion of Dryness that: 'The continuing failure to integrate expanding multicultural experience into a consistent understanding of culture and cultural engagement still bedevils the evangelical movement'; W. A. Dryness, 'Evangelical Theology and Culture', in T. Larsen (ed.) *The Cambridge Companion to Evangelical Theology*, Cambridge: Cambridge University Press, 2007, p. 155.

3 J. Webster, *Holiness*, London: SCM Press, 2003, pp. 3–5.

4 D. W. Hardy, 'Worship and the Formation of a Holy People', in S. C. Barton (ed.) *Holiness Past and Present*, London: T&T Clark, 2003, p. 487.

5 References to Wesley's sermons are to the text as published in A. C. Outler (ed.) *The Bicentennial Edition of the Works of John Wesley*, vols 1–4, Nashville, TN: Abingdon Press, 1984, 1985, 1986, 1987; abbreviation: *Works*.

6 J. Telford (ed.), *The Letters of the Rev. John Wesley*, London: The Epworth Press, 1931, vol. 8, p. 238. For a full list of similar references see H. B. McGonigle, *Sufficient Saving Grace: John Wesley's Evangelical Arminianism*, Carlisle: Paternoster Press, 2001, p. 242.

7 See the sermon published in 1770, 'On the Death of George Whitfield', §III.4, *Works*, vol. 2, p. 343.

8 See the sermon published in 1748, 'Upon our Lord's Sermon on the Mount: Discourse the Third', §IV.1, *Works*, vol. 1, p. 530.

9 R. L. Maddox, *Responsible Grace: John Wesley's Practical Theology*, Nashville: Abingdon Press, 1994, pp. 157–8.

10 Sermon published in 1765, 'The Scripture Way of Salvation', §I.2, *Works*, vol. 2, p. 156.

11 'Scripture Way of Salvation', §I.4, *Works*, vol. 2, p. 158.

12 Ibid. Thus he describes justification as 'what God does *for us* through his Son' and sanctification as 'what he *works in us* by his Spirit' (sermon published in 1746, 'Justification by Faith', §II.1, *Works*, vol. 1, p. 187, his italics). Cf. this use of the *favour* and *image* of God: 'By justification we are saved from the guilt of sin, and restored to the favour of God; by sanctification we are saved from the power and root of sin, and restored to the

image of God' (sermon published in 1785, 'On Working Out Our Own Salvation', §II.1, *Works*, vol. 3, p. 204).

13 Wesley typically describes this as 'sin properly called' (e.g. in his 'Plain Account of Christian Perfection', T. Jackson (ed.) *The Works of the Rev. John Wesley A.M.*, London: John Mason, 1872, vol. XI, p. 396) and defends it as the scriptural understanding of sin (e.g. in the sermon published in 1785, 'On Perfection', §II.9, *Works*, vol. 3, p. 79).

14 'The Scripture Way of Salvation', §III.18, *Works*, vol. 2, p. 169; cf. the more detailed version of this argument in the sermon published in 1784, 'On Patience', §§11–12, *Works*, vol. 3, p. 177.

15 Ibid.

16 Wesley makes this expedient argument explicitly: see *Journal* entry for 15 Sept. 1762, *Works*, vol. 21, p. 389, and 'Large Minutes', Question 56, *Works* (Jackson), vol. VIII, p. 329. From a historical perspective, Henry Rack points out that the rise in testimonies of perfection corresponds with a change in Wesley's preaching to encourage expectation of instantaneous sanctification; H. D. Rack, *Reasonable Enthusiast: John Wesley and the Rise of Methodism*, Peterborough: Epworth, 2002, p. 335.

17 R. Newton Flew, *The Idea of Perfection in Christian Theology: An Historical Study of the Christian Ideal for the Present Life*, London: Oxford University Press, 1934, pp. 332–41.

18 Maddox, *Responsible Grace*, p. 19.

19 A phrase first coined in relation to Wesley by E. G. Rupp, *Principalities and Powers: Studies in the Christian Conflict in History*, London: Epworth Press, 1952.

20 McGonigle, *Sufficient Saving Grace*, pp. 318, 328.

21 Maddox, *Responsible Grace*, p. 67.

22 'The Doctrine of Original Sin: According to Scripture, Reason and Experience' (1757), Preface §4, *Works* (Jackson), vol. IX, p. 194; cf. sermon published in 1759, 'Original Sin', §III.3, *Works*, vol. 2, p. 184.

23 Wesley does not use the more typical term 'total depravity', but does use similar terms on a handful of occasions, e.g. 'entire deprivation' (sermon published in 1759, 'Original Sin', §III.1, *Works*, vol. 2, p. 183) and 'universal depravity of our nature (in which dwelleth no good thing)' (sermon published in 1786, *Of the Church*, §II.21, *Works*, vol. 3, p. 53). Outler and Maddox both give a full account of Wesley's relationship to a Calvinist understanding of depravity: Outler, 'Introduction', in *Works*, vol. 1, pp. 80–1, and Maddox, *Responsible Grace*, p. 82.

24 'Doctrine of Original Sin', Part II, §ii, 17, *Works* (Jackson), vol. IX, p. 283; this phrase is a quotation from p. 149 of Taylor's treatise.

25 Wesley argues that by the last judgement it is within the power of the grace of God to go further than just to cover over our corrupt nature, but actually to accomplish 'the renewal of the soul "in the image of God wherein it was created". ... The imagination that faith supersedes holiness is the marrow of antinomianism', sermon published in 1791, 'On the Wedding Garment', §§17–18, *Works*, vol. 4, p. 148.

26 A comparison to Tom Greggs' chapter is again apparent here; he uses a similar position to describe the relation between evangelical soteriology and eschatology (see p. 155 of this volume).

27 Wesley was ambivalent about this term, and tended only to use it when engaged in polemics over such issues; addressing Taylor he writes of: 'this infection of our nature (call it original sin, or what you please)' (*Works* (Jackson), vol. IX, p. 274); for a full tracing of his use of 'original sin' and 'inbeing sin', see Maddox, *Responsible Grace*, p. 74.

28 Article IX, 'Of Original or Birth-sin', *Book of Common Prayer* (1662).

29 'Scripture Way of Salvation', §I.1, *Works*, vol. 2, p. 156.

30 Ibid. §I.2.

31 Letter to John Mason, 21 November 1776, J. Telford (ed.) *The Letters of the Rev. John Wesley, A.M.*, London: Epworth, 1931, vol. 6, pp. 239–40. This is usually recognized as

Wesley's clearest expression of the universality of prevenient grace; for example, McGonigle, *Sufficient Saving Grace*, p. 327 and Maddox, *Responsible Grace*, p. 75.

32   Sermon published in 1785, 'On Working Out Our Own Salvation', §I.4, *Works*, vol. 3, pp. 199–200.

33   Ibid., §III.4, *Works*, vol. 3, p. 207.

34   Ibid., §1.2, *Works*, vol. 3, p. 200; cf. 1 John 2:2.

35   Sermon published in 1782, 'On the Fall of Man', §II.8, *Works*, vol. 2, pp. 410–11.

36   Wesley's use and adaptation of this concept is attributable to a variety of sources from Christian tradition, but most clearly to the theological extension of a Lockean epistemology in Peter Browne's *The Procedure, Extent and Limits of Human Understanding (1729)*. For a full account of Wesley's relation to Browne and Locke see R. Brantley, *Locke, Wesley and the Method of English Romanticism*, Gainesville: University of Florida Press, 1984, pp. 1–101. Cf. a brief summary of alternative accounts of the roots of Wesley's 'spiritual senses' in Maddox, *Responsible Grace*, pp. 27–8, and a detailed analysis stressing the influence of Greek patristic sources in H.-J. Lee, 'The Doctrine of New Creation in the Theology of John Wesley', Unpublished PhD Dissertation: Emory University, 1991, pp. 129–42.

37   'An Earnest Appeal to Men of Reason and Religion' (1743), §12, *Works*, vol. 11, p. 49.

38   Ibid., §6, *Works*, vol. 11, p. 6.

39   Ibid., §35, *Works*, vol. 11, p. 57.

40   'A Farther Appeal to Men of Reason and Religion', Part I, §I.3, *Works*, vol. 11, p. 106.

41   'Plain Account', §19, *Works* (Jackson), vol. XI, p. 406.

42   S. J. Jones, *John Wesley's Conception and Use of Scripture*, Nashville, TN: Abingdon Press, 1995, p. 96; as an example of this over-emphasis on experience he cites G. Croft Cell, *The Rediscovery of John Wesley*, New York: Henry Holt, 1935, p. 45.

43   Sermon published in 1767, 'The Witness of the Spirit II', §IV.1, *Works*, vol. 1, p. 293.

44   Ibid., §III.6, *Works*, vol. 1, p. 290.

45   Sermon published in 1750, 'The Nature of Enthusiasm', §25, *Works*, vol. 2, p. 55. Here I follow Jones' detailed account of Wesley's views on the purpose and nature of the interpretation of Scripture: Jones, *John Wesley's Conception and Use of Scripture*, pp. 104–10.

46   Sermon published in 1760, 'The New Birth', §§II.2–3, *Works*, vol. 2, p. 191.

47   Sermon published in 1746, 'The Means of Grace', §III.10, *Works*, vol. 1, pp. 388–9.

48   As Richard S. Briggs puts it: 'Text and action are bound together, we might say, in the transforming of the reader' (this volume, p. 25).

49   Recent work pursuing this point to which I have not already referred includes, for example, P. R. Meadows, 'Wesleyan Theology for World Context', in P. R. Meadows (ed.) *Windows on Wesley: Wesleyan Theology in Today's World*, Oxford: Applied Theology Press, 1997, pp. 20–52. Meadows draws out some themes similar to those here, but focuses more on Wesley's view of providence and its application in global perspective. With respect to an interfaith perspective see e.g. E. Harris, 'Wesleyan Witness in an Interreligious Context', in Meadows (ed.) *Windows on Wesley*, pp. 53–85; and R. L. Miles, 'John Wesley as Interreligious Resource: Would You Take This Man to an Interfaith Dialogue?', in M. Forward, S. Plant and S. White (eds) *A Great Commission: Christian Hope and Religious Diversity*, Bern: Peter Lang, 2000, pp. 61–75.

50   G. A. Lindbeck, *The Nature of Doctrine: Religion and Theology in a Postliberal Age*, Louisville, KY: Westminster John Knox Press, 1984, passim.

51   Cf. the description of 'pastoral theology' as: 'critical phenomenology, studying a living and acting faith-community in order to excavate the norms which inhabit pastoral praxis', in E. Graham *Transforming Practice: Pastoral Theology in an Age of Uncertainty*, London: Mowbray, 1996, p. 140.

52   Gerkin's work displays this more programmatic approach, and in some respects his approach is similar to the Wesleyan dynamic I have described: he defines 'practical

theology' as 'the critical and constructive reflection on the life and work of Christians in all the varied contexts in which that life takes place with the intention of facilitating transformation of life in all its dimensions in accordance with the Christian gospel,' in C. V. Gerkin, *Widening the Horizons: Pastoral Responses to a Fragmented Society*, Philadelphia, PA: The Westminster Press, 1986, p. 61.

Select bibliography

Primary sources

The Bicentennial Edition of the Works of John Wesley, vols 1–4: Sermons, A. C. Outler (ed.), Nashville, TN: Abingdon Press, 1984, 1985, 1986, 1987.
The Bicentennial Edition of the Works of John Wesley, vol. 11: The Appeals to Men of Reason and Religion and Certain Related Open Letters, G. R. Cragg (ed.), Oxford: Clarendon Press, 1975.

Secondary sources

Dryness, W. A., 'Evangelical Theology and Culture', in *The Cambridge Companion to Evangelical Theology*, Cambridge: Cambridge University Press, 2007, pp. 145–59.
Jones, S. J., *John Wesley's Conception and Use of Scripture*, Nashville, TN: Abingdon Press, 1995.
McGonigle, H. B., *Sufficient Saving Grace: John Wesley's Evangelical Arminianism*, Carlisle: Paternoster Press, 2001.
Maddox, R. L., *Responsible Grace: John Wesley's Practical Theology*, Nashville, TN: Abingdon Press, 1994.
Meadows, P. R. (ed.), *Windows on Wesley: Wesleyan Theology in Today's World*, Oxford: Applied Theology Press, 1997.
Rack, H. D., *Reasonable Enthusiast: John Wesley and the Rise of Methodism*, 3rd edn, Peterborough: Epworth Press, 2002.

Chapter 6

Reformation pessimism or Pietist personalism?

The problem of the Holy Spirit in evangelical theology

Simeon Zahl

Evangelical understanding of the work of the Holy Spirit has been shaped primarily by two distinct pneumatological developments. The first development dates back to the heart of the Reformation in the sixteenth century: the conviction that Scripture is the supremely privileged and authoritative instrument of God's Spirit in the world. Although the 'Scripture principle' is often discussed as a theological locus in its own right, historically it was first worked out mainly as a pneumatological designation, as we shall see. The second development is closely associated with evangelicalism's historical 'grandparent', European Pietism, and involves the importance of felt personal experience of Christ through the Spirit. This mediation of what is often referred to as a 'personal relationship with Jesus Christ', too, is primarily a pneumatological category: Christ is made known to us and dwells in us by the Spirit. These two pneumatological emphases are so integral to evangelical identity that Timothy Larsen counts them as two of the five determining criteria for defining what an 'evangelical' is.[1]

There is a basic problem with these two pneumatological criteria, however. Understood in light of their historical-theological heritage, the 'Scripture principle' and what I will call 'pneumatological personalism' stand in significant tension with one another. Specifically, the 'Scripture principle' was developed in its earliest stages precisely as a *critique* of an understanding of experience of the Spirit that is a foundational component of 'personalism', at least as it has tended to be understood from early German Pietism to the present. Put another way, there is a fundamental tension – bordering on contradiction – in evangelical thought and practice between the doctrine of sin and the doctrine of the Holy Spirit.

In what follows, I will explore the nature of this pneumatological tension and its potentially problematic consequences. Along the way, we will touch on several salient features of evangelical history and background. These will include Martin Luther's early debate with the 'enthusiasts' in the 1520s; the emphasis on 'personal experience', especially unmediated experience, generally present in Pietist and Methodist theology; John Wesley's defense against the charge of 'enthusiasm'; and the witness of a crucial figure in late nineteenth and early twentieth century Pietism and the pre-history of the Pentecostal movement, Christoph Friedrich Blumhardt. There is not room here to go into a great deal of historical and theological detail in relation to these themes, but a general overview will serve to indicate the basic contours of the problem. In the concluding section I will sketch one avenue evangelical doctrine of the Holy Spirit might follow, taking its cue from aspects of Johannine descriptions of the Spirit, in order to move beyond this problem, by holding together both the Reformation wariness about the deceitfulness of the heart (Jer. 17:9) and the affective and pastoral power of pneumatological personalism.

Martin Luther and the problem of spiritual self-deception

It is well known that Martin Luther emphasized the authority and centrality of the Bible over and against the ecclesial authority of the Roman Catholic Church. Less well known, but equally important, was his early rejection of the error of 'enthusiasm' on the same basis. Indeed, in The Smalcald Articles he understands the traditional view of papal doctrinal and spiritual authority to be a sort of 'sub-heresy' under the larger umbrella of 'enthusiasm'.[2]

What does Luther mean by 'enthusiasm'? The term – in German, *Schwärmerei* – has a long theological history, but it is Luther with whom it is most closely associated. In his view, 'enthusiasm' describes an erroneous understanding of the relationship between the Word of God in the preached text of Scripture,[3] and the activity of the Spirit in the inward life of a believer. The mistake of the *Schwärmer* is that 'they boast that the Spirit has come into them without the preaching of the Scriptures'.[4] The problem is not that they reject the authority of Scripture outright, which they do not. It is rather that they do not believe experience of the Spirit to be limited *exclusively* to the instrumentality of the Word preached. Luther explains what he means in his most extensive treatment of the problem of 'enthusiasm', the treatise *Against the Heavenly Prophets*:

> Now when God sends forth his holy gospel he deals with us in a twofold manner, first outwardly, then inwardly. Outwardly he deals with us through the oral word of the gospel and through material signs, that is, baptism and the sacrament of the altar. Inwardly he deals with us through the Holy Spirit, faith, and other gifts. But whatever their measure or order the outward factors should and must precede. The inward experience follows and is effected by the outward. God has determined to give the inward to no one except through the outward. ... Observe carefully, my brother, this order, for everything depends on it.[5]

For Luther, any claim to experience of the Spirit apart from the direct instrumentality of the 'external Word' (*verbum externum*) is false by definition.[6]

This view of the Word is strikingly high. The action of the Spirit in the world is tied so completely and directly to the scriptural text as to border on the magical. Luther is saying that in the post-apostolic church the Spirit will never act in a decisive way in a person's life apart from during a sermon or the reception of the sacraments. 'Damascus' experiences, for example, do not happen any more: God has chosen to speak instead through the Bible alone. The old joke, 'Father, Son, and Holy Scripture' is perhaps all too apt. Why would Luther resort to such drastic measures to safeguard the centrality of Scripture? Why is he so worried about experience not mediated exclusively by the 'external Word'?

The answer to this question brings us into the domain of *anthropology*, the theological understanding of human nature. Luther's insight into 'enthusiasm' was to perceive how intimately pneumatology must be connected with the doctrine of sin in Protestant thought. His concern was that human nature, in its irrepressible egoism, could not be trusted to perceive the unmediated action of God in itself with any clarity or reliability. Left to its own devices, human nature will actively pursue idolatry and evil, though often without realizing it.[7] Any 'spirit' not rigorously connected with the *verbum externum* will be a false one: 'the spirit of these prophets is the devil's spirit'.[8] The problem with the *Schwärmer* is that they are self-deceived, 'curved in' on themselves, unwittingly baptizing the impulses of their sinful flesh by attributing them to the direct personal activity of the Holy Spirit in their lives.[9] In Luther's view, the 'enthusiast' believes he or she is in direct personal communication with God, but in fact is talking only to themselves, or to the devil. As he famously put it, the *Schwärmer* have 'devoured the Holy Spirit feathers and all'.[10]

Because they allow for the Holy Spirit to speak outside of the preaching of the Word, when the 'fanatics' do read the Word they get nothing out of it: they 'understand nothing in the Scriptures', and 'neither seek nor find anything therein but their own dreams'.[11] In this critique, Luther is anticipating the powerful broadsides against Christianity by Feuerbach, Marx and Freud, who claim in their different ways that mighty unconscious forces, rather than reason or the conscious will, are the true, secret captains of the human ship. For Luther, who understood the Christian to be *simul iustus et peccator* (at the same time justified and a sinner), the possibility of radical egoistic self-deception cannot be ruled out in a given instance, even for the justified believer. When someone claims that God has told them something directly, or that they have encountered the Spirit in the profundity of the natural world or in a perceived providential coincidence, they are self-deceived. The Spirit does not act in this way, either to guide or to save: its true province of activity is via the vessel of the authoritative Word, an irreducible component of which is the scriptural text.

Luther's understanding of the Bible, then, is a *pneumatological* doctrine that is seen to be necessary for *anthropological* reasons. The preached Word as the sole instrument of God's saving Spirit in the world is the divinely ordained bulwark against the proclivity for self-deception that can never be ruled out in this world until the eschaton. Calvin, too, argued against the 'fanatics' that 'God bestows the actual knowledge of himself upon us only in the Scriptures',[12] and that 'the Word is the instrument by which the Lord dispenses the illumination of his Spirit to believers'.[13] Although theologians since Luther have not always agreed with every detail of his doctrine of the Word, the baseline for later Protestant and evangelical discussions about the precise nature of Scripture's inspiration and the mode of its effective work remains Luther's radical pneumatological prioritization of the Bible in Christian faith and practice. In other words, evangelical theology's distinctive biblicism is to a significant degree based in a classical Protestant wariness about human nature's ability to be self-deceived about direct personal experience of the Spirit apart from the Word, whether by the world, the flesh, or the devil.

The Pietist reaction

For a variety of reasons, Lutheran and Reformed theology developed in the century after the deaths of the magisterial Reformers in the direction of what has been called a Protestant 'scholasticism'. Confessional disputes within and between denominations over issues like the nature of the sacraments, the relationship between Christ's divine and human natures, and the problem of sanctification in light of 'forensic' justification, led to a very high premium within Protestant thought on doctrinal precision and 'orthodoxy'. As a result, before too long many Protestants began to perceive a growing spiritual 'coldness' in their churches – a sense that something crucial had been lost in the exhaustion of the confessional disputes. The various responses to this perceived spiritual poverty, starting in Germany in the seventeenth century but soon spreading through Europe and to the Americas, have been given the title 'Pietism', or, more broadly, 'the Protestant evangelical awakening'.[14] One of the more expansive definitions of Pietism calls it: 'a transnational and transconfessional phenomenon beginning in a post-Reformation crisis of piety rooted in the difficulties the Reformation churches experienced in realizing Christian life and activity'.[15] The influence of the Moravian Pietists on John Wesley played a vital role in giving birth to Methodism, helping to expand the 'awakening' beyond the borders of continental Europe. It is out of the dense seventeenth- and eighteenth-century matrix of revivals and spiritual quickenings that evangelicalism can be said to have sprung.[16]

Central to the Pietist reaction to Protestant orthodoxy was the second evangelical pneumatological 'move' referred to above – namely, a new focus on 'personalism', individual 'experience' of the divine, and the importance of the affective in spiritual life. John Wesley described the spiritual and theological 'Pietist impulse'[17] quite well when he called it 'the religion of the heart', which stands in contrast with 'a religion of form, a round of outward duties, performed in a decent, regular manner ... a system of right opinions'.[18]

An important component of the emphasis on the heart alongside (and perhaps over) right action and right confession is the category of unmediated personal 'experience' of God in the Christian life. According to Joachim Track: 'the intellectual and spiritual power, and the vitality, of Pietism and all related movements lies in their orientation towards experience'.[19] 'Experience' here covers a range of categories, including especially emotionally profound 'conversion experiences'; a general sense of intimacy with God in day-to-day life; and the conviction that God guides his people personally and directly, whether through illuminating a scriptural text to demonstrate its relevance to a particular contemporary situation, or through 'signs' in the world or mystical visions.[20]

Such 'experience' has often been described as *unmediated*. This is not because it is never mediated by Scripture or by 'signs' recognized in the world, which it often is, but in order to capture the sense of personal intimacy and directness Pietists and their successors often describe feeling in such experiences, and to convey the contrast with a strict *verbum externum* biblicism like Luther's. It is 'unmediated' in contrast to Luther's sense of mediation through the preaching of the Word. This is not to say that Scripture is not hugely important for Pietists. If anything, Pietists, like evangelicals after them, understood themselves to be more 'biblical' than their mainstream interlocutors, and to be restoring the Bible to its central place within Protestantism. Nevertheless, insofar as it allows for the possibility of personal 'experience' of God not tied exclusively to the preaching of the Word, Pietist biblical understanding is formally 'lower' than classical Protestant anti-enthusiastic views.

Historically speaking, it is as a result of the experiential aspect of their Pietist heritage that evangelicals believe in the importance of a 'personal relationship with God'. Personalism takes many forms, and some evangelicals reject versions of it espoused by other evangelicals. For example, a conservative Reformed evangelical might be extremely wary of the sort of ecstatic expressions of intimacy with God that might be found on the more charismatic end of evangelicalism, such as speaking in tongues or claims to direct prophetic visions through the Spirit. On the other hand, a charismatic evangelical might wonder how 'personal' a relationship with God one can have if one is consistently suspicious of subjective emotion as a constitutive component of spiritual life and worship, as might be the case with our Reformed friend. Both the charismatic and the Reformed evangelical would agree, however, that they understand a professed Christian faith to be somewhat suspect if it does not appear to be a 'lived' faith as well as a professed one – i.e., a faith characterized in some way by an on-going sense of God's activity and will in the spiritual life of particular individuals and congregations. In this sense, both our charismatic and our Reformed evangelical subscribe to a form of pneumatological 'personalism'.

As we have seen, evangelical pneumatology is characterized on the one hand by a commitment to the Bible as the sole reliable instrument and authority for discerning the relationship between God and the world, and on the other by a conviction of the living reality of God's presence in individual lives. The latter is closely connected with evangelical concern for evangelism and missions: the belief in personal eschatological judgement and the consequent importance of faith in Christ are predicated on a divine concern for individuals as individuals. This is central to the message: 'Jesus died for *you*'. The problem is that the same sinful nature that requires the atoning death of Christ renders human powers of discernment suspect. When we say that God 'speaks to us', when we say we have discerned his 'calling' in our lives, when a verse jumps out as if God is speaking directly to us – as when Augustine famously opened his Bible to Romans 13:13–14 in a Milanese garden – we are assuming that we are fundamentally capable in some way of discerning God's personal will and action in our lives. 'Personalism' presupposes the ability to recognize reliably the presence of the invisible God in the world, at least in certain contexts. By contrast, the 'Scripture principle' assumes that our ability to discern that presence is fundamentally and profoundly suspect. As Luther pointed out so long ago, in Christian praxis, there is a serious theological question to be resolved concerning the relationship between hamartiological pessimism and pneumatological optimism. One of the fundamental questions in evangelical theology is how to trust encounters with the Spirit in light of the problem of sin without resorting to Luther's almost superstitious limiting of the Spirit to the written and preached Word.

Evangelical responses to the tension: Wesley and Edwards

The problem of how Christians are to 'test the spirits' (1 John 4:1) in light of these concerns has been approached in a number of different ways. Luther's method, as we have seen, was a rigorous limitation of the action of the Spirit to the instrumentality of the Word. Because of the importance of 'experience' and personalism in evangelical theology, however, evangelicals have tended to approach the problem somewhat differently. John Wesley summed up the key features of common alternative approaches to the tension between hamartiology and pneumatology in one sermon in particular, 'The Nature of Enthusiasm'. It is worth spending some time with this text to see how successful he is in resolving the tension.

Wesley and his followers were often accused of being 'enthusiasts'. Wesley responds to this charge in 'The Nature of Enthusiasm' by taking issue with the traditional definition. He proposes an alternative understanding of 'enthusiasm' in order to distinguish between his views and true 'enthusiasm', which he rejects. According to his new definition, enthusiasm is no longer any claim whatsoever to experience of God apart from the mediation of the proclaimed Word. Rather, it is:

> a religious madness arising from some falsely imagined influence or inspiration of God; at least from imputing something to God which ought not to be imputed to Him, or expecting something from God which ought not to be expected from Him.[21]

Enthusiasm is falsely attributing an experience, influence or communication to God that is not from God at all.

As far as it goes, Luther would agree with this definition. The crucial difference, however, is that Wesley does not equate experience apart from the 'external Word' *directly* or *necessarily* with false attribution of this kind. As he puts it: 'There is a real influence of the Spirit of God, there is also an imaginary one: and many there are who mistake the one for the other.'[22] Similarly, although one should not normally expect to hear from God in 'visions or dreams', God 'does, in some very rare instances' communicate in this way.[23] Although the difference between this position and the Lutheran one may seem quite small, it has significant theological implications. Because Wesley opens the door, however cautiously, for experience apart from the *verbum externum*, the problem of discernment of the Spirit is put on a completely different footing. Unlike Luther, Wesley's pneumatology requires him to distinguish between true 'influence of the Spirit' and false influence in countless cases Luther would have rejected outright.

In order to aid in this discernment, Wesley offers two general criteria. The first is evidence of sanctification.[24] If the person claiming to have experienced God directly (in this case, a person who claims to have had a 'New Birth' experience) does not demonstrate an increased and increasing holiness of character, their experience must have been false: 'That they are not Christians, is clear and undeniable. ... For Christians are holy; these are unholy: Christians love God; these love the world: Christians are humble; these are proud', etc.[25] According to this criterion, holiness and sanctification are discernible to other Christians. In order for the criterion to be meaningful, the process of distinguishing between a Christian and a non-Christian, a holy person and an 'unholy' person, must for the most part be a straightforward operation. If the difference were not somewhat clear, the criterion would not be very useful.

In appealing to demonstrable sanctification as a mark of the true work of the Spirit, Wesley is voicing a common evangelical view. Another important theologian for the evangelical tradition, Jonathan Edwards, offers a helpful qualification to this view, and it is a qualification with which Wesley would not entirely disagree, though he might state it more mildly. In his treatise *The Distinguishing Marks*, Edwards argues that 'great imprudences and irregularities' of behaviour – i.e., sinful behaviours – are 'no sign that a work wrought amongst a people is not from the Spirit of God'. This is the case even if 'there be not only imprudences, but many things prevailing that are irregular, and really contrary to the rules of God's holy Word'. The 'irregularities' are instead to be explained as part of the 'exceeding weakness of human nature' that persists even in those who are 'subjects of the saving influences of God's Spirit, and have a real zeal for God'.[26] In other words, just because someone commits obvious sin, whether public or private, it does not necessarily follow that they do not have the Spirit in them or that they are not saved.

Confusingly, however, Edwards goes on to list certain 'positive' 'distinguishing marks' of the Spirit that seem to contradict this view, at least to a certain degree. It is not entirely clear how someone experiencing a 'spirit' that operates 'against the interest of Satan's Kingdom' and 'men's worldly lusts',[27] which gives a person 'greater regard to the Holy Scriptures' and confidence of their 'truth and divinity',[28] and which 'operates as a spirit of love to God and man ... winning and drawing the heart with ... motives and incitements to love',[29] is to be distinguished from a spirit that accomplishes demonstrable sanctification in a person. What are sanctification and holiness if not increase in 'love to God and man'?

In expressing these two somewhat contradictory views, Edwards demonstrates an internal confusion on this subject that one often finds in evangelical theology. If the reliable distinguishing mark of the Spirit is holiness and increase in love, then what are we to make of on-going sin in the Christian life, of 'great imprudences' that are 'really contrary to the rules of God's holy Word'? What is the difference between an 'irregularity' that does *not* discount the possibility of true presence of the Spirit, as Edwards argues, and the sin, pride and 'love [for] the world' that does indeed demonstrate the absence of holiness and therefore the presence of the Spirit? In practice, the criterion of holiness proves highly subject to arbitrary interpretation. The same 'datum' – some obvious sinful behavior or attitude – can signify *either* the on-going reality of sin in the life of a true believer *or* the opposite, the absence of the Spirit in that person, depending on one's interpretation. This arbitrariness is exactly the sort of problem Luther sought to avoid with his instrumental connecting of Spirit and the preached Word. The whole problem of the discernment of the spirits is still present, unresolved, in the question of whether a given manifestation of sin should or should not be seen as proof of a false claim to experience of the Spirit.

Perhaps Wesley's second criterion for discernment will fare better than the holiness criterion. In most cases, according to Wesley, God will not communicate himself in an immediate and supernatural way, because his primary mode of communication remains Scripture:

> But how is a sober Christian ... to know what is the will of God? Not by waiting for supernatural dreams ... not by looking for any particular impressions or sudden impulses on his mind: no; but by consulting the oracles of God.[30]

The 'oracles of God' here refers to the Bible. '[Y]ou are to know what is the will of God ... by applying the plain Scripture rule.'[31] Even more than holiness, the 'Scripture rule' is perhaps the best-known criterion for discerning between true and false spirits in evangelical theology. Edwards, too, explicitly understands his list of 'positive marks' in *The Distinguishing Marks* to derive from Scripture, above all from the *locus classicus* on spiritual discernment, 1 John 4.[32] In short, we can learn from the Bible what the will of God in general is, and this in turn will help us to discern in specific situations whether the spirit at work is a true or a false one. One hears this criterion at work in the classic evangelical refrain: 'Sure, but is it biblical?'

Before we proceed to discuss this criterion, it is important to understand the difference between Wesley and Edwards' Scripture criterion and Luther's understanding of the *verbum externum*. At work here are two slightly different ways of 'being biblical'. To put it most simply, for Luther the final guarantee of the authority of Scripture is God's continued living activity through it in the world. Luther is more interested in the inspiration of our *reception* of Scripture than in questions about an *original* inspiration that took place during the acts of writing and gathering the biblical texts. This is not to say he would deny the latter, just that what is pneumatologically decisive for him is God's present, rather than his past, activity through Scripture. The view of Scripture espoused by Wesley and Edwards in the works we have been discussing, on the other hand – and here we are painting with only the broadest of strokes – is more focused on the authoritative *content* of Scripture. The original inspiration of the text guarantees that the truths within it are divinely authoritative for all time. Scripture 'works' because it is full of revealed truth, not just because it is the primary divinely designated pneumatological instrument. It would not be too far off the mark to say that in this view God's ordained pneumatological vessel is *the 'truths' authoritatively revealed within the Bible* rather than the Bible as such. Again, none of these theologians would view these two ways of understanding pneumatological mediation as mutually exclusive; we are referring here mainly to two different emphases rather than to necessarily contradictory doctrines.

We see the difference between the two views at work in the different ways that Luther and the more pietistically oriented theologians apply their Scripture principles to the problem of enthusiasm. For Luther, the bulwark against enthusiasm is Scripture in general, as a sort of 'means of grace'.[33] In this view, the Spirit can be relied upon to be present whether you 'feel' it at work or not, as long as the Word is being proclaimed in sermon and sacrament.[34]

For Wesley and Edwards, on the other hand, Scripture protects against enthusiasm by providing within itself certain revealed guidelines for how the Spirit works. For example, one criterion Wesley finds in the Bible, in 1 Thess. 4:3, is that 'the will of God is our sanctification'.[35] If an experience leads to or is oriented towards 'our sanctification', then it is probably the true Spirit of God at work. Similarly, Edwards believes that his principle that 'If the spirit that is at work among a people operates as a spirit of love to God and man, 'tis a sure sign that 'tis the Spirit of God'[36] is directly revealed in Scripture in the discussions of God's love in 1 John 4, 'from the seventh verse to the end of the chapter'.[37] Enthusiasm is combated by means of specific content within Scripture, which indicate God's own guidelines for determining the presence of the Spirit.

This latter view, which is by and large the dominant evangelical view, assumes that the Scriptures are clear enough that anyone reading them carefully will be able to identify the correct categories for discerning whether a 'spirit' is divine or not. It also assumes that right knowledge of those categories will more or less lead to right application of the categories – in other words, that as long as we know in our minds, thanks to biblical revelation, what to look for, we will be able to see accurately whether a 'spirit' is indeed oriented towards sanctification or love, or not.

Does this Wesleyan and Edwardsian version of the 'Scripture principle' hold up against Luther's great concern about radical self-deception in Christians? I do not think it does. Although Luther did have a certain confidence that the Scripture 'interprets itself', and is therefore for the most part basically clear,[38] he would have been highly suspicious of the idea that right cognitive knowledge of the principles that can be found in the Bible (in this case, principles for spiritual discernment) can be straightforwardly applied. In his view, our tendency will be to apply the principles as and where we want to, and to avoid applying them when it is inconvenient for us – though we may not be aware we are doing this. Gerhard Forde states it well when he explains Luther's understanding of the 'bondage of the will' in terms of the domination of reason by our fleshly desires, which are far more powerful: 'We all do what we want to do! That is precisely our bondage.'[39]

Feuerbach, Marx and Freud would all critique Wesley and Edwards' basic hermeneutical optimism in a similar manner. They would argue that although we think we are reading the Word objectively, really our conclusions are being determined unconsciously by projection, by issues of class and power, or by subterranean neurotic desires and mechanisms. As we have seen, Luther's 'enthusiastic' opponents, as he portrays them, believed they were interpreting the Bible correctly, but really they 'neither seek nor find anything [in the Scriptures] but their own dreams'.[40]

Resolving the tension

We have now observed more clearly the tension that I argue exists between the two primary evangelical pneumatological doctrines. Evangelical biblicism goes back to a concern that we might baptize our feelings, experiences and impulses by attributing them falsely to the Holy Spirit; to combat this problem, the claim is that God has given us the Bible to be the primary privileged instrument of the Spirit in Christian faith and practice. On the other hand, evangelical pneumatological 'personalism' depends precisely on a reliable ability to discern when it is God acting or communicating in our lives and when it is just the voice of the world, the flesh, or the devil. Neither of the two criteria that have usually been given in evangelical theology for resolving this conflict stands up very well to a more radical anthropological pessimism. The 'holiness' criterion is arbitrary, given the phenomenon of recidivism and moral failure in the Christian life. The evangelical version of the 'Scripture principle', while perhaps a stronger criterion than the holiness principle, still assumes that the act of biblical interpretation is to some degree exempted from the on-going power of original sin. Neither criterion fully resolves our pneumatological difficulty.

There are two further theological options for resolving this tension, both of which are in my view equally problematic. One is Luther's rigorism of the Word, which essentially rejects the 'personalism' element that is central to the 'Pietist impulse'. The affective and personalist contribution of Pietist and evangelical pneumatology is crucial if Christian life is not to be reduced to cold confessionalism or theological abstraction. The Pietist protest against Protestant scholastic orthodoxy has an enduring theological, biblical and pastoral legitimacy.

Similarly problematic is the other option – favored by most evangelicals – which is simply not to worry so much about radical self-deception. In other words, one could subscribe to a less pessimistic anthropology of the Christian than Luther. In this view, the Bible is basically clear and sanctification is basically discernible, as long as one is careful to run one's conclusions by other Christians, especially biblical or ecclesial authorities, and to take the whole Bible into account in one's interpretation. If one applies the right set of criteria in this way, then the anthropological problem we have identified is largely a theoretical one, and nothing to be too concerned about.

There are myriad issues with this option. For our present purposes, however, I wish to focus on just two of the more significant ones. The first is what we have been alluding to throughout our discussion to this point – the powerful critiques of Christianity and of the possibility of objectivity that have been launched in critical theory and philosophy in the past 150 years. These critiques are not just limited to Feuerbach, Marx and Freud: the whole linguistic problem falls into this category, for example. To ignore the conclusions of these critiques of objectivity is to plug one's ears against the most profound (and most interesting!) insights of modern and postmodern philosophy and critical theory. A post-critical evangelical theology must take into account the problem of radical self-deception and of unconscious coercion by external structural forces in its hermeneutics and pastoral practice, or else risk naive co-option by the world, the flesh and the devil.

The second reason not to avoid this sort of critical pessimism is more fundamental and pastoral. It is that evangelicalism and evangelical Christians have so often found themselves taken off guard, and indeed, undone, by the reality of on-going sin in the Christian life. We see this in the surprise and consternation one observes when a public evangelical leader turns out to have a darker 'other life', but also more commonly in the private frustrations of so many sincere Christian people at their inability (and that of their peers) to conquer persistent problems and pattern sin despite prayer, accountability, Bible-reading and otherwise 'doing everything right'. The response to such recidivism, all too often, is a doubling-down on law and guilt at the expense of love and joy – and the problem only gets worse. Where radically critical anthropology is not taken seriously, there is very little resource for making sense, for example, of the ubiquitous pastoral reality of addiction. However, this does not mean that the 'Christian pessimism' I am describing is a capitulation to the world, the flesh, and the devil. To the contrary, it is the necessary predicate for Christianity's most powerful transformative agent – a truly radical theology of grace.[41]

How then are we to resolve our pneumatological tension, if we wish to sacrifice neither personalism nor critical anthropology? I wish to propose one possible way forward, through a limited criterion of 'negative' experience in discernment of the Spirit.

'Negative' experience of the Spirit

Nineteenth-century preacher and charismatic healer Christoph Friedrich Blumhardt (1842–1919) spent much of the last few decades of his life wrestling with the problem of how to integrate a critical anthropology of the Christian with his lived experience of the power of the risen Christ in the world.[42] What he found, though he did not put it in so many words, was that the two can be brought together without contradiction in the unmediated personal experience of God's righteousness and judgement over and against human sin and egoism. Personal experience of divine judgement is both deeply personal and affective on the one hand, and critically clear about humankind's on-going 'incurvation' upon itself on the other. True personal encounter with God is most reliably discernible when it takes the form of the 'negative' – suffering, and the thwarting of the sinful human will. This is what he means when he says:

> Although [we] may find a kind of peace with God in [the authentic Christian life], the reliable mark of the Holy Spirit at work is not so much divine peace as birth-pangs, the anxiety and unsettled feeling that accompanies profound change.[43]

In developing this idea, Blumhardt draws particularly on certain Johannine language about the 'Spirit of truth', above all the statement in John 16:8 that 'when [the Advocate] comes, he will convict the world of sin and righteousness and judgment'.[44] A crucial and often ignored role of the Spirit is in the conviction of sin and the destruction of the old self. Where this work is taking place, one can trust that the Spirit is present. Blumhardt described the experience of the Spirit in the Spirit's role as judge and convictor as 'birth-pangs' – another term picked up from John 16, with resonances of Romans 8:18–25.

In Blumhardt's view, although God does sometimes give the feeling of 'a kind of peace with God', and does communicate with his people in a personal and guiding way, God's primary way of doing so is through 'negative' experiences, in which our guilt and the true limits of our supposed autonomy are made manifest. Through these experiences of the Spirit, we die to ourselves again and again, in such a way as to pave the way for transformation and new life. Blumhardt's watchword during one of the most important phases of his development was: 'Die, so that Jesus may live!'[45]

In light of the core tension we have been identifying within evangelical theological identity, Blumhardt's pneumatological proposal possesses great intellectual and pastoral power. A criterion of 'negative' experience of the Spirit contains within itself a robust self-critical component that stands up far better to the self-deception problem than the traditional evangelical alternatives. Such experiences are less susceptible to deception and co-option than are 'positive' personalistic experiences, because they contradict rather than conform to our will and desires. We are not likely to make them up, to be forging them in our unconscious to meet some secret need, because the Spirit works against the forces unknown to us as well as those that are known. Excluded here, therefore, would be any masochistic appreciation of negativity, because such masochism would really be a veiled or indirect 'positive' experience. A truly 'negative' experience of the Spirit drives directly against our egoism no matter how subtle a form that egoism takes. This is why the thwarting of the will, including *especially* the sub-conscious will, is a very helpful way of describing what is taking place when the Spirit is active in this role. If an experience is easily assimilable into a comfortable category or pattern of control, it is not 'negative' at all. One thinks of Peter's strange reaction to the miraculous catch of fish in Luke 5. Paradoxically, it was the miraculous gift of what he had been toiling for all night that was so utterly unsettling to the fisherman: 'But when Simon Peter saw it, he fell down at Jesus' knees, saying, "Go away from me, for I am a sinful man!"'

One way of understanding the pneumatological criterion of 'negative' experience is simply as conviction of sin that produces repentance. This is not to be confused with the common and superficial use of the term 'conviction' in evangelical parlance – 'I really felt convicted about not witnessing more to my colleagues at work.' True 'conviction' is the kind that kills and make alive, that converts us and causes us to be undone at our core. It is much closer to the addict's admission of powerlessness, which is deeply, almost impossibly difficult, and yet the only true foundation for hope. Only the power of God by the Spirit can bring us to this divine and cruciform powerlessness. Too often, preachers and pastors believe it is their role to be the 'convictor' of sin, and in this we usurp most dangerously the role of the Spirit described in John 16.

What we are talking about here could be called a 'charismatic theology of the cross'. 'Positive' experiences of God in peace and joy are not excluded, but they are viewed with wariness. God is present personally and affectively in our life, but first and foremost in our darkness and our difficulties, because of the degree of our basic opposition to him and interest in ourselves that persists (to whatever degree) in the Christian life. If God appears to become 'silent' in our prayer life, for example, the discomfort and anxiety this experience produces is a far surer sign of divine presence – 'birth-pangs' – than any direct and comforting guidance or ecstasy might be.

The hope we have in such experiences, grounded in the hope secured in Christ's resurrection, is that the 'negative' word is not the final Word, and that the God of Jesus Christ is at work here, through the Spirit, for our good, both in this life and in the life to come.

Notes

1 T. Larsen, 'Defining and Locating Evangelicalism', in T. Larsen and D. J. Treier (eds) *The Cambridge Companion to Evangelical Theology*, Cambridge: Cambridge University Press, 2007, p. 1.
2 '[Enthusiasm] is the source, power, and might of all the heresies, even that of the papacy and Mohammed.' The Smalcald Articles (1537), *The Book of Concord*, Minneapolis: Fortress Press, 2000, III, 8:9–10 (p. 323).
3 For Luther this category includes the sacraments of baptism and the Eucharist, which he believed to be physical forms of the preaching of the Word, because of their scriptural sanction.
4 Ibid., 8:6.
5 M. Luther, *Against the Heavenly Prophets in the Matter of Images and Sacraments, 1525, Luther's Works 40*, Philadelphia, PA: Muhlenberg Press, 1958, p. 126. Henceforth, Luther's works will be cited as *LW* with volume and page.
6 For Luther, the 'oral word of the gospel' signifies quite literally listening with the ears to preaching based on a biblical text. Although 'Gospel' and 'Word' are quite complex categories in Luther's thought, orality and textuality are a *sine qua non* for the true and

effective 'Word'. See P. Althaus, *The Theology of Martin Luther*, Philadelphia, PA: Fortress Press, 1966, pp. 35–42.

7 M. Luther, *Luther: Lectures on Romans*, vol. XV, Library of Christian Classics, London: Westminster John Knox Press, 1961, pp. 218–19, 225.

8 Luther, *LW 40*, p. 110.

9 Luther's particular concern about enthusiasm's susceptibility to sinful human nature was that it would lead to a return among Protestants to justification by works. See ibid., p. 90.

10 Ibid., p. 83.

11 Ibid., p. 92.

12 J. Calvin, *Institutes of the Christian Religion*, vol. 1, London: Westminster John Knox Press, 2006, 1.vi.1.

13 Ibid., 1.ix.3. Although Calvin is greatly concerned in the *Institutes*, in a manner quite similar to Luther, to emphasize 'the kind of mutual bond' by which 'the Lord has joined together the certainty of his Word and of his Spirit' (ibid.), his exposition of their interconnection is not quite so rigid as Luther's. Nevertheless, he does not go so far as to allow explicitly in his main exposition on Scripture in Book 1 for the viability of experience of the Spirit apart from the Word.

14 W. R. Ward, *The Protestant Evangelical Awakening*, Cambridge: Cambridge University Press, 1992.

15 Carter Lindberg, 'Introduction', in C. Lindberg (ed.) *The Pietist Theologians: An Introduction to Theology in the Seventeenth and Eighteenth Centuries*, Oxford: Blackwell Publishing, 2005, p. 3.

16 Larsen, 'Evangelicalism', pp. 5–7.

17 This term is taken from C. T. Collins Winn (ed.) *From the Margins: A Celebration of the Theological Work of Donald W. Dayton*, Eugene, OR: Pickwick Publications, 2007.

18 J. Wesley, 'The Nature of Enthusiasm (Sermon 37)', in *Sermons II: 34–70*, Nashville, TN: Abingdon Press, 1985, p. 46.

19 J. Track, 'Erfahrung III/2', in Gerhard Müller (ed.) *Theologische Realenzyklopädie 10*, Berlin: Walter de Gruyter, p. 121.

20 See Larsen, 'Evangelicalism', p. 12.

21 Wesley, 'Sermons II', p. 50.

22 Ibid., p. 53.

23 Ibid., p. 54.

24 These themes are explored further in ch. 5 in this volume, by George Bailey.

25 Ibid., p. 51.

26 J. Edwards, 'The Distinguishing Marks', in C. C. Goen (ed.) *The Great Awakening*, London: Yale University Press, 1972, p. 241.

27 Ibid., p. 251.

28 Ibid., p. 253.

29 Ibid., p. 256.

30 Wesley, 'Sermons II', p. 54.

31 Ibid., p. 59.

32 Edwards, 'Marks', pp. 248–9.

33 For a description of this category of scriptural understanding, see J. Webster, *Holy Scripture: A Dogmatic Sketch*, Cambridge: Cambridge University Press, 2003, pp. 24–5.

34 For further discussion of Luther's understanding of proclamation as constitutive of what is proclaimed, and the way he grounds his doctrine of assurance and his understanding of real presence in the sacrament on that basis, see G. Forde, *Theology is for Proclamation*, Minneapolis, MN: Augsburg Fortress, 1990, pp. 147–78; and O. Bayer, *Martin Luthers Theologie: Eine Vergegenwärtigung*, Tübingen: Mohr Siebeck, 2003, pp. 46–53.

35 Wesley, 'Sermons II', p. 54.
36 Edwards, 'Marks', p. 255.
37 Ibid.
38 This famous dictum of Luther's has tended to be interpreted somewhat superficially. Notger Slenczka has recently shown that what Luther has in mind is more the fact that Scripture 'works' – that it is a reliable pneumatological vessel, as we have discussed – than that the content is always straightforwardly easy to understand. See N. Slenczka, 'Das Evangelium und die Schrift. Überlegungen zum "Schriftprinzip" und zur Behauptung der "Klarheit der Schrift" bei Luther', in *Der Tod Gottes und das Leben des Menschen*, Göttingen: Vandenhoeck & Ruprecht, 2003, pp. 44–55; see also G. Forde, *The Captivation of the Will: Luther vs. Erasmus on Freedom and Bondage*, Cambridge: Eerdmans, 2005, pp. 28–30.
39 Ibid., 37.
40 Luther, *LW 40*, p. 92.
41 For one of the best accounts of this dynamic, see P. F. M. Zahl, *Grace in Practice: A Theology of Everyday Life*, Grand Rapids, MI: Eerdmans, 2007.
42 For a more in-depth study of Christoph Blumhardt and the category of 'negative' experience, see my, 'The Holy Spirit between Wittenberg and Azusa Street: Pneumatology and Theology of the Cross in the Preaching of Christoph Friedrich Blumhardt', PhD Diss., University of Cambridge.
43 C. F. Blumhardt, *Damit Gott kommt: 'Gedanken aus dem Reich Gottes'*, Giessen/Basel: Brunnen Verlag, 1992, p. 179.
44 The NRSV reads 'prove the world wrong about', but lists 'convict the world of' as an alternate translation. The latter is more consistent with Blumhardt's reading of the verse, which comes from the original Luther translation, where the verb '*strafen*' is used.
45 C. F. Blumhardt, *Sterbet, so wird Jesus leben! Predigten und Andachten aus den Jahren 1888 bis 1896*, vol. II, Erlenbach-Zürich: Rotapfel-Verlag, 1925.

Select bibliography

Bayer, O., *Martin Luthers Theologie: Eine Vergegenwärtigung*, Tübingen: Mohr Siebeck, 2003.

Blumhardt, C. F., *Damit Gott kommt: 'Gedanken aus dem Reich Gottes'*, Giessen/Basel: Brunnen Verlag, 1992.

Edwards, J., 'The Distinguishing Marks', in C. C. Goen (ed.) *The Great Awakening*, London: Yale University Press, 1972.

Forde, G., *Theology is for Proclamation*, Minneapolis, MN: Augsburg Fortress, 1990.

Luther, M., *Against the Heavenly Prophets in the Matter of Images and Sacraments, 1525. Luther's Works 40*, Philadelphia, PA: Muhlenberg Press, 1958.

Moberly, W., *Prophecy and Discernment*, Cambridge: Cambridge University Press, 2006.

Wesley, J., 'The Nature of Enthusiasm (Sermon 37)', in *Sermons II: 34–70*, 46–60, Nashville, TN: Abingdon Press, 1985.

Zahl, P. F. M., *Grace in Practice: A Theology of Everyday Life*, Grand Rapids, MI: Eerdmans, 2007.

Chapter 7

Feeding and forming the People of God

The Lord, his Supper and the Church in Calvin and 1 Corinthians 11:17–34[1]

Ben Fulford

By placing the story of the institution of the Lord's Supper in the context of Jesus' celebration of Passover and near the beginning of the passion-resurrection sequence, the synoptic writers leave us in no doubt as to the importance of the practice of memory Jesus of Nazareth instituted for his disciples and its close connection with his passion.[2] As evangelical theologians begin to take renewed interest in the theology of the church and its life, attention must therefore be paid again to the Lord's Supper, so often marginal to the spirituality, theology and worship of evangelicals.[3]

One way of focusing such attention is to ask, with Christopher Cocksworth, what is 'the *real value* of the Eucharist over and against that of hearing and believing the Word'?[4] To this end I return both to a Reformation source of evangelical tradition, John Calvin, and to the norm of all Christian theology, the Scriptures. I do so by reading Calvin's commentary on 1 Corinthians 11:17–34, and by seeking to supplement his account through fresh theological engagement with the biblical text. Reading Scripture leads Calvin to identify the Supper, in answer to Cocksworth's question, as an intensified moment of covenant with God in soul-nourishing union with Christ and one another, intensified because of the instrumental role of physical signs. Yet he pays relatively little attention to the importance of the life of the visible church community in the meaning of the Supper in Paul's argument. By exploring this ecclesial dimension further, I argue, we see the practical, ethical and missional implications of the Supper's meaning for the church.

Calvin on 1 Corinthians 11:17–34

In 1 Cor. 11:17–34, Calvin notes in his *Commentary* of 1546, Paul addresses the abuse of the Lord's Supper in the Corinthian church. Once (adapting Jewish and Gentile practice) poor and rich had eaten in common at the expense of the latter. Now, 'while the rich indulged themselves sumptuously, they appeared, in a manner, to reproach the poor for their poverty'.[5] Paul corrects this abuse by recourse to Christ's institution, 'a sure rule' from which they have erred and to which he recalls them. Calvin's concern, with an eye to contemporary Roman and Protestant theologies and practices of the Supper, is to return with Paul to the *principium*, the 'origin and first principle' of the Supper.[6]

The Supper as covenant, memorial and Eucharist

The wider purpose of the Supper Calvin finds first indicated in the narrative framing of the words of institution: 'on the night when he was betrayed' (11:23). For this temporal circumstance 'teaches us the end of the mystery: that the benefit of Christ's death might be confirmed in us'.[7] The Supper, he adds, is a 'covenant', which Christ gave to his apostles just before his sacrifice, so that the apostles 'might soon perceive the fulfilment in his body of that which was represented to them in bread and wine'.[8]

Next, Calvin explains Christ's action of thanksgiving (11:24) as directed towards his Father for his merciful works and the inestimable benefits of redemption. The Lord thus 'invites us by his example, as often as we approach the sacred table, to raise ourselves to the recognition of the boundless love of God for us, and to kindle ourselves to true gratitude'.[9] In the Supper, then, we have an action of Christ toward us, to confirm by covenant the benefits of his death. But there is also a counter-action of ours in response: to give thanks for the inexhaustible love of God shown toward us in the same. The Supper is at once covenant and Eucharist.

This eucharistic dynamic of lifting the mind to recognition of God's great mercy and kindling the heart to thankfulness is the purpose of the memorial dimension of the Supper for Calvin. The command to 'do this in remembrance of me' (11:24) is given in respect to our weakness, that the Supper may recall to us Christ's death.[10] Calvin goes on to explain when commenting on v. 26 that this is a remembrance 'with thanksgiving'.[11] It bestows knowledge of Christ's death, Calvin continues, which is to excite us to the confession of praise: 'to declare before human beings what we sense within in the presence of God.'[12] This is the more precise doxological and confessional sense in which the Supper is a Eucharist, for Calvin. This helpful memorial, moreover, belongs to the epistemological conditions of the eschatological tension in which we live, between Christ's ascension and return: 'the extension to us of some symbol of his spiritual presence is necessary, by which our minds may exercise themselves.'[13] This idea brings us to the relation of sign to reality in the Supper.[14]

The spiritual presence of Christ our food

Calvin understands Christ to refer to the bread when he said, '*This is my body*' (11:24) as is clear from the parallel, '*This cup is the new covenant in my blood*' (11:25).[15] The expression, Calvin claims, is to be understood as a metonym: 'the name "body" is assigned to the bread, because it is its sign or symbol.'[16] In this sacramental way of speaking, 'the Lord assigns the name of the signified to the sign'. The reason for the metonymy brings us to the question of presence.

Calvin explains that 'the name of the thing signified is not imposed upon the sign because it is [merely] a figure of it, but rather because it is a symbol, by which the thing is displayed'.[17] For whereas worldly symbols are but empty representations, the bread is the body of Christ 'because it attests with surety that the body which is

represented is presented to us, or that the Lord, by extending to us visibly this symbol, at once also gives to us his body'.[18] The reason comes down to the faithfulness
of the sign-giver: 'Christ is not false, to feed us with empty figures.'[19] The reality,
he says in the commentary, is here 'conjoined with the sign', or what amounts to the
same thing: 'we shall be truly participants of Christ's body, in respect of spiritual
strength, who feed on the bread.'[20] As we shall see, Calvin sees Christ's words
together with the signs here as having illocutionary force: by calling the bread his
body and the wine his blood given for us, Christ assures us that he feeds us with his
flesh. But this performative character of his speech and action requires that the
symbols of bread and wine signify not merely a past event but the spiritually present reality of Christ's own flesh as food, or Christ would be false to his promise.[21]

This point takes us to the soteriological heart of Calvin's account of the Supper.
For here he argues that it is not sufficient merely to say that 'we are made participants in all the goods which Christ acquired for us in his body when we embrace
Christ as crucified for us and risen from the dead'.[22] For 'we only participate in the
good of Christ when we obtain Christ himself'.[23] Christ, Calvin implies, works salvation in himself for us. Thus the *Institutes* explain that the whole course of Christ's
obedience is salvific, but especially in his death, resurrection and ascension we are
freed from the power and penalty of sin, reconciled to God, mortified in our flesh,
restored to righteousness and new life and the way is opened for us to heaven.[24] The
flesh of Christ, indwelt by the Word, does not live of itself but 'is pervaded with
fullness of life to be transmitted to us'; hence is life-giving, like a rich and inexhaustible fountain of life from God.[25] Therefore we need to lay hold of Christ himself, not merely the truth about him, if we are to enjoy that benefit (a point
sometimes obscured even in high evangelical doctrines of the Supper).[26]

We obtain Christ, Calvin argues in the commentary:

> not so much when we believe him to have been sacrificed for us, but when he
> dwells in us, and is one with us, when we are members of his flesh; in short,
> when we are (so to speak) united with him in one life and substance.[27]

We need union with Christ himself. More precisely, we need to feed upon his flesh.
For this is what Christ's words of institution mean, that 'Christ does not offer to us
only the benefits of his death and resurrection, but his very body, in which he suffered and rose'.[28] Here Calvin makes central what was entailed in the affirmations
of real presence by medieval theologians like Aquinas and by Luther. Thus far
Calvin stands in continuity with them and over against Zwingli, without affirming
the presence of Christ's body in the elements themselves.[29] So he concludes quite
carefully that 'the body of Christ is really (as is commonly said), that is, truly given
to us in the Supper, that he may be healthy-bringing food for our souls' (*and* our
bodies, which his flesh quickens even now).[30] 'Really given' does not mean 'present in the elements' but 'truly given'.[31]

Thus we are united with Christ: 'the substance of his body nourishes our souls,
so that we are made one with him.' In other words, 'that vivifying strength from

Christ's flesh is poured into us by the Spirit, although separated from us by a great distance, nor mixed with us.[32] By talking of the Spirit pouring the vivacious force or strength of Christ's flesh into us, Calvin rules out a physical mastication of that flesh or the local presence of the same that it would involve, or any confusion of us with Christ (we are not 'mixed'), and at the same time affirms that the Spirit's action effects our being nourished with Christ's body and so united with him.[33] This language needs to be understood alongside and not in place of Calvin's realistic assertion that we are truly, really given Christ's body to eat.[34] After all, we derive vivifying strength from the 'substance' of food just by eating it. Calvin's is not a comprehensive theory, and he elsewhere denies that he could explain Christ's presence; his account should not therefore be pressed to yield too clear an answer where none such was thought possible.[35]

Calvin here distances himself from those who, like Luther, affirm that Christ's flesh is received orally. The heart of the issue is the relation of Christ's presence in the Supper to his absence in virtue of the ascension. Calvin confirms the sense in which Christ is absent in the Supper in connection with the command to remember him (11:24). Christ is absent in the sense that he is 'not visibly present, nor distinguished with the eyes, as are the symbols which arouse our remembrance by representing him in figure'.[36] When he communicates to us 'the virtue of his flesh', he does so from heaven and without change of place, he adds. Christ is absent in the sense that his body is not in the same place as ours, nor is it visible to us, and his presence is the presence of one absent in this way. For Calvin Christ's body is really present, we may conclude with Brian Gerrish, in its power and efficacy.[37]

How can Christ's body be so present when thus absent? Christ's 'communicating himself to us is the secret capacity of the Holy Spirit, who is able ... to unite in one things separated by distance of place', Calvin asserts.[38] This is a spiritual presence, as Killian McDonnell points out, 'only because it is effected by the Holy Spirit'.[39] We should not, Calvin adds, seek 'to measure [the Spirit's activity] by the small standard of our intelligence'.[40] Instead, we partake of this nourishment by faith (not with our mouths). We rise heavenward to apprehend what our senses cannot perceive by believing Christ when he tells us in the words of institution that the bread is a symbol of Christ's body and thus that his 'body is given to [us] as spiritual food'.[41] (The ontological transcendence of heaven here implied mitigates considerably the impression that for Calvin Christ is separated from us within a common dimension of space.)[42] The Spirit actualizes a dynamic participatory encounter in which we feed on Christ's flesh by believing, grasping the invisible through the visible.[43]

Yet the reception of the elements remains indispensable in the Supper, for they teach us that Christ's body has been given for us, so sealing his promises in the gospel, and show us the benefit of this: the Supper, Calvin likes to say, is a mirror which represents Christ crucified for us.[44] The role of the signs is not to be containers of the spatial presence of the body and blood, for these are not locally present, but neither are the elements merely illustrative of a present reality. For the implications of Calvin's account are first that Christ offers us his body as food *through* the symbol of the bread, because of our weak capacity to perceive spiritual realities. So Calvin speaks elsewhere in this context of the bread and wine as instruments by which Christ distributes his body and blood to us.[45] Second, it follows also that we in faith perceive that proffered spiritual nourishment by way of those same symbols and that in this same way we are enabled to receive them. The symbols of bread and wine, as symbols, are instrumental to the gift of Christ's body in the Supper *and* its reception by faith.

Covenant, communion and incorporation

Calvin's comments on the cup-word (11:25) integrate this account of the elements as symbols, the real nourishment they attest and the real presence it entails with the covenantal context of the Supper. He first notes that what is said of the cup applies also to the bread. The bread is the body to us, 'that it may be a Testament in his body: that is, a compact ratified once by the sacrifice of his body, and now ratified by eating, when believers feast on that sacrifice'.[46] The same is true of the blood, which 'was poured out to reconcile us to God, and is now drunk spiritually by us that we may be participants in that reconciliation'.[47] We partake in the reconciliation Christ achieved by partaking in him, and this participation is confirmed in the Supper. Thereby we have assurance both of our sharing in Christ and in the salvific benefits that flow from him.

This covenantal dimension of our participation in Christ's body also brings us back to the Supper's eucharistic character. If the sacraments are covenants, Calvin explains, then 'they contain promises, by which consciences are roused to confidence of salvation'.[48] It is in this context that Calvin goes on to say in relation to 11:26 that the remembrance to which the Supper recalls us 'seals the virtue of Christ's death in our consciences', and that this knowledge kindles us to the confession of praise in respect of which the Supper is called the Eucharist. Here the symbols are crucial to this arousal of our gratitude. As Calvin says elsewhere, nothing spurs us so keenly as when Christ 'makes us, so to say, see with the eye, and touch with the hand and manifestly feel a blessing so inestimable, that we feed upon his substance'.[49] We may conclude, therefore, that this arousal and enflaming of the soul to gratitude comes not from simply a rational apprehension of a cold fact, but from a living participation by faith in Christ's own saving flesh, perceiving the spiritual reality signified and offered and received by means of the symbols of the meal.

There is, finally, a corporate dimension to Calvin's understanding of the Supper, that relates directly to the participatory manner in which it is covenantal. He refers to this dimension in passing when commenting on the command to take and eat the bread, which is found in some manuscripts of this text (11:24).[50] In these words, Calvin claims Christ is saying: '"By sharing in the breaking of the bread according to the order and rite received from me, you shall also be participants in my body."'[51] He explores the same point when commenting on Paul's appeal to the Supper in his exhortation against the Corinthians' participation in idolatrous pagan cultic meals in 1 Cor. 10:14–17. Calvin pays particular attention to verse 16: 'The cup of blessing that we bless, is it not a sharing in the blood of Christ? The bread that we break, is it not a sharing in the body of Christ?' This *koinōnia*, says Calvin, denotes the kind of unity that believers have through the blood of Christ as one body.[52] The same holds true, he adds, in respect of the bread, and in this sense Paul says that we are all one body who partake of one bread (10:17). 'For we must be incorporated (so to speak) into Christ first, that we may be united with one another.' This reading, Calvin adds, makes sense of Paul's argument, which appeals to the spiritual union between Christ and believers to conclude that it is an unbearable sacrilege for the Corinthians to be polluted by communion with idols (10:21). Thus, 'the *koinōnia* of his blood is the community we have with Christ's blood, when at once we are all incorporated in his body, so that he lives in us and we in him'.[53] We may infer that faithful sharing in the Supper binds together the participants not merely in a common rite, but in their common participation by the Spirit in the reality it represents – Christ's own body.

Calvin on the Supper for evangelicals

Calvin was later quite clear, in the 1559 *Institutes*, that we do not only receive Christ in the Supper; we receive him through the gospel 'but more clearly through the sacred Supper'.[54] The nourishment we there derive, moreover, is not restricted to the time of the rite, but continual. Nevertheless, Calvin here asserts the Supper's significant distinctiveness in the greater clarity with which we receive Christ there. For this greater clarity of the Supper has the effect of confirming God's promises in Christ to us, since there we are made to see through symbols his nourishment of us and the sealing of his covenant with us. We may also infer that the greater clarity of the giving of the gift encourages a more intense enjoyment of it, and may arouse a deeper gratitude. Furthermore in the Supper our incorporation into Christ is most clearly displayed to us visibly. And in his earlier *Short Treatise in the Holy Supper* (1541), Calvin tells us that the Supper is also a 'vehement incitement to holy living, and above all to observe charity and brotherly love amongst us', as those incorporated into the same body, not merely by the external sign representing that unity, but also by the impartation of his Holy Spirit to give efficacy to the ordinance and assist our growth in charity.[55] In all these respects and more Calvin's theology of the Supper has much to offer evangelicals.

In addition, Calvin's account connects together the accomplishment of redemption by Christ with its appropriation and application to us by way of our participatory union with Christ's own body as the redeemed human being. Calvin considers as concrete, particular and embodied the grace that we so often speak of in the abstract. It also militates against any docetic leanings to relate to Christ merely as God, and not as incarnate in human flesh. In this connection, Calvin offers evangelicals a view of the Supper as a visible instantiation of the gift of his Son in whatever time and place the Supper is celebrated, and particular to those who gather to celebrate it. Such a theology draws us away from prioritizing the individual and individual interiority by turning our attention outward through symbols to the givenness of Christ for us. It grounds our affective experience of and response to God's grace in the symbolically objectified gift of his Son by his Spirit. And it encourages us to recognize in our actions our corporate unity in him in the very act of eating together, and to practise Christ-like charity toward one another. However, Calvin gives relatively little consideration to this last dimension of the Supper, and does not greatly illumine the theological significance of the irreducibly social setting and character of that meal. This lack also relates to an omission in his reading of 1 Cor. 11:17–34.

Calvin's theological interpretation of I Cor. 11:17–34

We may characterize Calvin's use of 1 Cor. 11:17–34 as follows. Calvin, we saw, seeks to understand Paul's appeals to the institution narrative and earlier to the character of the Lord's Supper, in their rhetorical contexts and the circumstances they addressed. In this respect, his approach differs from modern historical approaches only in the relative paucity of the theoretical and technical resources and wealth of knowledge he could bring to bear. But for Calvin, the norms Paul appeals to are normative for Christian practice in his own time. In order to realize their normative force, Calvin seeks to understand what they imply about the reality with which we have to do in the Lord's Supper, and to inquire into what we might call its operating conditions: that which actualizes this reality (an account of which renders it more intelligible).[56] This move makes Calvin's exegesis theological insofar as he seeks those conditions in God's activity and identity.

This procedure is quite sophisticated, involving a number of moves. When, for example, Calvin interprets the bread and cup-words, his first move is to identify them as a kind of speech-act – in the light of their covenantal content, they are promises – involving metonymic figures. Next, he interprets the force of the metonyms in light of their promissory character, and the character of the one who makes the promise (Jesus Christ, who does not lie). This move already involves Calvin's assent to Scripture's testimony about Christ, going beyond a merely philological *explication du texte*. Calvin's next step is also made within a deeper commitment, namely the belief that not only the practices but the realities their meaning implies apply to us also, a belief warranted by the experience of Christ in the Eucharist to which Calvin also appealed.[57] Thus he concludes that Christ's flesh, 'given for us' on the cross, is truly given to us and partaken of when we eat the bread and drink the wine. Calvin then inquires after the conditions of the operation of this gift and participation, by framing the hypothesis he believes most consistent not only with what Paul's argument directly implies, but also with the wider witness of Scripture (and the best insights of tradition) – his account of true presence. The final move of the procedure, not explored above, is to apply the now theologically illumined norms Paul uses to reform the Christianity of Calvin's day.

This procedure rests ultimately on a confidence that Scripture is a lens by which, illumined by God's Spirit, we may discern the realities of God's ways with the world and especially with human beings.[58] It is also an approach that is thoroughly rooted in the biblical text and accountable exegetically within the terms of properly theological assumptions basic to Christian confession and practice. In those terms, much of Calvin's reading of the passages in question seems robust and is defensible, even exegetically attractive: for example, he can find a way to hold on to the apparent realism of Paul's language of participating in Christ's body and blood together with the covenantal and communal dimensions denoted by *koinōnia*.[59]

Calvin's procedure, then, has much to commend it, but there seems to be a crucial omission in his reading of 1 Cor. 11:17–34. For, although he carefully attends to the circumstances implied in verses 17–22, he does not go very far to relate the meaning of the institution narrative Paul recounts as a reparative rule to the problem to which it was applied. This omission is borne out in his reading of verses 27–34 as directed against a general unworthiness, not specific to the abuses of the Corinthians, which prevents recognition of Christ's body (though the counsels on self-examination in the 1559 *Institutes* mitigate this omission).[60] Here Calvin's reading fails to do justice to the logic of the text which, as we shall see, relates the institution narrative and the conclusions it licenses in 11:27–34 directly to the issues in Corinth. I turn therefore to sketch a Calvin-like reading of the passage that takes account of these features. Here the force of Scripture takes us beyond Calvin, not least in the ethical implications of the Supper, presenting fresh challenges for evangelicals.

Rereading 1 Corinthians 11:17–34

In verses 17–22, Paul lays out the reasons for his disapprobation of the way the Corinthians have failed to keep to the traditions he handed on to them. The Corinthians do not come together 'in assembly' (*en ekklēsia*) for the better, but for the worse; they meet amidst internal divisions (11:18–19). It seems reasonable to understand verse 20 as explicating what he means.[61] When the Corinthians assemble, it is not to eat the Supper in honour and in the presence of the Lord (the *kyriakon deipnon*).[62] Rather, he explains in the following verses, at the given time each goes ahead with his or her *own* supper (the *idion deipnon*), and the result is that 'one goes hungry and another becomes drunk'. So Paul upbraids them: they have homes in which to eat and drink, otherwise they are showing contempt for the church (the *ekklēsia*) and humiliating those who 'have not'.

There is some disagreement as to whether the 'have-nots' are distinguished from those Paul criticizes by their social status and superior food (so Gerd Theissen and others), or simply by arriving before their fellow poor and consuming all the elements in their hunger (so Justin Meggitt).[63] We cannot resolve the dispute here, but it does highlight the speculative character of these reconstructions, and the outcome seems to make little difference to the force of Paul's argument as an appeal to mutuality. For at the least he condemns an unequal distribution and consumption of the available fare, resulting in several, unequal, semi-private meals.

In 11:23 he introduces the tradition of the institution as though by way of justifying his rebuke (*gar* here seems to signals a connection of this kind). Therefore we must infer that the institution narrative gives reasons for thinking that the Corinthians' behaviour is unfitting to the Lord's Supper. At the other end of the passage, verses 27–32 appeal to the tradition to assert the accountability of the Corinthians for the body and blood of the Lord and counsel self-examination before participation on the grounds that failure to discern 'the body' results in the consumption of judgement and hence the sickness and even death of some of the Corinthians. Verses 32–34 give practical counsel that relates directly to the issues identified in 11:20–22, which indicates that the assertions of 11:27–32 have them in view also, and that therefore that accountability for the Lord's body and blood, failure to discern them and the consequences that follow are directly related to the distorted practices decried in 11:17–22. So what understanding of the institution narrative can best do justice to the role it plays here? A satisfactory answer to this question must be able to tie together the meaning of the Supper in that narrative, on the one hand, and the social form of its celebration, on the other, so as to explain the gravity of the distortion of the latter in terms of the former.

This connection is the reality implied by the text. The question we need to ask next is: 'What wider understanding would make that reality more intelligible and lend it greater clarity?' Calvin's reading of the words of interpretation, supported and supplemented by that of 1 Corinthians 10:16–17, offers us a starting point: believers have unity with one another through their common participation in Christ's flesh by the Spirit and thus in the covenant with God that he secured. The strengths of this reading have already been noted above. To test it further and improve upon it, we need to consider the connections we have in view and how they might relate to the institution narrative in light of other related patterns in the epistle. What we are looking for is some indication that the outcome of Christ's saving work, through the activity of the Spirit, is the formation of a particular new kind of sociality. Several patterns of thought in the epistle point in this direction.

First, similar connections between relation to Christ and his saving work and the visible life of the community are in evidence elsewhere in the epistle. Paul addresses the Corinthians as the church of God (1:2), the *ekklēsia tou theou*: 'those sanctified in Jesus Christ and called to be holy together with all those who in every place call on the name of our Lord Jesus Christ.' They are, his language implies, sanctified in Christ as a people, like ancient Israel, and called in continuity with her to be a holy people: being 'in Christ' pertains to a community and their common life.[64]

Something of the same force of implication is carried by the subsequent declaration (1:9) that the faithful God has called the Corinthians into the fellowship (*koinō nia*) of his Son, implying a bond with the Son and through him with others that is manifest in mutual relations, as Paul's appeal for unity which follows indicates.[65] That appeal hints at a connection with Paul's understanding of the Supper when Paul asks, aghast (1:13): 'Has Christ been divided? Was Paul crucified for you? Or were you baptized into the name of Paul?' These questions seems to assume that Paul and his readers suppose there to be a connection between Christ's crucifixion for us and their unity with one another in identification with him, whereby they are (we assume through baptism) his 'body'. Later, Paul's use of the images of the Corinthian church as the flourishing field of God, God's building and, most strikingly, his Temple in which his Spirit dwells (3:5–17) suggest that the community, in its visible life, is the fruit of the gospel by the Spirit's active presence, and as such God's dwelling place and sacred.

Second, these connections are illumined by another passage. In 1 Corinthians 12:1–11, Paul explains that the Corinthians' diverse gifts are for service of the same Lord and activated by the same God through the same Spirit who activates them all for the common good. As the body is one yet has many members, *so is Christ*, he continues (12:12). Paul thus closely but not totally identifies the Lord of the church with its members considered as an organic whole in order to make sense of how the diversity of Spirit-manifestations serves the common good. The implication is that union with Christ by the Spirit binds us into one community internally differentiated and related interdependently by the Spirit's gifts.[66] Paul's explication of this analogy (12:13) – we were baptized into one body 'in the one Spirit', and given that one Spirit to drink – reinforces the sense that it is the Spirit who unites us to Christ and to one another in this unity-in-differentiation and that the old markers of identity – Jew/Greek, slave/free (and elsewhere Paul adds male/female – Gal. 3:28) – should no longer divide us.[67]

The cross is not immediately evident in this passage. However, Paul's emphasis on the special dignity and care owed to the weakest members of the body (12: 22–26) recalls one strand of the argument of chapters 8–11:1, to the effect that the freedom of the strong should be laid down for the sake of the weak 'for whom Christ died', who are so closely linked to him that a sin against these members of one's own family is a sin against Christ (8:11–12); and that the strong should, with Paul, imitate Christ (it is implied) in his self-sacrifice (11:1). The argument of 1 Corinthians 13, that gifts are nothing worth without (Christ-like) love, recalls the same ethic, rooted in the cross. In this way 1 Corinthians 12–13 evinces a thematic connection with 1 Corinthians 11:17–34: the cross-bound imperative to have loving regard for the weak, the 'have-nots'.[68]

This thematic connection helps make sense of the appeal to the institution narrative, and why the Corinthians' behaviour offended against the body and blood of the Lord. For Paul appeals to the institution narrative, where the bread is interpreted as Christ's body 'given for you', in order to show how wrong it is, at the celebration of the Supper, to disregard the 'have-nots' of the community. In the pattern of thought just examined, the 'weak' are those for whom Christ died, with whom he is united. The Spirit who unites us to Christ thus binds us with the weak in a body where its members are mutually dependent, and which is called to unity by the exercise of those gifts for the common good *after the pattern of Christ's self-gift of his body*.

It seems reasonable to infer, therefore, that Paul appealed to the institution narrative because in his view sharing the bread and cup which symbolize Christ's body and the new covenant in his blood displays not simply the invisible unity we have in him, but expressively enacts its visible realization in community life. The elements symbolize the reality that is both the source and ethical norm of Christian community: Jesus Christ crucified and risen. In which case we must conclude that Christ's self-giving of his body on the cross 'for us' not only reconciles us to God and makes his humanity the source of life from God; this life from God involves the creation of the form of life of a distinctive social body, of which Christ's bodily humanity for others is the source, pattern and norm through the Spirit, and in anticipation of the age to come in the kingdom (1 Cor. 6: 9–11). The social form of the Supper, therefore, must be consistent with the full meaning of its institution. For Paul it is imperative that the church crystallizes, in the way it shares food at this meal, the ecclesial meaning of the bread and wine as signs by which Christ assures us of the gift of his body and blood.

Conclusion: operating conditions; practical, ethical, and missional implications

What might be the operating conditions of the Lord's Supper so understood? The first is that the work of Jesus Christ in his life, death and resurrection condemns and overcomes sin, enacts human obedience to God and defeats death in his person, so establishing his renewed humanity, righteous and ascended to God. Included within this condemnation, victory and righteousness is the judgement and overcoming of destructive and divisive sociality and the embodied *principium* and pattern of a redeemed sociality in Jesus himself.[69] Such a transformation is the outcome of the 'in-humanation' of God's Wisdom, so united to Jesus' humanity as to identify him uniquely through all he does, says, suffers and undergoes, so that salvation is worked out in him for us.

The second is pneumatological. Christ is irreducibly distinct from us in virtue of the life he leads to God, as Hans Frei put it, and his ascension underlines the transcendence of this life and thus his freedom over his presence to us.[70] Yet he lives this life for us, and in this regard the New Testament links the identity of Christ to the activity of the Holy Spirit, who serves and justifies Jesus' obedient intentions by energizing and transforming him as an embodied human being in his life (Lk. 3:21, 4:1f., 4:18f.) and his resurrection (Rom. 1:4). It is this Spirit whom the risen Christ breathes upon the disciples (Jn 20:21–22), and who is identified as the Spirit of Christ (Phil. 1:19; cf. 2 Cor. 3:17–18), whom God gives to his adopted children (Gal. 4:6). Scripture thus indicates that because the Spirit is inseparably active in Christ and the particular shape of his new life and yet free to indwell in the church, he effects in the church the plenitude of life in Jesus Christ. Because Christ embodies the pattern of redeemed sociality, by the Spirit he is the effectual shaping source of that sociality, binding us together *as a body* shaped by his identity. Of *this* union with Christ by the Spirit and all these benefits, the Supper is, by that same Spirit, the effective sign-promise, wherein and whereby Christ's transformed, embodied humanity is given to be the spiritual food that nourishes and orders us in a particular kind of community constituted in its union with him.

It follows that the church is called first to celebrate the Supper so as to display this meaning truthfully, and, second, to seek to fulfil and enter into all the Supper enacts dramatically in ordering the common life of its members. Those who celebrate the Supper are called to seek with careful discernment and Christ-like love the re-ordering of wider patterns of ecclesial sociality – formal and informal relations of power, exchange, activities of service and celebration, institutional structures, laws and administrative arrangements – without regard for differences of wealth, class, status or gender, after the pattern of Christ.

The Supper also has implications for the church's interactions with the wider world. God's activity in wisely ordering and empowering the life of the church in loving mutual dependence anticipates his final good purposes for creation, and the Supper includes this benefit in its meaning. Let us assume a missional account of Christian vocation, whereby every member of the church, as well as its institutional representatives and voluntary societies, is called to live out that hope for God's future by the way they contribute to the well-being of society – to be truthful signs of the coming of God's kingdom.[71] In the Supper, Christ gives us, in the breadth of its social and ethical meaning, a dense symbolic concretization of this missional sign-making. He thus offers the church in the Supper and its social form a norma-tive index not only for its own life, but for the missional participation of all its mem-bers in the world.

Such an account, I suggest, enriches Calvin through Scripture to offer evangeli-cals a more adequate answer to the question Cocksworth poses to them. And it does so in evangelical fashion – by drawing critically on evangelical tradition and renewing it by the theological reading of Scripture.

Notes

1 I am grateful to the members of the St John's Research Seminar and to Paul Jones for their helpful comments on this chapter.
2 See Mt. 26:17–35; Mk 14: 12–25; Lk 22: 7–23, cf. C. J. Cocksworth, *Evangelical Eucharistic Thought in the Church of England*, Cambridge: Cambridge University Press, 1993, p. 9.
3 For evangelical interest in ecclesiology see T. Bradshaw, *The Olive Branch: An Evangelical Anglican Doctrine of the Church*, Carlisle: Paternoster Press, 1992; S. Grenz, *Renewing the Centre: Evangelical Theology in a Post-Theological Age*, Grand Rapids, MI: Baker Books, 2000, ch. 9; M. Husband and D. J. Treier (eds) *The Community of the Word: Toward an Evangelical Ecclesiology*, Leicester: Apollos, 2005; and L. van Dyk, 'The Church in Evangelical Theology and Practice', in T. Larsen and D. J. Treier (eds) *The Cambridge Companion to Evangelical Theology*, Cambridge: Cambridge University Press, 2007, pp. 125–41. The marginality of the Supper for evan-gelicals is evident in its relative absence from much evangelical worship, song, and pub-lication on theology or spirituality, as well as from the often detailed statements of faith of bodies like that of the UK Evangelical Alliance (available at: http://www.eauk.org/about/basis-of-faith.cfm [accessed 15 Sept. 2008]).
4 Cocksworth, *Evangelical Eucharistic Thought*, p. 9, his emphasis.
5 J. Calvin, *Commentary on the Epistles of Paul the Apostle to the Corinthians by John Calvin*, Grand Rapids. MI: Eerdmans, 1948, p. 370.
6 Calvin, Comm. 1 Cor. XI.23. Unless otherwise indicated translations are my own, from:

Ioannis Calvini in epistolam Pauli ad Corinthios priorem commentarii, in *Ioannis Calvini in Novi Estamenti Epistolas Commentarii* I (1844).

7 Ibid.
8 Ibid.
9 Calvin, Comm. 1 Cor., XI.24.
10 Ibid.
11 Calvin, Comm. 1 Cor., XI.26.
12 Ibid.
13 Ibid.
14 Cf. Calvin, *Institutio Christianae Religionis* (1559), IV.17.1. Henceforth cited as *Inst.* (1559).
15 Calvin, Comm. 1 Cor., XI.24.
16 Ibid.
17 Ibid.
18 Ibid.
19 Ibid.
20 Ibid.
21 Cf. M. Tinker, *Churchman* 112:2 , 1998, 131–49.
22 Calvin, Comm. 1 Cor., XI.24.
23 Ibid.
24 *Inst.* (1559), II.16.1–16.
25 J. Calvin, *Institutes of the Christian Religion*, IV.17.9, Philadelphia: The Westminster Press, 1960, p. 1368. Henceforth, cited as *Inst.*
26 See e.g. Bradshaw, *The Olive Branch*, pp. 191–3.
27 Calvin, Comm. 1 Cor., XI.24.
28 Ibid.
29 E.g. Aquinas, *ST* 3a.76, vol. 58, Cambridge: Cambridge University Press, 2006; Luther, *The Large Catechism* (1530), XV (available at: http://www.iclnet.org/pub/resources/text/wittenberg/luther/catechism/web/cat-15.html [accessed 17 Feb. 2009]); Zwingli, 'On the Lord's Supper', in G. W. Bromiley (ed.) *Zwingli and Bullinger*, London: SCM Press, 1953.
30 Ibid.; *Inst.* IV.17.32, to which I was alerted by J. D. Nicholls, '"Union with Christ": John Calvin on the Lord's Supper', in *Union and Communion, 1529–1979*, London: The Westminster Conference, 1980, p. 42.
31 Cf. J. Tylanda, 'Calvin and Christ's Presence in the Supper – True or Real?', *Scottish Journal of Theology* 1974, vol. 27, 65–75.
32 Calvin, Comm. 1 Cor., XI.24.
33 K. McDonnell, *John Calvin, the Church, and the Eucharist*, Princeton, NJ: Princeton University Press, 1967, p. 242.
34 So McDonnell, *John Calvin*, pp. 244–5.
35 See Calvin, *Inst.* 1559, IV.17.7, 10.
36 Calvin, Comm. 1 Cor., XI.24.
37 B. Gerrish, *Grace and Gratitude: The Eucharistic Theology of John Calvin*, Edinburgh: T&T Clark, 1993, p. 179.
38 Calvin, Comm. 1 Cor., XI.24.
39 McDonnell, *John Calvin*, p. 239.
40 Calvin, Comm. 1 Cor., XI.24.
41 Ibid.
42 J. T. Billings, *Calvin, Participation, and the Gift*, Oxford: Oxford University Press, 2007, p. 138. Cf. T. J. Davis, *This is My Body*, Grand Rapids, MI: Baker Academic, 2008, p. 136.
43 Calvin, *Inst.* 1559, IV.17.5, cf. Nicholls, '"Union with Christ"' p. 39; Billings, *Calvin*, 129–41.

44 Calvin, *Inst.* 1559, IV.17.3–4; Comm. 1 Cor., XI.24; 'Short Treatise' II, in J. Reid (ed.) *Calvin: Theological Treatises*, London: SCM Press, 1954, pp. 144–5.
45 Calvin, 'Short Treatise' II, in Reid, *Calvin*, p. 147; cf. McDonnell *John Calvin*, pp. 234–5, 244; and Gerrish, *Grace*, pp. 165–9.
46 Calvin, Comm. 1 Cor., XI.25.
47 Ibid.
48 Ibid.
49 Calvin, 'Short Treatise' II, in Reid, *Calvin*, p. 148.
50 As in Mt 26:26.
51 Calvin, Comm. 1 Cor., XI.24.
52 Ibid., X.16.
53 Ibid.
54 Calvin, *Inst.* IV.17.5.
55 Calvin, 'Short Treatise' II, p. 149.
56 I have taken this notion of 'operating conditions' from D. W. Hardy, 'Karl Barth', in D. F. Ford and R. Muers (eds) *The Modern Theologians*, Oxford: Blackwell, 2005, p. 28.
57 'I experience it rather than understand it', *Inst.* IV.17.32.
58 Cf. Calvin's *Inst.* 1559, I.VI–VII.
59 On *koinōnia*, see W. L. Willis, *Idol Meat in Corinth: The Pauline Argument in 1 Corinthians 8 and 10*, California: Scholars Press, 1985, pp. 168–208, whose analysis of the term implies that it denotes not merely fellowship in covenantal allegiance, but such fellowship and allegiance in common participation *in something*: Christ's body and blood.
60 Calvin, Comm. 1 Cor., XI.27–9; *Inst.* IV.17.40.
61 So G. Fee, *The First Epistle to the Corinthians*, Grand Rapids, MI: Eerdmans, 1987, p. 539.
62 Ibid., p. 540.
63 G. Theissen, 'Social Integration and Sacramental Activity: An Analysis of 1 Cor. 11:17 34', in his *The Social Setting of Pauline Christianity: Essays on Corinth*, T&T Clark, 1983, pp. 145–63; J. J. Meggitt, *Paul, Poverty and Survival*, Edinburgh: T&T Clark, 1998, pp. 18–22, 189–93.
64 *Ekklēsia* is the term used in the Septuagint Paul read for the gathered people of God: see W. Meeks, *The First Urban Christians: The Social World of the Apostle Paul*, New Haven, CT: Yale University Press, 1983, p. 108. According to Hays, the calling to be 'holy' echoes God's call to Israel: R. Hays, *First Corinthians*, Louisville, KY: John Knox Press, 1997, p. 16.
65 Cf. ibid., p. 19, for whom the term denotes fellowship with both Christ and the community.
66 Cf. ibid., pp. 213–14: the metaphor of the body of Christ illumines the church's union with and participation in Christ, through the Spirit.
67 Ibid., p. 214.
68 As Fee also notes, *Corinthians*, pp. 612, 615.
69 I take this language from D. W. Hardy, *God's Ways with the World*, Edinburgh: T&T Clark, 1996.
70 H. W. Frei, *The Identity of Jesus Christ*, Phildelphia, PA: Fortress Press, 1975, p. 172.
71 In elaborating this account of mission and Eucharist I am indebted to Dan Hardy in the conclusion to his *Finding the Church*, London: SCM, 2001, pp. 238–59.

Select bibliography

Calvin, J., *Commentary on the Epistles of Paul the Apostle to the Corinthians by John Calvin*, trans. J. Pringle, Grand Rapids, MI: Eerdmans, 1948.

Calvin, J., 'A Short Treatise on the Sacrament', in J. Reid (ed.), *Calvin: Theological Treatises*, London: SCM Press, 1954.

Calvin, J., *Calvin: Institutes of the Christian Religion*, 2 vols. Philadelphia, PA: The Westminster Press, 1960.

Cocksworth, C. J., *Evangelical Eucharistic Thought in the Church of England*, Cambridge: Cambridge University Press, 1993.

Gerrish. B. A., *Grace and Gratitude. The Eucharistic Theology of John Calvin*, Edinburgh: T&T Clark, 1993.

Hardy, D. W. 'Conclusion: Finding the Church', in *Finding the Church*, London: SCM, 2001, pp. 238–59.

Chapter 8

Embodied evangelicalism
The body of Christ and the Christian body

Elizabeth Kent

The body in western society has become the focus of many contemporary preoccupations ranging from the search for identity[1] to the quest for immortality.[2] Bodies are celebrated in the magazines of the mass media, honed in gyms and health clubs, surgically enhanced in operating theatres; and sick bodies are treated by the medical profession or by recourse to alternative therapies. The understanding that every person experiences life as an embodied person seems almost too simple a statement to make, but its importance lies in the bearing that it has on our understanding of the place and significance of the body. Having a body is a shared feature of human existence, though the subjective experience of being embodied is unique to every person.[3] Since the Enlightenment, the societal conception of the body has been founded on the understanding of the body of the individual as autonomous.

Evangelical understanding is that in response to the gospel Christians pursue a life of active discipleship and that the sanctification of the believer relates to the whole of life. This includes our relationship with and use of our bodies. Many evangelical pronouncements about what should and should not be done with our bodies come from an individualist post-Enlightenment treatment of Scripture as a set of universal principles to be applied to all, regardless of their relationship or non-relationship with Christ. As such, the view of what bodies are for, and what behaviour is appropriate or permissible, has been reduced to a series of maxims. Taken out of the context of the community of faith who witness to the centrality of the risen Christ, these pronouncements may at times appear unconnected, arbitrary rulings for those within the church; and irrelevant, unintelligible dictates to those outside the church.[4] The complexities of embodied existence in contemporary culture call for a theological response from evangelicals which extends beyond textual abstraction and enables Christians to live in faithfulness to Christ, heeding Paul's encouragement to 'glorify God in your body'.[5]

This chapter contends that the traditional emphases on individual piety and rationality in a context of modernity lead to an impoverished account of how Christians live embodied lives. Evangelical theology at its worst has prized cognitive understanding of doctrine over the exercise of Christian practices, individual privatized commitment over corporate participation, and an emphasis on redemption at the expense of incarnation. As a consequence, evangelicals have concentrated theological interest heavily on what may be done or not done with one's body in relation to certain areas,[6] but have virtually ignored other aspects of embodied existence.[7] Indeed, emphases within evangelicalism which have stressed the salvation of souls rather than the salvation and redemption of the whole person have generated two opposing extremes. The first is a gnostic leaning towards viewing the matter of the body as corrupt and corrupting. This results in a retreat from, and suspicion of the body and a renewed pursuit of the 'safer ground' of the intellectual quest for doctrinal purity. In contrast to this negative view of the body, the second response is that identified by R. Marie Griffiths.[8] The body is seen as the canvas on which the state of the soul is displayed and therefore to be cultivated to an ideal of 'perfection'. This idolization of the body of the individual is as much a distortion of the tradition as the neo-gnosticism, and it is toward a third way which avoids both these extremes that this chapter is directed.

In his articulation of 'the sanctified body', Stanley Hauerwas argues that individual bodies should be interpreted in the light of participation in the body of Christ.[9] In engaging with this work, while not fully endorsing its conclusions, I seek to formulate how these insights might open evangelicals to a perspective which is faithful to the best parts of our heritage, but reinterprets them for today. A further development of this possibility looks at how participation in the body of Christ might form disciples who take as their example the incarnate Jesus revealed in Scripture and how our embodied existence may be shaped by his.

Bringing into dialogue the insights on the one hand of R. Marie Griffith in her reflections on the 'born-again bodies' of American Protestants,[10] shaped by evangelicalism, and the work of Robert Song[11] and Stanley Hauerwas[12] in their call to re-envision individual bodies in the light of the body of Christ, as stated in 1 Corinthians, I endeavour to illustrate how the evangelical emphasis on individual piety, rationalism and acceptance of the body as unaffected by its location in liberal western society are susceptible to a distortion which has implications for how evangelicals faithfully 'offer their bodies as living sacrifices'.[13]

Unmasking the body – who defines the body?

Any discussion of the human body necessarily acknowledges the complexity of meanings generated by the subject. The variety of interpretations of the body and embodied existence which influence any theological treatment of the body need to be named before embarking upon any discussion.[14] As someone culturally located in the UK I am aware that, in this society, the individual experiences life in a context where the body is more than a functional physicality; it is a signifier of identity, protected by law and laden with meaning. The first part of this section argues that the philosophical foundations stemming from the Enlightenment create a societal understanding of the body as the autonomous property of the individual, defined in the various languages of professional disciplines and separated into spheres of interest. The body and the influences upon it as defined in psychology may differ considerably from what is described in sociology. The consequences of this for how people relate to their own bodies and the bodies of others will be explored, and especially the fact that evangelical theology has often accepted the claims of Enlightenment thought in its own interpretation of the body and embodiment.

My contention is that, too often, evangelicals have failed to appreciate that the body is not neutral. By 'neutral' I do not refer to the theological sinfulness or redeemed nature of the body, whether evangelicals perceive their bodies as 'good' or 'bad',[15] but that, aware of it or not, evangelicals seeking to discuss the relationship of the body to Scripture carry with them unspoken assumptions about the notion of body which they have adopted from the culture around them. Most typically this will be adopting the prevailing view of the liberal political society that the body of the individual is autonomous and sacrosanct. That bodies are the autonomous domain of the individual is likely to be unquestioningly accepted and defended by the majority of evangelicals. Without this principle the political and legal constructs of society are threatened and the close allegiance of evangelicals to politics of the liberal state makes it difficult for some evangelicals to conceive of any other way of understanding the body.[16] That the body as understood by the state and the body as lived in the Christian community and defined by its relationship to Christ are not the same may cause discomfort among some, but it is on this basis that this chapter proceeds.

Within that larger, societal frame of reference evangelicals have often adopted the principles of individual autonomous bodies but disagreed with the use to which others have put those bodies. In this way, the evangelical community has both allied itself with the structure that defines the body but disagreed with its conclusions. The naming and defining of the body in terms which are inconsistent with the revelation of God constitute powers which exert influence over the body. The starting point for any opening up of evangelical body theology must be to recognize the existence of these underlying assumptions or powers and hold them to the scrutiny of God's revelation in Christ.

The extent to which the body is referred to in the language of modern medicine or concepts of sociology, psychology, anthropology or feminist thought frames the values and understandings attributed to it. Modern medicine has as its aim the relief of suffering and, as such, struggles to conceive of a situation where bodily suffering may serve a purpose or where the death of a patient can be anything other than failure.[17]

Feminism has highlighted the diversity of embodied experience, particularly making the case for the female body's experience of patriarchal oppression. The influence of feminist thought upon society includes raising questions about how the fact that we are embodied in an actual, physical body shapes our experience and understanding of the world around us.

Psychology's description of the relationship of the body and mind, or the constitution of the 'self', has become a dominant narrative in some quarters, defining how the world is for those who describe themselves by its language. The complex relationship between the body and the mind is not a new issue, but within popular culture there exists a willingness to accept the 'professional' opinion of the psychologist in defining the relationship of mind and body.

All these disciplines make claims about what the body is and to some extent express value judgements about it. The challenge for Christians in the midst of these competing truth claims is to decide which to accept and which to reject. It matters a great deal whether, when speaking of the body, we are thinking merely of flesh and bones or a living, breathing canvas of meaning which encapsulates the very essence of a person. Whether we speak of *having* a body rather than *being* embodied reveals our relationship to the body. In the first case, *having* a body takes a possessive stance which locates the nature of the *real* as us somewhere other than the body, rather than the understanding of *being embodied* which suggests an integrated personhood combining body, mind and spirit.

Many of the issues which have caused evangelicals the greatest ethical struggles have ultimately come down to questions about a theology of the body. Questions about food, gender, sex, life and death all arise because we know no other way of existing other than as embodied beings. The nature of evangelicalism, with its emphasis on practical response to the gospel, consequently causes evangelicals to value ordering one's behaviour in conformity with Scripture. As human experience cannot be separated from being embodied beings, this will naturally raise questions about the nature, theology and purpose of the body. It is therefore imperative that any discussion of the body is clear about the power language has in defining and controlling debate, and that it is important that Christians do not unquestioningly legitimate the prevailing cultural definitions.

My assertion is that the body in western liberal society bears a plethora of meanings and is subject to influences which Christians are often unable to name because of our complicity in the system which determines how the body is understood. In identifying ourselves so closely with the liberal state, which has prized bodily autonomy and privatized belief, we struggle to articulate a Christian response to views of the body and practices of the body with which we disagree because we are so firmly wedded to the notion of one's body as one's own inviolable kingdom. Pronouncements by the church about what should and should not be done with the body sound to the world at large like an unwelcome invasion from a place of assumed superiority into the autonomous world of those who, in the language of 'rights', have the right to do what they like with their bodies. In the midst of such forces, the responses of evangelicalism have too often been found wanting.

The assault on the body – from the body as given to fluidity and modification

As someone located in the UK I am aware that I live in a culture whose attitude toward the body borders on the obsessional. Alongside the challenges identified above in actually conceptualizing the body, there is the challenge that the issues surrounding bodies and embodiment are not static. Advances in medical research challenge the very notion of the body as it has historically been understood as bodies are increasingly described in and controlled by medical terminology. The ethical debates about the beginning and ending of life are often framed in terms of personhood, seeking to delineate when a 'person' and a body are no longer congruent.[18]

Aesthetic developments in body modification also bring into question the fundamental nature of the purpose and 'givenness' of the human body. Cosmetic surgery for aesthetic reasons is on the increase,[19] and the flexibility and fluidity of the bodily form is greater than ever before. Media speculation about an obesity crisis in the general population,[20] a rise in eating disorders among adolescents, and focus on the weight and body shape of celebrities, has heightened societal awareness of the body and placed its size and practices firmly on the political agenda.

Technological advances, most notably the internet, have initiated situations where it is possible to have a non-embodied relationship. Apart from needing a body to operate a computer, virtual communities operate where no face-to-face or bodily contact is required for instantaneous communication and a relationship of sorts to exist. While the internet has many positive uses and raises interesting theological issues, it is in its capacity to facilitate non-embodied or differently embodied existence that it is significant here. It is now perfectly possible to create a virtual existence with a virtual body radically different in gender, race or style to one's physical body and meet others doing the same. This raises questions of truthfulness in relationship and also the creation of a world where, being disembodied, we lose a sense of our vulnerability. The susceptibility of physical bodies to sickness is a feature of embodied life which can be eliminated in cyberspace. The loss of body transports us to a place of unreality which denies that part of faithful discipleship which is learning to be self-controlled in the face of temptation and patient in physical affliction, and to acknowledge our fallibility and temporality. Virtual existence allows us to escape embodiment and all that can be learned from it as a means of discipleship and, instead, to create a world in our own image where we are as we choose to be – namely, in control.

These are but a few of the challenges flowing from secular culture which seek to shape and define twenty-first-century bodies. To lay all blame at the door of secularization, however, would be a failure to accept the part that evangelicalism has played in generating a distorted view of the body. In an attempt to separate from the world and pursue individual piety within the confines of American evangelicalism, a disturbing picture has emerged of the ideal of bodily perfection becoming an all-encompassing pursuit. Rather than separating themselves from the culture, as is often the evangelical position,[21] American evangelicals have influenced societal aspirations and practices.[22] Over time, however, the failure to ground such practices in the life of the worshipping community in relationship with Christ has caused the evangelical pursuit of a sanctified body to collapse into an individual body project undertaken without reference to God.

Bodies in crisis

Writing from a North American context, R. Marie Griffiths contends that analysis of the culture in which she finds herself reveals that bodies are in crisis.[23] The drive to cultivate the 'perfect body', she believes, has become a consuming project within mainstream America. The combining of spiritual, moral, political and health beliefs has generated a culture where 'born-again bodies', as she terms them, are the form to which many aspire as the outward manifestation of an inward spiritual state of holiness. In a thorough and nuanced appraisal of factors influencing this situation, she concludes that this is not simply forces of secularization at work but that the Protestant heritage of the United States has been a significant factor in generating attitudes to the body: 'Rather than a logical outgrowth of religion's supposed dislodgment, American fitness culture is an end that Protestantism's specific American forms boldly pursued: a devotional project aimed at bodily perfectibility.'[24] Popular literature aimed at the evangelical market, such as Dr Deborah Newman's *Loving your Body*, make explicit the link between individual piety and the body: 'You'll realise that growing close to the Lord naturally creates a desire to care more for the body He gave you.'[25]

It is not only within the confines of the church that such material flourishes. Griffith identifies the three elements which originated as Protestant practices for individual spiritual growth and which have come to exert considerable influence upon the populace in general. Food abstinence, sexual restraint and phrenology (the idea that the visible exterior of the body or face reflects the spiritual reality within) are having an on-going influence over the bodies of Americans, and Griffith identifies the resulting outcome as a culture which is obsessed with a quest for a perfect body.

It can be seen that the pietistic strand within evangelicalism, both in the US and in Griffiths' examples from early Methodism in the UK,[26] provide fertile ground for focus on the individual body as the locus of holiness. Initially, the purpose of fasting and sexual restraint was framed clearly in terms of the individual believer's sanctification and the use of the body to glorify God. What developed over time, however, was a combining of a quest for individual piety with the privatizing of religious faith. What emerged was a situation where the traditional evangelical emphasis placed on personal commitment and personal growth became susceptible to an individualistic quest for holiness separated from other believers.

If the outworking of salvation is framed in terms of developing a 'born-again body', in the sense that the toned, disciplined body reflects the disciplined self, then the potential for two serious distortions exists. First, there is the possibility of censure of those within the church who do not conform to the 'healthy' bodily ideal. When the aesthetic value or fitness of bodies become the means by which a Christian's life is judged, even based on the justification that what is seen externally reflects the inner life, then we have lost the good news that salvation is a gift of God's grace. The second consequence of equating 'born-again bodies' with growth in holiness is a tendency to generate self-righteousness among those who achieve it. This is also a perversion of growth in holiness, as it ignores the grace by which we are saved.

The evangelical emphasis on personal conversion and individual commitment has often reduced questions about the body to a quest to get right 'what I do with *my* body'. The jump from biblical texts to application is made without seeking to understand the context and concepts unstated in the text, but which form the scaffolding around which they are built.

There are many similarities in attitudes toward the body between the UK and the US, but significant cultural differences can also be detected. These include historical, social and religious differences which have shaped cultural understandings. Although these differences ensure that the situation in the US will not be identically replicated in the UK, sufficient points of congruence exist to hold up a mirror to our own context in order that we might recognize some of the dangers within it.

Our locatedness in a particular time and context cannot be denied nor escaped from but undoubtedly shapes who we are and how we perceive the body. Our views about what is beautiful or natural or normal will, to some extent, have been influenced by the culture we inhabit. How evangelicals read the Bible and seek to discern the purpose and right use of their bodies in such a situation can be problematic. How then might we extrapolate ourselves from the situation Griffiths describes, where the quest for bodily perfection has become an all-consuming feature of individual holiness?

Recovering fragments – letting go of my body as my autonomous inviolable kingdom

The movement towards what is being termed postmodernity presents both challenges and opportunities in forming a Christian understanding of the body which is faithful to Scripture. As raised above, the increased interest in the body and pressures upon concepts of the body to respond to a changing and diverse context challenge Christians to live a story of embodiment consistent with the claims of faithful Christian discipleship.

Stanley Hauerwas understands 'postmodernism' to offer fertile ground for a re-imagining of holiness, including holiness related to embodied existence, because of the change in the way people understand the world to be.

> The loss of the 'self' and the appreciation of the significance of the body, and in particular the body's permeability, can help us rediscover holiness not as an individual achievement but as the work of the Holy Spirit building up the body of Christ.[27]

The assertion is that postmodernity entails a loss of the self. As people are confronted by a diversity of complex situations, they adapt to respond to the context in which they find themselves. Their identity in any given situation differs to the point of their existing in a number of different identities, thus breaking down an integrated, stable identity or 'self'. Without the constraints of tradition or inherited social convention to dictate behaviour, there is a fluidity of identity unknown by previous generations. This in part accounts for the focus on the body as a canvas of identity, since in an environment where others form their impressions only from what they see in the body before them,[28] the image projected by that body becomes increasingly important.

Rather than agreeing with Hauerwas that what exists in contemporary western society is a loss of the self, I find more convincing the analysis of Anthony Giddens: '[t]he reflexive project of the self, which consists in the sustaining of coherent, yet continuously revised, biographical narratives, takes place in the context of multiple choice as filtered through abstract systems'.[29] The self is not lost, merely continually redefined in the 'reflexive project of self-identity'. The body is necessarily drawn into this project in the way it is fed, nurtured, styled, dressed, used, sculpted, adorned, articulated and perceived.

Where the body was once an inviolable autonomous unit there is now an openness to otherness, and instead of rigidity there is flexibility. As we seek to form evangelical theology at the juncture between modernity and postmodernity the body becomes an example of many of the features of the paradigm shift proposed. What was once controlled, boundaried and individual is now more fluid, permeable and receptive to participation with the other. The opportunity this presents is for a relinquishing of understanding the body as the locus of individual piety, which, as Griffith demonstrates, has the potential to lure us away from dependence on the grace of God. Instead, while not denying the need for conversion in response to the love of God which reaches out to us personally, it is fitting that our understanding of the body moves beyond an individual response to participation with the other.

Bodies and the body of Christ

What the influence of postmodernity and the questioning of our understanding of the body may be leading us to is this: the embodied self is most truly who it is in relationship with God through Christ and in the community that is the body of Christ.

When Paul writes to the church at Corinth he writes to people concerned with how their allegiance to Christ determines their embodied relationship to food, sex and each other. It appears that they, too, were prone to understanding their individual identity and needs as their primary focus,[30] and it is in this context that Paul's use of the image of the body of Christ expresses something profound about the call to Christian living. In stating the proper end of bodies as glorifying God,[31] Paul challenges them, 'Do you not know that your bodies are members of Christ?'[32] and, to provide further emphasis, 'Or do you not know that your body is a temple of the Holy Spirit within you, which you have from God, and that you are not your own?'[33]

It has been symptomatic of the individualism we have embraced that the individual body as the temple of the Holy Spirit has been the dominant image when discussing the body in evangelical circles. Too often we have failed to heed the second part of that verse, that we are not our own, and have failed to recognize that relating to our bodies as members of Christ requires us to live in such a way as to reclaim embodied existence as fully participating with others in Christ. Consequently our thoughts, words and actions are to be shaped, not by the theological justification of the prevailing culture (which may have been influenced by a distortion of Protestant theology in the first place), but by faithfulness to Christ who became incarnate and who by his Spirit now lives in us.

Our bodies should not be an autonomous project of self actualization. The radical disruption of Scripture calls us to understand individual bodies as primarily part of the body of Christ. In sharp contrast to the secular culture which enshrines the autonomous individual body, and at variance with evangelicals who have appropriated that same concept, the challenge to view our own bodies through the lens of participation in the body of Christ subverts what we have been led to believe the body is for.

As Paul develops the reference to bodies and the body of Christ,[34] Hays notes the fact that, instead of equating the one body with many members and the church, Paul equates them with Christ. 'Instead by identifying the many members of the church directly with Christ, Paul seems to press beyond mere analogy to make an ontological equation of the Church with Christ.'[35] Whereas we are tempted to reduce this to a metaphor, to understand that the embodied people who follow Christ are in some way Christ's body has implications for our interpretation of our individual bodies.[36]

Most radically, to the ears of contemporary Christians, our bodies are not our own. The significance of conversion is not merely a conversion of the mind, an assent to a proposition that Jesus Christ is Lord. It is more than that – a submission of the whole person, body, mind and spirit to the Lordship of Christ and a becoming part of the body of Christ. That surrender to Christ involves a surrender of all that we are means that, in contradiction to the voice of the secular culture, I no longer own my body. If our bodies no longer belong to us but are first and foremost members of the body of Christ, our perception of those members and what may be done with them must be shaped by that understanding. Learning to interpret our bodies in the light of this gives us understanding of why condemnation of particular practices in Scripture matter. In our attempts to glorify God in our bodies the question changes from 'Is this the right thing to do with my body?' to 'How does my behaviour affect the life of the body of Christ?' To eat at communion while other bodies are undernourished demeans the body of Christ.[37] To unite Christ's body with a prostitute is unthinkable.[38]

The worth of the body which was previously expressed in its usefulness, health or beauty is now found in its participation in Christ. Experiencing embodied existence as part of the body of Christ releases us from the quest for individual bodily perfection in the present age (as defined and sought by particular sections of society). Participation in the body of Christ transforms our understanding of what bodies are and what they are for. Bodies speak of who we are, not as canvases exalting our individual personal moral choices, but participating in the body of Christ they are bodies shaped by worship of God and service of the other. In moving from interpreting bodies as individual projects of piety to emphasizing the relational nature of embodied discipleship within the body of Christ, our focus changes. It is less about whether or not it is permissible to have a 'WWJD' tattoo on one's body and more about doing what Jesus does.

The body of Christ speaks prophetically of what true embodiment might be, for there is room within the body of Christ for all types of body. In contrast to the secular culture or even the individual pietistic ideal, there is no pressure for bodies to look a particular way. The diversity of gifts within the body of Christ indicates that a diversity of bodies in terms of colour, ethnicity, disability and size is to be celebrated not ignored. Being embodied has a particularity to it which makes us gendered, sexual, racial beings. This has the tendency to create binary categories, neither of which fully explains the complexities of our human experience but which have the potential to generate barriers and false assumptions. When we perceive ourselves first and foremost as members of the body of Christ, our bodily particularity is no longer the primary marker of identity. It is not the particularity which defines us over and against other Christians, but our common identity as members of the body of Christ.

The radical disruption of Scripture for ethics and the body is seen truly when the body of Christ, the church, is the means by which the individual body is understood. A sharp contrast can be seen with the view undergirded by western liberal capitalist ideals, which seek to establish bodily autonomy over and against the bodies of others. In the body of Christ, the mutual submission of members reveals the interdependence of the 'strong' and the 'weak'. If one suffers, all suffer, and so the mutuality and care for the needs of others stems from the fact that they are also part of the body of Christ. The attentiveness to the weak, the poor and the suffering which this view of 'body' enables reflects the incarnate Christ's refusal to shun those whose bodies did not meet the standards of health and purity demanded by their society.

As the body of Christ, we seek together to discern the revelation of God in Christ and what that might mean for a Christian response to the many issues facing the body. As we worship, we are not merely a collection of individuals, but primarily we are the body of Christ, each member aware of and attentive to the others. In worship, as we pray for the sick, we suffer with them, for when one part of the body suffers, all suffer. In hearing and responding to Scripture we seek not what this might mean, first, for my body, but what this means for us as the body of Christ. In confession we open ourselves up, speaking truthfully of who we are, so that in receiving the forgiveness of others in the body of Christ we experience the forgiveness of God.

As we share in the Eucharist we are reminded of the body of Christ broken and his blood outpoured. In a culture which seeks to avoid suffering and brokenness, the Christian cannot escape the realization that it is Christ's body broken on the cross which is the focus of salvation and hope. In the mystery of the Eucharist the words 'this is my body, broken for you' remind us that our participation in the body of Christ is at his invitation, through his grace and by his broken body. Such remembrance reveals the futility of the secular quest for the perfect individual body and declares that the way of salvation is not in some construct of bodily perfection or purity, but in Christ whose broken body hung on a cross. As we break bread and share wine we participate in the mystery which sustains the body of Christ by remembering that it is Christ who saves and transforms our embodied selves. It is Christ, who, in becoming incarnate, revealed that holiness is not an escape from the body but a purpose of the body, practised in the mess and complexity of life.

In celebrating the resurrected Christ as we share in the Eucharist we give thanks that though our earthly bodies will die, in Christ there is the promise of the resurrected body. Though we do not know what form or substance the resurrected body will take, we trust the witness of the risen Christ and live our embodied existence in faith that death is not the end. Bodies which do not fear ageing or dying stand in sharp contrast to the myth of eternal youth portrayed in contemporary popular culture. The idolizing of youthful bodies and the careful sidelining of aged bodies in film, television, fashion and business speak of a society which sees ageing as a path to death and thus attempts to deny its existence. Within the body of Christ, the presence and acceptance of bodies which age serves as a witness to the world that, to the Christian, ageing is not the worst thing that can happen to one's body and death is not to be feared.

If this emphasis on the body of Christ as a community of Christians sounds more Catholic than evangelical, it should be noted that our heritage contains various examples of when we have sought genuinely to live our embodied existence not as a private individual quest but as open to others. This requires a depth of commitment to being the body of Christ found in some of the assemblies of the early evangelicals. Their commitment to being the body of Christ entailed openness and vulnerability, acknowledgement of sin, serving the poor, proclaiming the good news and, in a very real sense, living as the body of Christ. Through participation in the body of Christ discipleship was a communal activity and the shaping and actions of individual bodies formed a natural part of such participation.

It has been identified earlier that Griffith uses John Wesley's instructions to Methodists about fasting as a negative example of the pursuit of individual piety.[39] It is my assertion that early Methodist class meetings and band meetings are examples of being the body of Christ and pursuing embodied holiness which do not collapse into an individual quest or salvation by works. Wesley's consideration of the practicalities of discipleship reveal a concern for the pursuit of holiness which is grounded in the realities of eating, drinking and clothing the body. Rather than becoming a prescriptive moral code, however, these issues were considered in the context of a disciplined community of believers. The band and class meetings constituted an outworking of being the body of Christ as the bodies of early Methodists ordered themselves to receive the grace of God, to be accountable to one another and together, to pursue holiness.[40] Hauerwas alludes positively to the value of Wesley's understanding that the church should be a 'disciplined community',[41] a recovery of which would mark an evangelical return both to our heritage and to a place where understanding the body in the light of participation in the body of Christ could be a reality.

For evangelicals, participation in the body of Christ is the antidote to the quest for 'bodily perfection'[42] as promoted in western industrialized nations. The radical nature of Scripture subverts such ideals and instead the body of Christ is a place where 'bodily perfection' is neither a quest for eternal youth in an attempt to deny the onset of age (and with it death), nor a purely spiritual endeavour, denying the reality of embodied living. Instead, participation in the body of Christ allows for embodied Christians of all shapes and sizes to encounter Christ in community and, as they meet, to be transformed by his grace.

The body of Christ and the incarnate Christ

If it is through participation in the body of Christ that we understand the purpose and appropriate uses of our bodies, how then do we seek to reconcile this with our understanding of the place of Scripture? It is suggested that central to understanding our participation in the body of Christ is our attentiveness to the incarnate Christ revealed in Scripture and the risen Christ present in his church by the Holy Spirit.

Being people who are shaped by living in relationship with the risen Christ and participating in the community which is his body re-orientates our bodies. Being shaped and formed in discipleship means being faithful in worship and service, and as we encounter the incarnate Christ in the gospels we become more aware of the Christ present by his Spirit in his body, the church. It would be possible to identify many passages in Scripture where the body of the incarnate Christ witnesses to how the church as the body of Christ should be. The following example addresses just one aspect of how those who understand their own bodies as members of the body of Christ may engage with the incarnate Christ. In the gospels we see Jesus unashamed of his body as a woman pours perfume over his feet and wipes them with her hair. As the body of Christ we learn that being embodied is good, and that to experience physical devotion or affection need not be primarily sexual.[43] In our practice of discipleship we then become those who welcome the lonely and unloved, and witness to the love embodied in Christ which affirms the gift of physicality.

Conclusion

If, as evangelicals, we can relinquish the overemphasis on piety focused on the individual body and allow Scripture radically to disrupt our self-understanding that we are autonomous individuals who gather to be a collective of individuals called church, then we may be able to encounter a richer understanding of embodied existence, which flows from the experience of being participants in the body of Christ. In looking to the incarnate Christ, we see embodied existence where physicality is enjoyed and pure,[44] where the physical limitations of the body provide opportunities for encountering God's grace,[45] and where Jesus' use of touch demonstrates an affirmation of bodies deemed outcast by society.

Understanding our own bodies through their participation in the body of Christ enables us to draw some conclusions which are counter-cultural. They are not counter-cultural in the sense of what they stand against, which has been a feature of some evangelical attitudes toward the body. Instead they re-orientate our way of thinking about the body, what it signifies and what end it might pursue.

The conclusion therefore is that the Christian's body derives its value from the fact that it is part of the body of Christ, a fact to which other members of the body bear witness. Consequently, the relationship of that member with other members of the body of Christ means they seek only to do those things with their body which encourage and build up other members to maturity, rather than seeking personal fulfilment. This is to suggest that in approaching our bodies this way, evangelicals might become embodied people on the way to being more fully the bodies they were created to be. That is to understand the body not as something to be escaped from, nor something to idolize, but as integral to a disciplined life lived fully to the glory of God in participation with the community which is the articulation of his body on earth.

Notes

1   For example, see Wolf on how the notion of physical beauty has become an ideal held up to women by which to determine their identity. N. Wolf, *The Beauty Myth*, London: Chatto & Windus, 1990.
2   The rise in popularity of anti-ageing treatments for the body, including cosmetic surgery, can be seen as an attempt to stave off ageing and deny the finitude of human life.
3   It is acknowledged that some of the most contentious ethical issues can be discussed within the heading of 'the body'. Genetic manipulation, human sexuality, euthanasia and abortion all require discussion about the theology of the body, though the limitations of this piece preclude specific treatment of each of these issues.
4   Note for example the derision and disbelief with which abstaining from premarital sex is treated in a secular culture which assumes all young people will be sexually active.
5   1 Cor. 6:20.
6   Bodies which are male or female are gendered and sexual. The ethics of sexual practice have long been a topic for debate within evangelical circles, and in some circles one's stance on sexual ethics is counted as a defining mark of whether one is 'orthodox' or not.
7   Few evangelical publications during the twentieth century considered the discipline of fasting or the appropriate response of the Christian toward food.
8   R. M. Griffith, *Born Again Bodies*, London: University of California Press, 2004.
9   S. Hauerwas, *Sanctify them in the Truth*, Nashville, TN: Abingdon Press, 1998.
10 Griffith, *Born Again Bodies*.
11 R. Song, 'Genetic Manipulation and the Body of Christ', *Studies in Christian Ethics*, 2007, vol. 20.3, 399–420.
12 Hauerwas, *Sanctify them in the Truth*.
13 Rom. 12:1.
14 Even if there is insufficient space for analysis of the claims they make to define the body.
15 Though these binary distinctions do little to help our understanding of our bodies as being part of the on-going process of sanctification.
16 See here Andi Smith, in this volume, ch. 12.
17 Though suffering is something we seek to alleviate, the possibility that God may redeem something which is in itself bad is a sign of his goodness and grace.
18 This chapter does not engage in specific discussion of 'personhood', nor of the anthropological relationship between body and soul. Instead the focus is on the body as the physical manifestation of embodied existence.

19 In a press release dated 18 September 2008, the British Association of Aesthetic Plastic Surgeons reported a 275 per cent rise in the number of breast augmentation operations performed by their members between 2002 and 2007 (see URL: www.baaps.org.uk/content/view/404/6/ [accessed June 2008]).

20 For example the *Guardian Online* reporting on government measures to tackle obesity in the population (see URL: www.guardian.co.uk/uk/2006/jun/16/health.foodanddrink [accessed September 2008]).

21 Being in the world but not of the world.

22 Such as encouraging dietary restraint as an outworking of the moral virtue of self-control, and advocating exercise as a means of increasing the effectiveness of the body in service of God.

23 Griffith, *Born Again Bodies*.

24 Ibid., p. 13.

25 D. Newman, *Loving Your Body*, Wheaton, IL: Tyndale House, 2002 (back cover).

26 Griffith quotes John Wesley's advice to the early Methodists to fast weekly, as was the stated practice of the Anglican Church. See Griffith, *Born Again Bodies*, p. 13.

27 Hauerwas, *Sanctify them in the Truth*, p. 78.

28 Rather than by relationship to kin or social class or occupation as would have been the case in previous generations.

29 A. Giddens, *Modernity and Self-Identity: Self and Society in the Late Modern Age*, Stanford, CA: Stanford University Press, 1991, p. 5.

30 See Paul's condemnation of the Corinthians for their selfishness at communion in 1 Cor. 11:21–22.

31 1 Cor. 6:20.

32 Ibid., 6:15.

33 Ibid., 6:19.

34 Ibid., 12:12.

35 R. B. Hays, *First Corinthians*, Louisville, KY: John Knox Press, 1997, p. 213.

36 It is not clear how Paul would have understood the relationship between the individual bodies and the body of Christ. For further discussion, see Hays, *First Corinthians*.

37 1 Cor. 11.

38 Ibid., 6:15.

39 Griffith, *Born Again Bodies*, p. 13.

40 For further discussion, see B. Tabraham, *The Making of Methodism*, Peterborough: Epworth, 1995, p. 46.

41 Hauerwas, *Sanctify them in the Truth*, p. 80.

42 Namely having a body which is slim, toned, unblemished and conforming to a particular ideal of beauty.

43 Although in Jn 12:3, Mary's action in anointing Jesus' feet and wiping them with her hair is a highly sensual act which goes beyond what would be expected social interaction between a man and a woman. Jesus' reaction to this expression of bodies which are sexual is not condemnation but an implicit affirmation that to be a sexual being is part of being an embodied being.

44 See the anointing of Jesus' feet, Jn 12.

45 See Jesus asking for a drink as he meets the woman of Samaria in Jn 4.

Select bibliography

Giddens, A., *Modernity and Self-Identity: Self and Society in the Late Modern Age*, Stanford, CA: Stanford University Press, 1991.

Griffith, R. M., *Born Again Bodies*, London: University of California Press, 2004.

Hauerwas, S., *Sanctify them in the Truth*, Nashville, TN: Abingdon Press, 1998.

Hays, R. B., *First Corinthians*, Louisville, KY: John Knox Press, 1997.

Song, R., 'Genetic Manipulation and the Body of Christ', *Studies in Christian Ethics* 20.3, 2007, 399–420.

Tabraham, B., *The Making of Methodism*, Peterborough: Epworth, 1995.

Thiselton, A. C., *The Hermeneutics of Doctrine*, Grand Rapids, MI: Eerdmans, 2007.

Wolf, N., *The Beauty Myth*, London: Chatto & Windus, 1990.

Chapter 9

Embodied Christianity

Practice illuminating a biblical ecclesiology

Donald McFadyen

> Christianity is manifest in the world as a society; Christianity is embodied in social form.[1]

Evangelicals are ambivalent about the church. I suspect that Daniel Hardy's assertion above that the church is nothing less than the embodiment of faith in the form of a society makes many evangelical minds simultaneously uncomfortable and hopeful. We are uncomfortable because we have become accustomed to thinking about faith with direct reference to God rather than being that which is mediated through the church. To emphasize the church when we know from experience how unreliable it is compared to God is risky, if not wrong. On the other hand we find hope through Hardy's words. They hold out the possibility that Christian faith operating in the world goes beyond just proclamation, and always being slightly removed from the relationship-hungry world, and results in a new form of life together, embedded in its surroundings.

More penetratingly I think Hardy's words expose an unstated but nonetheless real evangelical conviction that Christianity is individualistic not social. In other words, our ambivalence about the church stems from a belief that what really counts in faith is the individual's life with God, not the shared life that faith makes possible. We believe the church has value but only insofar as it helps the individual sustain their walk with God, alone. Thus the church is incidental to faith, and not intrinsic to it, and amounts to individual Christians gathered as a simple aggregate 1+1+1+1. Hardy holds out the possibility that church life is richer than this, precisely because *human life, including life as the church, is intrinsically social*. This is important because it concerns the foundation of the church, and so affects it in all its aspects – worship, corporate life and mission.

Here I want to make the case for understanding the church to be a society, and to make a few suggestions about how that might affect church practice. First I will look at some of the features of the pervasive evangelical ecclesiology that is focused on the individual. I will then look at some parts of the Gospel of St John to show how they point to a social, rather than individual, picture of life. I will then build on these insights through the writings of a sixteenth-century theologian,

Richard Hooker, before looking at implications for local church life. My intention is to aid 'thoughtful doing' in the church, insights from Scripture informing our practice, but also our practice shedding light on the Scriptures as we read them.[2] This process of mutual illumination is illustrated by the personal story with which I begin.[3]

As a priest in the Church of England I served part of my curacy with Revd Peter Owen Jones in a village near Cambridge in England.[4] One day during our staff meeting Peter told me that the 650th anniversary of the church's consecration would be occurring later that year and I was to organize the celebration. 'I want you to throw a party for the village,' he said. At first his request simply did not make sense. My unspoken reaction was, why a party for the village? What has this anniversary to do with them? This is a church event, affecting only church-attending people. It was clear, however, that Peter saw possibilities that I did not.

In hindsight this was my 'St Peter and Cornelius' moment. In Acts 10 Peter's 'Us and them, Jews and Gentiles, clean and profane' distinctions are challenged and profoundly reordered. In a comparable way I was caught in a deeply boundaried 'us and them' way of thinking,[5] and it would not be a divine dream that would challenge me, but a nine-month process of meeting and listening to those who lived in the village. As I did so I started to understand why Peter had invited me to think more widely than the church. I discovered among many people living in the village a commitment to the church, a belief that it was the glue that kept the village together by giving it its sense of identity. Consequently, there was an eagerness to celebrate its anniversary that I had never expected. I had assumed that, because people did not attend Sunday services, they were completely uninterested in the church's life.

The question I now faced was what to do considering the villagers' commitment to the church. While it was unrecognizable as faith in traditional evangelical terms, it nevertheless seemed important and valid, and therefore appropriate to give it expression. This became the question with which our planning group wrestled, working out not how we as the church could put on a party for the village to attend, but instead how we could enable the village to come together to celebrate its common life built around the church.

This was not straightforward. Some church people were adamant that the celebration should only take place in the church building. Peter, however, was resolute: it would happen outdoors on the common ground in the village. Some village people were equally antagonistic. When tickets went on sale one woman's response was, 'Why should I buy a ticket? What's the church ever done for me?' I began to worry that her view might spread to others so that the whole event would fail.

As it turned out it we sold all 500 tickets and had the truly village-wide party – the '650 Festival' – that Peter had envisioned. It went on all day and into the night. It started with a parade through the village, led by residents driving their vintage cars, followed by many others walking in costume. Then all afternoon we played – bouncy castles, a goal-scoring game provided by Cambridge United Football Club, many traditional stalls selling food and drink, or offering games with prizes, an inter-road tug of war, all against a background of music provided by a local string quartet. The day culminated in a hog roast, fireworks and live rock music played by a village-based band. The food people had already paid for in their ticket price ran out. I expected a riot, but nobody complained; they said the experience of being together as a village more than compensated for the lack of food. As the evening ended, three generations of villagers danced together under the stars. It was profoundly moving, a party on a scale I had not imagined possible, with people drawn close together who had in common simply their village and the church within it. In the days following it was remarked that people in the village seemed kinder to one another. It felt as if by celebrating our shared life we had tasted a little bit of heaven.

But what was I as an evangelical to make of the festival? Where did it fit in with my understanding of God, Christian faith and church life? There was no event asking for 'decisions for Christ'. Even if there had been it would have seemed inappropriate, not to say churlish, to judge the day's celebration only of value if it resulted in people finding faith, because all that had happened between the people of the village so clearly had value. In other words, the 650 Festival was not *for* anything; it was an end in itself, and that end was what had happened between people. I wanted to find a way to understand and articulate this social meaning.

My challenge in doing so was made more complicated when, a few weeks later, we had the 'official' church celebration of the anniversary. It was a good occasion attended by our bishop, at which the significance of the anniversary was remembered, prayers of thanksgiving for the past and of hope for the future were said, and Holy Communion was celebrated. But it was hard to see the connection this celebration had to do with the party that had taken place earlier. It was attended mainly, though not exclusively, by 'church people', and lacked the passion and vitality of the village-wide party. I was left wondering which of the two had more meaning, which more closely approximated the Kingdom of God.

The problems with evangelical ecclesiology

Before we consider how the Bible might help us to understand the sort of 'people-enriching' event that the 650 Festival was, I want to try to diagnose the problem in evangelical ecclesiology that we are addressing. I have suggested that evangelicals tend to read the Bible as if people live as disconnected individuals and come to God in the same state. What I realized through the 650 Festival was that such an individualistic view also had the effect of separating church people from the world around them, rather than carrying them towards it – the basic dynamic of mission. I suggest, therefore, that evangelical ecclesiology is characterized by 'individualistic separatism'.

In terms of individualistic separatism, our way of being the church includes these aspects:

1   *Corporate life* means an individual, capacitated by grace to receive the truth, 'becoming a Christian' and joining the church. The joy of new life in Christ

bestows responsibilities to act in certain ways towards others, but not a radical unity with them. Conversion occurs as an isolated individual; the matter is primarily between the person and God.

2   *Mission* (often no more than evangelism by another name) means taking the truth of God out into the world and telling it to people there so that they will come out of the world and into the church. There is little room for the notion of discovering truth in the world, or of enjoying people in the world. Mission happens from a position of strength: Christian proclamation is complete, sealed even; people must simply be told the good news.

3   *Worship* consists often of praise songs written to enable the individual worshipper to respond to God's invitation to a deeper personal relationship with him. Such intimacy is inherently individualistic, for the songs address God in the first person ('I' or 'me', not 'we' or 'us'), and is inhospitable to other aspects of worship, most seriously Holy Communion.[6]

Taken as aspects of corporate life, mission and worship, none of this is wrong. Life-changing turnings to Christ, energetic outreach and renewed and deep worship are all good for the church, of course. But as presently practised they are insufficient because they lack explicit social (i.e. corporate) implications. As ways of practising faith they therefore do not carry us very far when we try to articulate what the church is because they do not tell us how faith affects the social bonds between people. That something is missing from our understanding becomes acutely apparent when we encounter situations outside this individualistic understanding, such as that in my story above, where people are together in ways that are much richer, more joyful, and therefore perhaps more biblical than those we usually experience.

My contention is that we need deliberately to design church practice that has as its goal bringing about such richness of life together. I believe this is a biblical aspiration, in ways that individualistic separatism is not, and turn now to John's Gospel to show how this is so.

The social condition of life in John's Gospel

If we go to the Bible expecting to find a fully fledged doctrine of the church we will be disappointed. Like the doctrine of the trinity, it is not there.[7] We cannot move directly from the Bible to the church. What we do find, however, are the 'conditions' that allow us to develop our understanding of the church by going beyond but not away from the Bible. Reading the Bible to unearth those conditions requires a 'deep reading' that gradually builds our understanding of the way God has ordered human life in the world. It requires taking Scripture more seriously not less, as we search for the deepest truths, puzzling away at Scripture, and allowing ourselves to be puzzled away at by Scripture, so that the truth of God and the world may over time emerge.[8]

I have chosen some texts from St John's Gospel partly because its author addresses the fundamental conditions of creation in his prologue, and partly because its third chapter contains the dialogue between Jesus and Nicodemus that functions as something of a hermeneutical key for evangelicals to understand the way faith, and by implication the church, operates. Its use can contribute significantly to the idea that God calls solitary individuals into relationship with him (individualism) and that the scope of this call barely reaches beyond the *ecclesia*, as if, 'God so loved the *church* that he gave his only Son' (separatism). Here I want to offer a reparative reading by looking at several other parts of the gospel to show that the writer sets this dialogue in the wider context of the conditions of human existence in the world. There we find elemental truths about the way the world is, how its character reflects that of its creator, and how that in turn means the world, far from being individualistic, is relational throughout.

> In the beginning was the Word, and the Word was with God and the Word was God. He was in the beginning with God. All things came into being through him, and without him not one thing came into being. What has come into being in him was life, and the life was the light of all people ... to all who received him, who believed in his name, he gave the power to become children of God.
>
> (John 1:1–4, 12)

Here, we are told the way in which creation relates to its triune creator. By starting his gospel in this way the writer of John is signalling that his subject is utterly primary, the words 'in the beginning' deliberately evoking the opening words of Genesis. Moreover, he is telling us that implicated in creation was 'the Word'. Without this Word the creation would not be: the Word 'gives birth' to all that is. There is nothing for which the Word is not responsible, nothing in which the Word is not involved. All creation, therefore, carries the hallmark of the Word, the being of God. Exactly how this is so is not explained here but the point to highlight is that the world and God's Word are essentially 'compatible' by nature. They are not like oil and water, which cannot by nature be mixed together because they always separate themselves from each other. Instead, they are deeply and intricately woven together. God does not keep himself separate from the world, but through his Word is with it, to the extent that people made in his image may be reborn as members of his family. (The implication is that the image of God in people may be badly defaced but has not been obliterated.)

> And the Word became flesh and lived among us, and we have seen his glory, the glory as of a father's only son, full of grace and truth. ... From his fullness we have all received, grace upon grace. The law indeed was given through Moses; grace and truth came through Jesus Christ. No one has ever seen God. It is God the only Son who is close to the Father's heart, who has made him known.
>
> (John 1:14, 16–18)

Here is the clearest indication of the extent to which God and the world are together, indeed God's complete commitment to the world. But this commitment is especially so towards human beings, for when God's Word 'happens' in the world, it happens as a human being. Here we find the clearest 'joining place' between human beings and God – his Word. We are made in the image of this Word who is God. The advent of Christ shows us that, as triune creator, God has the human within himself, identified as God's Word, intrinsic to who God is. Jesus therefore can be seen as the presence of humanity within the Godhead: 'Jesus Christ himself [is] intrinsic to the identity of the unique God.'[9] So, just as Genesis tells us that there is compatibility between God and creation, John tells us there is the 'highest' level of compatibility between God and human beings.

Jesus Christ, then, is God's Word made flesh who radiates God's glory and truth. It is easy for us to misread this text as saying that Jesus came to substitute the law with grace, whereas it says he came in succession to the law-giver, Moses, to bring grace and truth.[10] I shall return to this important relationship between law and Christ, but for now I suggest the most helpful notion is of Christ refreshing the law rather than replacing it, by way of being, as verse 18 puts it, the one 'who is nearest to the Father's heart' (NEB), or 'in the bosom of the Father' (KJV).

> Now there was a Pharisee named Nicodemus, a leader of the Jews. He came to Jesus by night and said to him, 'Rabbi, we know that you are a teacher who has come from God; for no one can do these signs that you do apart from the presence of God.' Jesus answered him, 'Very truly, I tell you, no one can see the kingdom of God without being born from above.' Nicodemus said to him, 'How can anyone be born after having grown old? Can one enter a second time into the mother's womb and be born?'
>
> (John 3:1–4)

Here, we are taken deep into the profound nature of God's call: to a condition as fundamental as birth itself. Jesus speaks to Nicodemus of another sort of 'in the beginning' – the emergence of new human life from within the life of another human being. We should dwell on these words. Anyone who has seen a human birth will testify to its wonder, its mystery, its miraculous nature. Jesus' invitation to think of a second birth thereby takes us into the heart of this mystery, one life emerging out of the life of another, this time of spiritual life emerging from the life of God. The relationship is 'inner' in both cases: just as our fleshly birth means we emerge from inside our mother's womb to be born of our mother, so our spiritual birth entails being born of God. But of course to a Jew to be born of a Jewish mother's womb is to be born of God, because you are born as one of, and into, God's chosen people. Nicodemus is not just pointing to the biological absurdity of returning to a mother's womb after being born. He is questioning the spiritual necessity of rebirth. To Nicodemus, to be born a Jew is enough, is complete, whereas to Jesus the completeness comes only through rebirth by water and the Spirit, which is normative. Thus Jesus is dismayed that this teacher of Israel does not understand this spiritual birth to be as necessary, obvious and natural as physical birth. This is elementary, the basic requirement for seeing the kingdom of God.

But it is an invitation to intimacy with God through the Spirit for life as God's people, not as isolated individuals.

> On the third day there was a wedding in Cana of Galilee, and the mother of Jesus was there. Jesus and his disciples had also been invited to the wedding.
>
> (John 2:1–2)

Having begun his gospel with a deliberate allusion to the beginning of Genesis, the writer of John makes a further allusion to Genesis by situating Jesus' first miracle at a wedding. In the celebration of a man and a woman becoming one flesh (Gen. 2:24) John points us again to beginnings, this time the union that, as with Adam and Eve, has the potential to generate a society. Unity is fruitful.

> I ask not only on behalf of these, but also on behalf of those who will believe in me through their word, that they may all be one. As you, Father, are in me and I am in you, may they also be in us, so that the world may believe that you have sent me. The glory that you have given me I have given them, so that they may be one, as we are one, I in them and you in me, that they may become completely one, so that the world may know that you have sent me and have loved them even as you have loved me.
>
> (John 17:20–23)

Here, as in marriage, is the notion of unity generating a society as Jesus prays that the unity of his disciples will spawn believers in the world. The quality of this unity is no less than that between Jesus and his Father. It is more than being 'with' Jesus and each other; it is unity made possible by Jesus being *in* them and them *in* him. Thus St Paul writes:

> No one ever hates his own body, but he nourishes and tenderly cares for it, just as Christ does for the church, because we are members of his body. 'For this reason a man will leave his father and mother and be joined to his wife, and the two will become one flesh.' This is a great mystery, and I am applying it to Christ and the church.
>
> (Eph. 5:29–32)

The primal unity found in marriage is the best way Paul can find to speak of the unity between Christ and the church. Just as how a man and a woman can become one, a unit, is ultimately beyond understanding, and therefore a 'mystery', so with Christ and the church: their unity can never be explained but is real nonetheless.

Richard Hooker on law

Here, then, in the Gospel of John is the 'law' of people's life in the world as it lives connected to and reliant upon God to create, order and sustain it. This law is quite different from that of 'individualistic separatism' that characterizes so much of our church life. The profound unity of the relationships described in these passages – in creation, in marriage, in the church – are of fundamental significance when it comes to understanding our experience of life with others in the world and church.

How, though, are we to move from the inchoate church of the New Testament to church life today? We need to 'flesh out' these texts to see how they can enrich our contemporary church life. To help us, I will draw on the writing of the sixteenth-century theologian, Richard Hooker.[11] Hooker writes to address a particular social situation very different to our own, but, in refuting the views of his opponents, he addresses the area of concern to us: how to relate the Bible to the church.

Hooker's opponents' response was to say the laws of Christ directing the life of the church are there in the Bible in black and white: we must simply obey them. Hooker maintains that the situation is not so simple and sets out an alternative view that, far from being less true to the Bible, is, he maintains, more securely anchored in it. In doing so he sets out what the church is and how it works in a foundational ecclesiology. Its scope goes beyond conventional notions of human beings, society and the church, to something higher, richer and more inspiring. He gives us nothing less than a vision of what the church can be.

In a post-Luther church, 'law' is an ambivalent word. It can be taken as antithetical to grace and the whole thrust of Jesus' mission, yet Christ was at pains to say he came not to abolish the need to fulfil it, but to make obedience to it possible. However, even to say that much means we are in danger of begging the question by assuming that by 'law' the Bible writers mean rules imposed on the world by a coercive God. Perhaps, though, law is something different, not antithetical to grace and Christ's mission, but conformable to them? To explore that possibility we must find the provenance of law and what it connotes.

In his use of law Hooker effectively gives us the most fundamental way to talk about life in the world, applicable to everything simply by virtue of it being part of the creation. Everything that exists, including human beings, follows laws that dictate their working. The specific role of law is to guide life to its fulfilment or completeness. Law therefore functions between creation and eschatology, ensuring that life in the world is not haphazard, but has a regularity in its working that sustains it and moves it forward. To speak of law is as fundamental as speaking of existence. There is no language more primary. While this may be to us a somewhat alien way of thinking, law is nonetheless a familiar biblical word, designating the instruction of God by which the world, and particularly human beings, should live. To us law often has a negative connotation, as an Old Testament idea that constrains and is to be contrasted with God's grace in the gospel of freedom.[12] However, Hooker sees things differently. He says that these laws are not stultifying rules imposed on us from outside by God, but rather, as internal to creation, are a way of speaking about what it means to live in the world: this is the way creation is made, free to be self-regulating. How does creation become this way? It is because God's most fundamental character is to be lawful, that is to say, constant in all he does. There is complete consistency between God being who he is and doing what he does.

Hooker puts it succinctly: 'The being of God is a kind of law to his working.'[13] The significance of this insight is that it establishes the link between God and the ongoing life of the world. Law links being and working in God and in all else besides. God is not a god who creates the world and then stands apart from it. His lawfulness means that in his freedom he has chosen to limit himself to complete faithfulness to it. Connectedness to the world is natural for God. That is to say, God by nature is with the world.

It is God's nature that gives to human beings their nature. A fundamental aspect of this nature is its 'sociality',[14] the state of being social. Just as God is by nature with the world and church, so human beings, made in his image, are by nature with one another and God. Of course, there is freedom involved: we choose whether to act according to this law, but to put things this way is to say that for human beings to move in the direction of completion or flourishing entails moving towards one another not withdrawing from one another, not just for superficial friendship but for deep levels of relating:

> Forasmuch as we are not by ourselves sufficient to furnish ourselves with competent store of things needful for such a life as our nature doth desire, a life fit for the dignity of man: therefore to supply those defects and imperfections, which are in us living, single, and solely by ourselves, we are naturally induced to seek communion and fellowship with others.[15]

Living in societies, then, is intrinsic to human existence, so people cannot reach their God-intended perfection alone. Hooker continues:

> Two foundations there are which bear up public societies, the one, a natural inclination, whereby all men desire sociable life and fellowship, the other an order expressly or secretly agreed upon, touching the manner of their union in living together.[16]

In other words, for people to live together as a society of any sort there have to be two conditions: first, an inclination or desire to be together and, second, a way of agreeing how that should happen. Without these conditions social life is impossible. Furthermore, not only is there a law concerning human beings individually, and a law concerning them as they are linked to form a society, but there is also a law concerning the joining of societies, 'the Law of nations'. The human desire for communion with other human beings, stemming from 'a natural delight which man hath to transfuse from himself into others, and to receive from others into himself especially those things wherein the excellency of his kind doth most consist'[17] does not observe national boundaries but causes people to seek fellowship with those of other societies:

> Civil society doth more content the nature of man than any private kind of solitary living, because in society this good of mutual participation is so much

larger than otherwise. Herewith notwithstanding we are not satisfied, but we covet (if it might be) to have a kind of society and fellowship even with all mankind. Which thing Socrates intending to signify professed himself a Citizen, not of this or that commonwealth, but of the world.[18]

So, contends Hooker, there is a limitless impulse in human beings for relationship with others. Desire for universal relationship is not based on a common Christian belief, but on a common humanity. This desire for 'society and fellowship' is what the church builds on, for it finds its highest expression in our desire for God:

Then are we happy therefore when fully we enjoy God, as an object wherein the powers of our souls are satisfied even with an everlasting delight: so that although we be men, yet by being unto God united we live as it were the life of God.[19]

Hooker's key insight that Law is intrinsic to God finds echoes in the description of wisdom in the Old Testament. In Proverbs 8, wisdom is personified as one who was with God in the beginning of creation: 'Ages ago I was set up, at the first, before the beginning of the earth' (v.23). Wisdom is also one who works in earthly leaders when they rule in a righteous way: 'By me Kings reign, and rulers decree what is just' (v.15). At the end of Book 1 of the 'Laws' Hooker celebrates the existence of law in the world:

Of law there can be no less acknowledged, than that her seat is the bosom of God, her voice the harmony of the world, all things in heaven and earth do her homage, the very least as feeling her care, and the greatest as not exempted from her power, but Angels and men and creatures of what condition soever, though each in different sort and manner, yet all with uniform consent, admiring her as the mother of their peace and joy.

Hooker here describes law in the same terms that the Bible uses to describe wisdom. Rowan Williams points out that Hooker is evoking law:

in terms very close to those of the great hymns to Wisdom in the sapiential books. ... The sudden transition here to the feminine pronoun would alert any scripturally literate reader to the parallel with the divine Sophia of Proverbs, Job, and (most particularly) the Wisdom of Solomon; what is claimed here for 'Law' is what the Bible claims for Wisdom.[20]

And by saying, 'her seat is the bosom of God' Hooker is also evoking the Prologue of John's Gospel. Thus, there is the bringing together of the notions of wisdom, law and the Word. When these 'happen' in the world, the result is 'harmony' and 'peace and joy', hallmarks of the Kingdom of God.

The Word is implicated in all that Hooker has been saying. The very working of the world has its provenance in the working of God through his being or Word. This Word has been made known by taking flesh as Jesus Christ. Jesus is not anomalous to the world, an unconformable stranger in it, for the world, made through him, is his home, even if that which owes its very existence to him and works according to his being rejects him and puts him to death. In Hooker's terms, Jesus is not antithetical to law, he is law: Jesus is the law of the world. As such he is behind all possibilities of harmonious, peaceful and joyful life together, be it in the world or the church, and it is his goal that all people be reunited as brothers and sisters in the family of God that is the church.

What is most significant about Hooker for us is that he enables us to see this connection between Christ and human social life, and the unlimited scope of Christ's work. That we may have failed to see this exposes our inability to think in a fully godly, that is to say trinitarian, way, to understand that the life and work of God is present in the life and work of his Word, Jesus Christ. We see in the life of Jesus, the Word made flesh, one who, far from living a life of individualistic separatism, gives himself to God and other people to the maximum extent, so that his church may do the same. Jesus lives a deeply sociable life, judged by the religious leaders to mix with the wrong people, in the wrong places. He lives in dependence on others whom he calls friends, unafraid to rely on them. As God's life in the world he exemplifies the human existence spoken of by Hooker that gives itself into the other, ultimately through the bread and wine of Holy Communion.

Hooker, then, helps us to go beyond the church characterized by individualistic separatism to a much richer notion of the church as a social body characterized by people coming together in unity. I call this, 'dynamic social truth'; *dynamic* because it is not describing a state of affairs but a movement in a given direction; *social* because that direction is towards one another and God; *truth* because human unity is central to the Kingdom of God.

These two ideas of the church have different starting points. If we start with the assumption that the individual is what counts in matters of faith, then we end up with what might be described as 'the parts of the whole'. Here, the church is organized mechanically, starting with the parts of the church with the aspiration that they can be put together to make the whole. This does not begin with a clear sense of what the church as a whole is, but works with the assumption that the whole is the aggregate of the parts. To see the church as corporate because people are already in some sense together by way of their shared humanity in Christ is to see the whole of the church as present in every part. It might be described as 'the whole in parts' such that each person is a part of the whole in which the whole is contained.[21] Or, to put it slightly differently, the whole Church is latent in its parts. Thus the aggregate that we earlier thought of as 1+1+1+1 is replaced by a single, unified one of which the individuals are a part.

The difference between these two views can be illustrated by way of a family. The first view thinks of the family as only 'happening' when its constituent members are assembled. They are individuals who, when brought together, make the family. On the second view the family as such has existence all the time within each person who is a member of it. When they come together they do so not as a collection of individuals, but as parts of the single family.

Practising dynamic social truth

If the church is to be characterized by dynamic social truth, then we have to let go of conventional quantitative measurement as our way of determining the success of church practice – 'bums on seats' – and aim at something that is fundamentally qualitative. This qualitative difference lies in the bonds that exist between people made active by faith. We might call it, 'Life together Plus'. Within this understanding of church life numbers will feature, but as a measurement of the extent to which a community is being gathered before God. In this final section I draw on personal experience to describe briefly some practical ways in which I and our local church have experienced the deepening and strengthening of bonds between people in the church's worship, corporate life and mission, the interrelated aspects of its life spoken of earlier.

Mission

As a priest I live in a vicarage with a large garden. Even in a post-Christian village people see the vicarage as an extension of the church and therefore as quasi-ecclesial. In the summer for the last three years we have held the 'Big Village Gig'. We are fortunate in having within our congregation a woman whose father played bass guitar in the rock band The Kinks. Together with his two sons he now plays with various bands, including The Zombies, and this summer all except one of the band members played in our garden one August evening. Hundreds of villagers came – children, parents, grandparents – armed with picnics, blankets, lanterns and chairs. We had a wonderful time together as the music filled the garden. It was a carnival atmosphere, a sense of being a village family. A man whom I'd first met when we'd been watching our sons play football, and subsequently when he and his wife asked me to baptize their second child, approached me at the end of the evening. He was really moved by the event, surprised that the church would organize such a thing. 'This is so great! I wish I could have all my family here, all my friends here, to experience it!' I was deeply moved by his response, for it seemed so rare and so precious, like the pearl of great price that Jesus spoke of. Without individualistic separatism a sense of deep togetherness, rich social life, had been given space to flourish and he was embracing it.

In the days following people who previously avoided me because I was the vicar and so they would not know what to say came up to me in the school playground and told me how much they had enjoyed the music and meeting other villagers they had seen before but never talked to. Barriers had been broken down and people had connected with one another, and through me with the church, and in some sense with God. What made this possible was the location: the vicarage garden is *of* the church but not *in* it. The bonds between the church and village were strengthened, and so as a church we are seen and heard differently, as an agency that belongs firmly within the community and brings people together as one village.

Worship

I recently attended an all-age communion service at a Christian summer camp, together with more than 3,000 adults and children. For the intercessions the worship leaders encouraged the children to pray using, of all things, balloons. Each child was given one, and asked to think of different situations about which they should pray as they blew each time into the balloon. When the balloons were fully inflated the children held them up to release them together. They were the type that made a screeching sound as the air rushed out of them. On the count of three everyone released their balloon, to symbolize the prayers going up to heaven. It was an unexpectedly moving sight as hundreds of balloons spun up to the roof in one movement. It was a corporate act, greeted with spontaneous joyful applause, an experience of communion quite different to any I had experienced before, the intercessory counterpart of sharing bread and wine. It greatly enhanced our sense of being one body of Christ.[22]

When as a church we celebrated Harvest this year, we publicized it in the newsletter that goes to everyone in the village as a whole weekend celebration. On the Saturday we invited people to come and help decorate the church in the morning; in the afternoon to sell home-produced food at stalls in the churchyard, and have cream teas in the vicarage garden while a village tractor enthusiast was giving rides to children; in the evening to come to a barbecue in the churchyard where we had wine, burgers and beer available on a donation basis. On the Sunday we had morning worship focused on living lives aware of God's provision in creation. By the end of the weekend we had enabled more of the village than before to be together in contact with the church, aware of its dependence on God for all that sustains us.

With a similar motive of enabling the village to express its spiritual aspect we put substantial resources of time and money into our Remembrance Sunday service, making good use of soldiers from our local army barracks to embody the message of solemn thanksgiving. This year we introduced the option of villagers laying a poppy cross at our war memorial within the service.

Corporate life

Our church has a long-standing link to the Mothers' Union, which was struggling to find its contemporary role within the village. In partnership with its leaders, my wife began a new group called MUMA (Mothers' Union Mothers Active). It is held in the vicarage as a mutual support group, including spiritual support. It is proving to be a natural place for young mothers (some part of the worshipping life of the church, others not) who otherwise would be isolated to come to build friendships and receive appropriate Christian teaching. Again, its location in the vicarage seems a key ingredient to its success, a place of 'public hospitality'.

The MUMA leaders recently organized an event called 'Esther's Spa', this time in the church building. Inspired by the Old Testament character, the church invited the women of the village to come to be made beautiful on the inside and outside. Local beauty therapists offered their time and talents within a church decorated to be comfortable and welcoming. A stall of carefully selected books was available. Again, what struck those who came was the experience of unity, under the aegis of the church.

Conclusion

The above are but a few examples of an approach to being the church that puts into practice what this chapter has been about – discovering afresh the social aspect of Christian faith in order to be an embodiment of God's mission to the world. It requires the church to stand, not outside its surroundings (as if it ever could), but within them, becoming deeply involved in people's lives, to 'lift' them from within to their creator.[23] To do so requires putting aside ambivalence about the church, and embracing it as intrinsic to faith, nothing less than Christian faith in social form. Then we can fully apply ourselves to the vision for the church attributed to Archbishop William Temple who said: 'The church is the only cooperative society in the world that exists for the benefit of its nonmembers.'

Notes

1 D. W. Hardy, 'The Sociality of Evangelical Catholicity', in his *Finding the Church*, London: SCM Press, 2001, p. 80.
2 This theme is also attended to in the chapter in this volume by George Bailey.
3 An extended story, containing some of the most inspiring material on thoughtful church practice is contained within A. Michonneau, *Revolution in a City Parish*, London: Blackfriars, 1951. Concerning a Roman Catholic parish in Paris, France in the middle of the last century, it is a textbook example of how to rethink church life in the face of a changed mission to working class, inner city parishioners.
4 Peter has always been dissatisfied with the status quo, believing that there is more to life with God than we often experience, and actively searching for it. See his BBC television series 'Extreme Pilgrim', first broadcast in 2007.
5 This theme is unpacked further in terms of eschatology in the chapter by Greggs in this book.
6 For a fuller discussion about the efficacy of Holy Communion for the church, see the chapter 'Feeding and forming the People of God' by Ben Fulford in the present volume.
7 It is arguable whether we should be looking for a *doctrine* of the church as such to place alongside other Christian doctrines because that implies something finished and complete which the church as contingent practice never can be. Rather, we are looking for the conditions that make the church even a possibility.
8 If we fail to read Scripture in this deep way, which is to do theology, we risk doing nothing more than 'going through the motions' in a way that does not affect our church practice. R. Williams, *Arius: Heresy and Tradition*, London: DLT, 1987, p. 236, highlights the inherent danger of doing so, and offers a corrective:

> Theology is not only legitimate but necessary. The loyal and uncritical repetition of formulae is seen to be inadequate as a means of securing continuity at anything more than a formal level; Scripture and tradition require to be read in a way that brings out their strangeness, their non-obvious and non-contemporary qualities, in

order that they may be read both freshly and truthfully from one generation to another. They need to be made more *difficult* before we can accurately grasp their simplicities.

9 R. Bauckham, *God Crucified*, Carlisle: Paternoster Press, 1998, p. 27.
10 For the implications of Jesus' embodying grace and truth and bringing these as gifts into the world, see a sermon preached by Tom Wright, Bishop of Durham, on Christmas Day 2006. Available at: www.ntwrightpage.com/sermons/Christmas06.htm (accessed 5 January 2009).
11 Hooker lived in England, 1554–1600, and wrote an eight-volume work, *Of the Laws of Ecclesiastical Polity*. Here we do not need to explore the background to his writing; its value to us lies in his aim to unearth the foundations of the church universal which makes it strikingly contemporary in its message and tone. For recent debate on the wider significance of Hooker's writing see papers from a symposium collected within *Anglican Theological Review*, fall 2002.
12 That such a view may be a misrepresentation of Scripture is explored by Ellen Charry in 'The Law of Christ All the Way Down', *International Journal of Systematic Theology*, 2005, vol. 7.2, 155–68.
13 R. Hooker, *Of the Laws of Ecclesiastical Polity*, Cambridge: Cambridge University Press, 2002, p. 54.
14 A term used extensively by Dan Hardy, for example in 'Created and Redeemed Sociality' in his *God's Ways with the World*, Edinburgh: T&T Clark, 1996, pp. 188–205.
15 Hooker, *Laws* 1.10.1. Here is the antithesis of the Enlightenment view that the goal of human existence is the strong, self-reliant self.
16 Ibid., 1.10.1.
17 Ibid., 1.10.12.
18 Ibid., 1.10.12.
19 Ibid., 1.11.2
20 R. Williams, *Anglican Identities*, London: Darton, Longman & Todd, 2004, p. 41.
21 Thus credal churches describe themselves as parts of the one, holy, catholic and apostolic church.
22 Unhappily, though, the sung praise in the service had not engendered communion because we were nearly always singing 'I' or 'me' rather than 'we' or 'us'. The individualistic and the social were in conflict.
23 Such a vision of the church's role in society is well described by Coleridge. He coined a new term for this aspect of the church's life, the 'enclesia', that was called *in* to its surroundings, rather than called out, the meaning of 'ecclesia'. See S. T. Coleridge, *On the Constitution of the Church and State*, Princeton, NJ: Princeton University Press, 1976, p. 45.

Select bibliography

Coleridge, S. T., *On the Constitution of the Church and State*, Princeton, NJ: Princeton University Press, 1976.

Hardy, D. W., *Finding the Church*, London: SCM Press, 2001.

Healey, N. M., *Church, World and the Christian Life*, Cambridge: Cambridge University Press, 2000.

Hooker, R., *Of the Laws of Ecclesiastical Polity*, Cambridge: Cambridge University Press, 2002.

Jenkins, T., *Religion in English Everyday Life*, New York/Oxford: Berghahn 1999.

Michonneau, A., *Revolution in a City Parish*, London: Blackfriars, 1951.

Ramsey, A. M., *The Gospel and the Catholic Church*, London: Longmans, Green & Co., 1936.

Chapter 10

From glory to glory

The transfiguration of honour and giving in the light of the glory of Christ[1]

Jason Fout

Charles Wesley's hymn 'Love Divine, All Loves Excelling', well-loved by evangelicals, concludes thus:

> Finish, then, thy new creation;
> pure and spotless let us be.
> Let us see thy great salvation
> perfectly restored in thee;
> changed from glory into glory,
> till in heaven we take our place,
> till we cast our crowns before thee,
> lost in wonder, love, and praise.

This verse, in part quoting 2 Corinthians 3:18, is just one indication of how evangelical Christians have had on their lips and in their minds the glory of God and its interaction with the human. Given its prominence in first-order language about God, in prayer, praise and worship, it is all the more surprising then that it has been so little considered in evangelical theology over the last century.[2]

In this chapter I provide an account of divine glory as it relates to human agency, showing that this interaction is not one in which the human is overawed or evacuated of agency, but rather one which constitutes and establishes human agency in a manner consistent with the identity of the Lord. Put another way, God's glory – God's surpassing excellence and unrivalled praiseworthiness – correlates with human flourishing and sociality, and these both in relation to God and in relation to others. This glory is only seen fully eschatologically, but is known now by humans as it constitutes them as teleologically oriented towards God's glory.

This chapter aims at expounding this thesis and breaks down into five sections. First, I examine several basic issues surrounding doctrinal consideration of the glory of the Lord, with a particular focus on the common problem of heteronomy. A heteronomous concept of divine glory would be one which is only imposed 'from outside', overwhelming human agency (rather than enabling it). One troubling implication of such a heteronomous account is that, since human agency is evacuated, God's glory is thus unable to be known in history and life.

Next, I take a detour through anthropology, in order to present the classic exposition of 'the gift' by Marcel Mauss. I do this so that I may then shed some light on certain historical, socio-cultural notions of honour, such as were taken for granted at the time the New Testament was written. Giving is a primary means by which honour and identity – of both persons and groups – is established, maintained and reinforced, and is also an expression of sociality. This, in turn, helps to illumine the sorts of things the Apostle Paul has to say about honour and gift-giving, particularly in 2 Corinthians, to which I turn in the third part of the chapter.

But I also turn to this analysis with the conviction that God is part of the real, with all its stubborn untidiness and conceptual variety, with the upshot that no discourse or area of life, no matter how seemingly distant or unrelated, is theologically barren. In this way, theology is not then a matter merely of exegesis of texts, in isolation from the twists and turns of life, but is more a matter of, as Paul Ricoeur puts it, a 'believer seek[ing] to understand himself [before] the texts of his faith'.[3] To that I would elaborate only by adding 'in the presence of God'. This chapter is a partial and exploratory assaying of what such a theology might look like.

In the third section, then, I turn to Paul's second letter to the Corinthians, with the goal of exploring what he says about honour and giving. Although I draw on recent social-anthropological work to illumine what Paul says, I intend to go beyond it as well, for Paul himself (in the light of Christ) is intent on going well beyond what the expectations of honour and giving would be. That is to say, for Paul, honour and giving are transfigured to reflect better the Lord, whose honour and glory are surpassing, and whose primal gifts are at the source of all that is truly human, particularly in the form of creation and redemption.

The fourth section explores in greater theological detail the difference that Christ makes for transforming human honour. This is also, through the lens of the specificity of Paul's exposition of Christ and his centrality and importance, a more general exposition of the particular shape of the glory of God.

A final, fifth section closes with some elaboration on how the glory of God relates to human agency, particularly human obedience to other humans or to human mediation of God's commands.

Glory, heteronomy, and the 'I'

Why an account of glory? I have chosen glory as it is prominent in first-order discourse about God, particularly among evangelical Christians. It appears throughout Scripture when God is spoken of, particularly in praise of God in the Psalms; it is also spoken of in narrative and epistolary literature. Particularly strikingly, it is often referred to in Scripture in especially intense manifestations of God to people.[4] It also figures in the historical worship forms of the church, in hymns, anthems and canticles.[5] It is often mentioned in prayer, both extemporaneous and liturgical. It seems fair to say, on the basis of the witness of the tradition, that the glory of God is an important part of the level of the confession, the originary level of faith[6] – that it is somehow elemental to who the Christian God is.

Given the prominence of glory at this basic level of the discourse of faith, it is somewhat surprising that it has not figured more widely in second-order discourse, particularly in evangelical systematic theologies or theological monographs in the last hundred years. Yet when it does figure in at these levels – indeed, at times even when evangelical believers give voice to it in first-order discourse – it can tend to be spoken of as heteronomous, as externally imposed in a way which overwhelms human agency.

A contemporary theological example of this is found in an essay by Wolfhart Pannenberg, drawing on the work of Edmund Schlink.[7] In what is otherwise a fine essay sifting through the issues related to analogical language for God, Pannenberg at one point elaborates on the function of such language, saying that its intention is not:

> to provide theoretical definitions of the being of God ... [rather, it is] charac-terized throughout by what Schlink has termed a 'doxological' structure. They express adoration of God on the basis of his works. All biblical speech about God, to the extent that its intention is to designate something beyond a partic-ular deed, namely, God himself and what he is from eternity to eternity, is rooted in adoration and is in this sense doxological.[8]

Language, when used of God himself, glorifies God and speaks of him as glorious (although this glory may be parsed out in many different ways – as merciful, holy, etc.). Elaborating on this 'doxological' form of theological statements, Schlink says:

> If in the doxology the divine 'Thou' gives way to the 'he' the 'I' of man who utters the doxology is bound to disappear as well. ... In doxology [the worship-per] neither asks for anything for himself, nor does he give thanks for God's dealings with him. He does not pay attention to himself as the person who is offering praise. Neither the 'I' of the worshipper nor his act of worshipping is explicitly mentioned in the words of the doxology. Thus both the individual human 'I' as well as the 'we' of the congregation lose their prominence, though without vanishing altogether. Yet the absence of the 'I' ... indicates utmost devotion. For although the 'I' of the worshipper does not occur in the text, it is contained in the actual performance of worship. The 'I' is sacrificed in doxol-ogy. Thus doxology is always sacrifice of praise.[9]

There is something quite right about this, as it acknowledges that glorifying God, praising God – doxology – has the effect of opening one up to the other, to God, and of giving God a central status and place. Further, there is the strong connection drawn from God's acts back to God's being: doxology is connected with the acts of God. This helps to make explicit the reasons for doctrinal formation. The church confesses God to be glorious not on the basis of supposition or rumour, but because of the character of his acts – God delivering Israel from slavery to Egypt and giving them the promised land, for example. Yet this account of doxology, for all its helpful use in discussing analogy in theological language, critically overlooks one aspect of doxology in Scripture.

Schlink is correct in saying that in the language of the Bible God is praised without reference to the one praising. There is no sense of instrumentality in Scripture's doxology, no sense of praising God in order to achieve something other than praising God, whether in terms of merit with God, or some more immanent goal – say, material gain. Nor is there any sense of status for the one praising, and so there is rightly no reference to the worshipper. But if the life of the worshipper beyond this simple act might be more broadly characterized as one of doxology, filled with and directed towards the praise of God, the matter of the worshipper's 'ego' being absent or sacrificed becomes quite deeply problematic and heteronomous. God's eminent praiseworthiness becomes necessarily disconnected with the shape of human life, unrelated to human flourishing.[10]

Yet the reality of the matter in Scripture is more complex than the worshipper's 'I' simply being sacrificed. On the one hand, Schlink is certainly correct to maintain that the 'I' fades in a certain way in the direct statements of praise of God. On the other hand, Schlink misses the frequency with which these direct statements are themselves situated in a broader narrative, giving the reader a third-person perspective on the praising. So, for example, to take one of the citations provided by Schlink, Isaiah 6:3 does indeed constitute doxology, and in this expression of worship the seraphs do not assert their own place or status but only God's. Further, Isaiah himself is shown as overawed by the vision of God in the temple. Yet the reader finds the literary context as the act of God to call a prophet for God's people Israel. Isaiah is not simply overawed and left cowering and despondent: he is purified, given a mission and sent out. Far from Isaiah's 'I' being absent, this encounter actually constitutes him as a person. This is not to say that Isaiah could have anticipated this, or that the doxology was instrumental in any way; nevertheless there is here a correlation between doxology and human flourishing.[11]

This is the case in non-narrative examples of doxology as well. To take another example cited in Schlink, Romans 11:36; here Paul summarizes, with a note of surrendering adoration, the acts of God in Jesus Christ. Yet in the very next sentence, 12:1, Paul writes 'I appeal to you therefore ... to present your bodies as a living sacrifice, holy and acceptable to God, which is your spiritual worship.' If recounting the acts of God has led naturally into doxology, then doxology has led (seemingly every bit as naturally) into discussing the shape of human life in light of that glory. In the broader context, doxology is seen to be related to human flourishing and sociality; it does not completely bracket the 'I' of the worshipper, but constitutes it in a certain way, giving a distinct shape to life.[12]

In this I have begun to show that divine glory – the praiseworthiness glorified in doxology – is not heteronomous, as intimated in some modern accounts, but instead manifests a dynamic of nonheteronomous dependence.[13] The glory of God de-centres the human, moving her out of self-absorption and self-satisfaction: but this is not through 'de-selfing' her, removing her ego and insisting on wooden obedience and conformity.[14] Rather, the glory of God, far from dispensing with the self, actually *constitutes* a self that is capable of glorifying God. Indicating how this is so in a way consistent with a non-heteronomous dependence constitutes the remainder of this chapter; to get there, I shall take a detour through anthropology, focusing on gift-giving and honour.

Glory, honour and the gift

Discussion and often intense debate rages today on the nature of 'the gift' and gift-giving, stimulating an almost bewilderingly multidisciplinary discourse, ranging over anthropology, sociology, cultural studies, ethics, political science, economics, gender and feminist theory, philosophy and, not least, theology.[15] I shall examine the work which stands at the fountainhead of this discourse, Marcel Mauss's *The Gift*.[16] Following this overview of Mauss's major ideas and some initial reflections on them, I shall then turn in the next section to an exploration of the theological reasoning of the Apostle Paul as it relates to gift-giving, honour and, above all, the glory of God, particularly as these are found in 2 Corinthians.

Mauss's The Gift: major concepts

The French anthropologist Marcel Mauss's work on gift-giving in what he termed 'primitive' cultures, first penned 85 years ago, serves as the wellspring for the on-going discourse related to the gift and gift-giving. In it, he examines gift-giving, and particularly what is known as 'potlatch', a feast and celebration within a tribe, or between clans or families, in which goods[17] are exchanged – re-distributed, really – on a massive scale and done so with great extravagance. Mauss called the potlatch 'total services' or a 'total system of giving';[18] commentator Mary Douglas explains this, saying 'each gift is part of a system of reciprocity in which the honour of giver and recipient are engaged'.[19]

Since 'honour' will become a key term, allow me briefly to gloss the word. Biblical scholar Bruce Malina explains that, in the biblical world honour was 'a claim to worth that was publicly acknowledged'.[20] Shame, on the other hand, was 'a claim to worth that is publicly denied and repudiated'.[21] It is a social term, concerned with claims to worth and identity.

In the ancient Mediterranean world in particular, this public or social identity would have been quite important, and the desire to maintain honour and avoid shame would have been a key factor in determining one's behaviour.[22] Thus social groups reinforced prohibitions and prescriptions by ascribing honour to those who acted in a way to embody society's ideals and dishonour to those who transgressed them. As DeSilva summarizes:

> 'Honor' becomes the umbrella that extends over the set of behaviours, commitments, and attitudes that preserve a given culture and society; individuals raised with a desire for honour will seek the good of the larger group, willingly embodying the group's values as the path to self-fulfillment.[23]

The practice of gift-exchange is one means by which honour of individuals or groups is expressed, deepened and reinforced.

Within the system of gift exchange, Mauss noticed three distinct but related obligations: (1) a duty to give, (2) a duty to receive, and (3) a duty to reciprocate. There is an obligation to give, and thus express one's honour publicly; honour unexpressed is honour unrecognized: in short, it is not honour. In response to the giving, there is an obligation then to receive the gift given; to refuse a gift would be an open insult and a public contesting of the claim to honour which the gift represents. In the social groups which Mauss examined, refusing a gift would have led to conflict and possibly war. Finally, upon receiving a gift there is a duty to reciprocate; as Mauss says: 'The unreciprocated gift ... makes the person who has accepted it inferior, particularly when it has been accepted with no thought of returning it.'[24] To accept from another what amounts to his own claim to honour, but to fail to respond with one's own claim to honour through giving is tantamount to admitting one has no such honour, no such claim to worth.

This exchange of gifts maintains relationships and expresses the identity of the givers and receivers, whether an individual or a community. This means that a gift is never simply an object, but an exchange within a larger social context. Indeed, since the obligation to reciprocate becomes itself an act of giving which elicits a duty to reciprocate, this describes an on-going process of exchange. Thus, giving, receiving and reciprocating are practices which establish, express and reinforce social relationships. In the time of the New Testament and among the tribes which Mauss studied, this would have been expressed most naturally in terms of honour, a means of designating publicly recognized worth and identity.[25]

Mauss: critique and considerations

Given this account of the gift, its relation to honour and the system of gift-giving as described by Mauss, I would like to call attention to two aspects in particular. First – and this is the difficulty that most subsequent observers have worried about, notably Jacques Derrida[26] – if this account is substantially true then it seems to make a gift impossible: gifts are given by obligation, rather than freely; they are given with reference to the giver as much as the recipient; reciprocal obligations devolve onto the recipient, which means that there is nothing 'given' which does not redound to the giver. To put it bluntly, in these terms, there is no such thing as a free gift, or indeed a gift of any sort.

To attempt a response, one must surely note three elements of Mauss's account which seem unappreciated by his interrogators. The first such element is this: Mauss does not envision gift-exchange, ultimately, as a one-off occurrence. Rather, as I have already noted, a reciprocation of a gift is itself a gift, and so any one cycle of exchange is the isolation of one element of a much larger on-going system, which began before that particular moment and will continue after it. Simply to focus on the single event of gift–receipt–reciprocation isolates one moment for consideration, but does not do justice to the overall on-going system of gift-exchange. To put it in different terms, even if the giving of a gift is a public claim to worth – that is, an expression of the giver's honour, as much or more than an expression of esteem for the recipient – the giver only arrived at that moment of giving as a moment of reciprocation. The gift always precedes the giver, and so the giver always is only actually one who reciprocates in some way.[27]

Second, Mauss speaks about the exchange of gifts as both obliged *and* free. But he does not see this as a tension to be resolved or explained away, so much as the conditions of the whole of life.[28] One freely participates in social obligations, yet this free/obliged participation itself produces something else besides the individuals' interaction: it creates and reinforces identities and the various bonds of sociality as an effect of this exchange. Indeed, it is hard to see how else this might be done apart from such a structure of obligation and freedom.

Even if one were to concede that the giving of a gift is a public expression of honour, redounding to the giver, it is still also the occasion for a response of a public expression of honour by the recipient. Even if the gift is thought of as chiefly about the giver and his public claims to worth, the response of the recipient is then chiefly about her public claims to worth – and the initial giver would give offence if he did not 'make room' for her claims, and receive her gift.

This segues to the third and final element of his account, which I think is not fully appreciated: for Mauss, gift-exchange establishes and deepens sociality. Even if there are no 'free gifts', this is not the same as saying that gift exchange is superfluous. Even if the gifts exchanged are of equal value, and the exchange expresses primarily the public claims to worth of two individuals, nevertheless it is the *occasion* for those claims and for their mutual recognition. This is a sociality which at its fullest allows the other to be other, and to show herself as the one she is, while also allowing space for one's own claims to be aired, all within a structure of both freedom and obligation.

Nevertheless, there are other aspects of Mauss's account which might raise concerns, to which I would like to turn briefly. If Mauss is substantially correct in what he says, then the system of gift-giving, a gift economy, is inherently conserving. Since gift-giving is bound up with the ability to give, with access to means of gifting, then clearly the greater degree of honour will be able to be expressed by those with more. Indeed, it would be fairly easy to see how the public demands of gift-giving and expression of honour might give rise to a systemic view which simply correlated the presence of honour with the possibility of its expression.[29]

Moreover, the way honour was conceived was also intrinsically agonistic. Honour was considered a scarce resource, such that claims of honour were conceived of as being in competition. Thus, to push the conventions of honour in the biblical world to their conclusions, every social interaction, among those who had honour, was a potential conflict or contest to win honour from the other, or else to lose it.[30] While this is a historical description and not a suggestion for the way things ought to be, nevertheless one might wonder if this is the only way by which honour might function. The Apostle Paul, for one, seemed to redescribe the dynamics of honour and honouring, a topic to which I now turn.

Glory, honour and gift-giving in 2 Corinthians

The Apostle Paul seems to have something other than the conventional wisdom in mind in what he says about gift-giving, honour and honouring in 2 Corinthians. What he says about these topics both confirms and significantly qualifies Mauss's – and other, contemporary social anthropologists' – observations about gift-exchange and honour. This is the more significant because people in the first-century Mediterranean world were keenly aware of the 'politics' of honour and gift-giving – to the extent, in some cases, of setting out manuals on them.[31] Yet even apart from such writings, most people from most walks of life – and not merely the literate or those interested in social climbing – would have had at least tacit knowledge of the social conventions associated with honour and gift-giving. Paul does not just reinforce this knowledge.

Against this background, Paul's account of the ways of God with humanity through Christ draws repeatedly on the language of honour, social standing and gift.[32] He shows awareness of these sorts of social conventions and expectations, and, in broad outline, they parallel the social dynamism which Mauss described as attaching to gift-giving. In this way, he 'confirms' Mauss.

Yet he is not at all content to leave the conventions untouched. One finds that Paul is willing to draw on them to some degree for his purposes, but that his use of them is not strictly conventional. On the contrary, Paul sets forth a gift-economy and an (implicit) account of honour which is transfigured in the light of the glory of God. This transformed social dynamism, implicit in Paul's writings, is both recognizably continuous with the gift-economy of his time (it does not simply dispense with the notion of honour, for example), and also changed in important ways to take account of the reality of God in Christ.

In 2 Corinthians, on the face of it Paul seems concerned about his reputation, his honour, and seeks to counter inroads into the Corinthian church made by others (whom he styles 'super apostles'). From the text of Paul's letter, we can ascertain a few details about these others: they may have charged or otherwise taken offerings for their ministry among the Corinthians (2:17, 11:7ff., 12:14). Further, they likely came with letters of recommendation (3:1), and perhaps observed more exalted standards of rhetoric and oratory than Paul (11:6). We may also descry hints from Paul's emphases that likely these 'super apostles' were thought important or powerful by the Corinthians – and may have boasted about themselves as important as well, even perhaps taking credit for what was not their own doing (10:15). At a minimum, on these grounds, we might say that the 'super apostles' exhibited a high or exalted status, attested by others, in such a way that it made the Corinthians feel honoured to host high-status people and learn from them. These 'super apostles' dealt in terms of the conventional honour of the day. In Mauss's terms, they gave gifts to the Corinthians, even if the gifts were themselves and their eloquent presence, and these 'gifts' expressed the honour of the 'super apostles' themselves, a claim to honour which the Corinthians themselves received (thus honouring the 'super apostles') and reciprocated through payment and writing letters of recommendation (3:1).

As David DeSilva writes: 'Paul's overarching goal is to teach the Corinthians about the true basis for honour. ... [Paul] expends much effort to defend his honour while at the same time maintaining the new definitions of what constitute honour in the eyes of God.'[33] Rather than counter the 'super apostles' by simply making opposite counter claims (as if to say 'Don't listen to them, listen to me!'), Paul instead attempts to trump their claims by pointing not to himself but to Christ, and to the relationship of Christ, Paul and the Corinthians. If the 'super apostles' were peddlers of the Word of God (2:17), if they curried favour in order to gain letters of recommendation (3:1), if they commended themselves to the Corinthians or others (10:12, 18), then their honour and reputation has found its horizon in themselves, not God. Their gifts really were only about building up their own honour.

In contrast to this, Paul does not boast in himself (except ironically), but rather glorifies Christ and boasts in the Corinthians (1:14, 7:14, 9:2). His honour is not found in himself, in conventional, human terms – or as he styles it, 'according to the flesh' – and he does not labour to build up his honour on these grounds, nor does he view others on these grounds (5:16, 11:18). Rather, his reputation comes from Christ and finds its fruition in the Corinthians. His honour is established in honouring others, rather than in being honoured. In this way, Paul's honour is found in God and in those he serves (3:2, 3). In this one sees a de-centring of the self as Paul lives and works 'for' others.[34] There is a fragility in this, too, as Paul relies entirely on Christ and the others of whom he boasts for his own status; the risks of this fragility are seen clearly in the occasion for this letter.

Paul's honour, service and identity are made possible by the act of God, an act which opens him up towards others in love. His honour and identity are established through this and thus he is free to honour others without fearing for himself, fearing that he will get a smaller share of the scarce supply of honour. He does not need to protect himself or strive against others to secure his honour, which puts him in a non-agonistic relationship with others: he is free to honour and bless them without worry for himself.[35]

Further, Paul wants for the Corinthians to be freed in this way too, to imitate him imitating Christ, and maintains that his honouring the Corinthians be 'paid forward', rather than paid back. He does not need the Corinthians' property or goods, nor letters of recommendation from them (12:14). He does not seek to benefit himself through them. If Paul gives to them (in preaching, in ministry), and they receive his gift, he does so not to constitute an obligation on their part to reciprocate to him and build up or confirm his honour. He does it out of his freedom and obligation arising from God's gift, and with the hope that the Corinthians might bless others through what Paul's gift (on the basis of God's gift) makes possible.

That is to say, the work Paul does with the Corinthians is fulfilled in its being shared with others. Paul mentions two such ways that the Corinthians can do this, by supporting the collection for the saints in Jerusalem (8:4, 9:1) and by sponsoring work that Paul does in another place, so he can work and not be a burden to others (10:16, 11:8, 9). These are not charges or fees, and in a very real sense are not 'for' Paul himself at all. They are offerings to be given according to the Corinthians' ability (9:12–15), and out of gratitude to God and for God's glory (4:15). Paul invites the Corinthians to be not patrons of his (and therefore having a status above him), nor clients of his (and therefore having a status below him), but to share in 'this grace' (8:7)[36] or more specifically, 'this ministry to the saints' (8:4). Paul's honouring of the Corinthians is not for the sake of his own honour (so that he can be built up), nor even purely for the honour of the Corinthians (so that they are built up only for themselves), but instead is intended to be worked out in the honouring of yet others, for the honour and glory of God.

This does not dissolve gift-giving; there is no hint here of modern individualism or Stoic withdrawal from the demands of sociality. But neither does he simply comply with the conventions of the day: Paul seems not to need to rush to defend cultural expectations as worthwhile in themselves. Paul's exhortations recognize the power of social construction through honour and gift-giving. These are dynamisms within societies, in both majority cultures and subcultures, which allow communities to be established and maintained; within these cultures and in the interactions with other persons and cultures, people are constituted in their identities. Hence, the self is not self-caused and self-constituted but instead given and negotiated in a complex dynamism involving both individual and community.

Or, to return to the question at hand and transpose this into Mauss's duty-terms: Paul is obliged and free to give; the Corinthians are obliged and free to receive; and the Corinthians are obliged and free to reciprocate; but this reciprocation is not to Paul, but to others, and through others, ultimately to God's glory.

The glory of God in the face of Jesus Christ

Why might Paul recast honouring in these terms? The answer to this has been elegantly summarized by R. W. L. Moberly:

> Because his message is 'Jesus Christ is Lord', its corollary is that Paul's role entails not mastery over others, but rather service of them ... to proclaim the lordship of Christ entails a revaluation of human priorities in the way of Christ, the renunciation of self-will and self-aggrandizement and the embrace of self-emptying and self-giving for the welfare of others. This is only possible for Paul because he has 'seen the light' – the light of God's glory revealed in the person of Jesus; it is this knowledge of God that determines Paul's priorities.[37]

It is because of the glory of God – seen in the particular, human face of Christ, expressed through the paradox of the one of surpassing honour embracing the humiliation of the incarnation and cross, bringing justification and reconciliation. This is a primal gift, given by him whose honour and glory are manifest yet magnified through such expression. The radical nature of this gift, the grace of God, has always lain at the heart of evangelical faith.

The grace of Christ is a gift which cannot be repaid but – along with the similar gift of creation – is the condition with which our very being and the possibility of our gift-giving and honouring begins. Persons are honoured through being gifted by God; moreover, they honour God through acknowledging and receiving this gift. Further, they incur an obligation, which is also a freedom, to reciprocate the gift, but this reciprocation is not fulfilled in 'paying back' God, but in 'paying forward' to others, and being able to receive the same back from them. In this is the possibility of a sociality of honouring, renewed in accordance with God's grace.

In the light of the glory of God, gift-giving is transfigured in such a way that all gifting is also reciprocating to others for these primal gifts. This transfigured sociality leads to the correlative increase of thanksgiving to God, to God's glory. Thus the glory of God is both primal and, in this renewed sociality, it may become the teleological end for human agency.

To return briefly to my observations about Mauss's gift-economy, on this Pauline account, one can see that God becomes the primal giver within this on-going process and cycle of gift exchange, a process which is highly adapted in all earthly cultures in very different forms. Yet this in no way reduces God to a finite term in a finite process, or infringes on God's wise, free initiative. It is in just this sense that all subsequent gifts are, in various ways, both expressions of an individual's honour, and a reciprocation of that individual being honoured by God, a divine honouring which extends through human agency in ever-unfolding ways.

Gift-exchange establishes sociality in the way I suggested earlier, but now with a triple agency of giver, receiver and God, with the mutually implied reciprocal givings of creatures also conveying the honour and gift of God. With God acknowledged as the surpassing source of honour and the primal source of honouring, there is the potential for subverting the merely conventional and conserving structures of honour, seeing all creatures no longer 'according to the flesh', in Paul's terms.

In this way gift-exchange might be transfigured, in accordance with the surpassing abundance of God's glory particularly as encountered in Jesus Christ. God's acts of creation and redemption are primal gifts which honour those created and redeemed, and create an elemental, inexhaustible obligation, as well as the freedom of response. This is an obligation and a freedom to honour God, that is, to reciprocate the gift, but the gift is reciprocated not by paying back to God but rather through 'paying forward'. To honour others in this way is no longer a threat to oneself, as the 'supply' of honour, as with its source, is endless. And so one may 'pay forward' the honour of God in loving service to others, thereby honouring one's brothers and sisters, one's neighbours, the stranger, the outcast, as well as the enemy and all those who, in conventional systems of honouring, are unjustly dishonoured.[38] This has the potential not only to enrich evangelical theology, but also to dislodge our (dismayingly common) sense of a privileged status in God's Kingdom, in favour of embodying the love and grace of God in a manner which spills over our too easily drawn boundaries.[39]

From glory to glory: the overflow of human response to God's grace

To return to the task I set earlier: how does this show that the glory of God is not heteronomous?

Turning briefly to Paul's letter, it is striking how often he uses the word 'overflow' and its cognates.[40] In each case, it describes the effect of the gift and grace of God on humans in sociality: through Christ, consolation for others overflows in the face of suffering; encountering God's grace causes thanksgiving to overflow to God's glory; the grace of God causes the Macedonians to overflow in joy in the face of hardship, an overflowing which is accompanied by generosity; the Corinthians' giving to the saints does not merely meet their needs but occasions the overflow of many thanks to God. This logic of overflow in human response to God's grace is one of excess; the response is not readily containable. It thus cannot simply be a matter of wooden obedience to a (humanly mediated) command, in which the result is anticipated in the directive.

On the contrary, the Macedonians' response to Paul and Paul's counsel to the Corinthians reveals a different sort of possibility, one more in accord with a transfigured sociality of honouring. In talking of the opportunity for the Corinthians to give to the collection for Jerusalem, continuing the commitment they made earlier, Paul specifically denies this is a command. Rather, it is a 'test' (8:8). Moreover, the Macedonians, in accepting Paul's request, gave 'not merely as we expected' (8:5). They gave more than a simple answer to a command: their response was excessive, overflowing, embracing the possibilities that were present to them and surprising Paul and his companions in the process.

In the wake of this, if there is still a place in Christian ethics for human command and human mediation of God's command, then in accord with this overflow it will be transfigured into something other than 'doing exactly as this person says'. It will be broadened to include the recipients' discerning consideration of the command, as well as their own 'performance' of it, which may well look unlike what the one who commanded had in mind. The one who commands will also be engaged in honouring the other in accord with the gift of God, and together they may hope to see the Spirit-empowered excess which God makes possible.

Paul's gift – that is to say, God's gift, which Paul was a part of 'paying forward' – established the Corinthians and others as able to respond, and this response was not an identical repetition, not simple obedience to a command. This gift does not overwhelm the recipient but empowers her to respond and is the very condition of that response. This is not heteronomy, as it genuinely enables the person's agency with no sense of the self being eliminated. Neither is it autonomy, as it acknowledges that human agency is radically dependent on the prior act of God, and recognizes the human as de-centred from her world in a certain way. Rather, it is a non-heteronomous dependence in which the human is established by another, and in which human flourishing is never self-focused but social. Moreover, the one who God 'gifts' in grace and establishes in this way as one who is empowered by the

Spirit to respond in thanks, love and honouring of others, is constituted thus as a self who may act in accord with God's glory (8:9), who may act teleologically for God's glory (1:20, 4:15, 8:19), and who may grow from glory to glory (3:18).

Through this, the gracious, glorious acts of God become the basis of a renewed sociality, in the church and through that in the world, in anticipation of the eschatological kingdom. This experience of gratitude to God and subsequent bearing witness to the grace of God has always been at the centre of the evangelical life of faith, a gratitude and a bearing witness which have historically taken many varied forms. If this is the case, then for the church to live faithfully, obedience cannot be a matter of precise, identical repetition, but instead involves careful discernment, joyful engagement and openness to possibilities of overflow in accord with the glory and grace of God. In this light, faithfulness becomes more a matter of non-identical repetition, or 'improvisation'.[41] Thus is the 'I' which God's glory constitutes and establishes opened up to the possibility of 'paying forward' honour in freedom and obligation in accord with the gracious, glorious primal gifts of God.

Notes

1 Dedicated to the memory of Professor Daniel W. Hardy.
2 The work of John Piper constitutes a partial exception to this, although the very conservative reformed perspective he takes substantially differentiates his work from mine.
3 P. Ricoeur, 'Towards a Hermeneutic of the Idea of Revelation', in L. Mudge (ed.), *Essays on Biblical Interpretation*, Philadelphia, PA: Fortress, 1980, p. 75.
4 For example, Exodus 33, 34; Isaiah 6; Ezekiel 1.
5 For example, *Gloria in Excelcis* and *Te Deum Laudamus*.
6 I am indebted to Paul Ricoeur for this way of conceiving these confessions as an 'originary' level of faith. See Ricoeur, 'Towards a Hermeneutic of the Idea of Revelation', p. 74.
7 W. Pannenberg, 'Analogy and Doxology', in *Basic Questions in Theology*, London: SCM, 1970, pp. 211–38; E. Schlink, *The Coming Christ and the Coming Church*, London: Oliver & Boyd, 1967.
8 Pannenberg, 'Analogy and Doxology', p. 215.
9 Schlink, *The Coming Christ*, p. 22.
10 That this 'ego' which is not absent is also not disembodied or individualistic is helpfully reinforced by Liz Kent's chapter, 'Evangelicalism and the Body'.
11 That I do not intend 'flourishing' to mean something like 'prosperity' or conventionally defined success should be clear by the nature of Isaiah's mission – to preach and not be heard, to make the mind of Israel dull, and to do so until cities lie waste (6:9–11).
12 It might be objected that the move I make here conflates doxological statements with other statements in Scripture – and so for example Romans 11.36 is doxological, but 12:1 is prescriptive. But this distinction ignores the way that doxological statements work in Scripture, leading to further narrative or prescription.
13 The phrase 'nonheteronomous dependence' is from P. Ricoeur, 'Towards a Hermeneutic', p. 117.
14 To clarify, by this last phrase I mean 'wooden obedience and conformity' to other people, or in our own thinking. Certainly, evangelicals would confess that one ought to obey God – yet our own thinking about this faithful obedience might itself be wooden or heteronomous. As we wrestle with what might be the most faithful form of obedience,

will we dare to be engaged in this task prayerfully and imaginatively, dare even to embrace *surprising* – not surprising to God, but to us – forms of faithfulness?

15 For a helpful overview, with special attention to current theological debates, see S. Coakley, 'Why Gift? Gift, Gender and Trinitarian Relations in Milbank and Tanner', *Scottish Journal of Theology*, 2008, vol. 61, 224–35.

16 M. Mauss, *The Gift: Forms and Functions of Exchange in Archaic Societies*, London: Routledge, 1990.

17 Although the potlatch has primarily to do with goods-exchange, gift economies themselves are more broad-based in what might count as a gift, not limiting themselves to tangible goods.

18 Mauss, *The Gift*, p. 8.

19 Ibid., p. xi.

20 B. Malina, *The New Testament World: Insights from Cultural Anthropology*, 3rd edn, Louisville, KY: WJK, 2001, p. 29.

21 J. Plevnik, 'Honor and Shame', in J. Pilch and B. Malina (eds), *Biblical Social Values and Their Meaning: A Handbook*, Peabody, MA: Hendrickson, 1993, pp. 95–6.

22 D. DeSilva, *The Hope of Glory: Honor Discourse and New Testament Interpretation*, Collegville, MN: The Liturgical Press, 1999, p. 2.

23 DeSilva, *Hope*, p. 3.

24 Mauss, *The Gift*, p. 83.

25 Consideration of the continuities and discontinuities of western notions of honour, worth and identity with biblical and tribal notions is beyond the scope of this chapter.

26 In J. Derrida, *Given Time: I. Counterfeit Money*, Chicago: University of Chicago Press, 1992.

27 Of course, literally speaking, the duty to reciprocate is to the one who gave, but there are all sorts of ways we are 'gifted' which we cannot repay (through parents and family, through our 'people', ethnically, nationally, socially, and so forth, not to mention situations where the giver dies or leaves), which give rise to an obligation (of sorts) to give to others, not simply as an honour-claim but as a means of reciprocating for what we have been given but cannot 'repay'.

28 'Let us adopt as the principle of our life what has always been a principle of action and will always be so: to emerge from the self, to give, freely and obligatorily.' Mauss, *The Gift*, p. 91.

29 Mauss contemplates just this, averring that wealth confers honour and prestige (ibid., p. 11).

30 See, for example, Malina, *The New Testament World*, pp. 36, 106.

31 See, for example, Seneca, *De beneficiis*, on the matter of patronal relationships. DeSilva points out the preponderance of both Greek and Jewish collections of advice designating certain actions as honourable or shameful (*Hope*, pp. 3, 28 fn2).

32 For example, 2 Cor. 4:7, 8:9, 9:15. These often also draw on economic imagery, but maintain the essential asymmetry between God as giver and humanity as recipient.

33 DeSilva, *Hope*, p. 121.

34 Paul repeatedly emphasizes the way in which his work is 'for' the Corinthians or others: 1:24, 2:10, 4:5, 4:15, 5:13, 11:7, 12:19.

35 There is one obvious way in which this is qualified: as mentioned above, the occasion of his letter is to counter the inroads made by the 'super apostles', and in this way Paul is obviously, in a certain way, protecting his honour and identity. Yet as Moberly has convincingly argued, Paul is setting out criteria by which the Corinthians themselves might discern true apostleship. In this way, he is not so much striving against the 'super apostles' encroaching on his 'turf' as giving the Corinthians the tools to discern truly. R. W. L. Moberly, *Prophecy and Discernment*, Cambridge: Cambridge University Press, 2006, pp. 179–208.

36 Here and elsewhere, the NRSV consistently translates this usage as 'this generous under-
    taking', gaining clarity at the expense of losing the analogy between this gift/'grace'
    (*charis*) and the grace (*charis*) of God.
37 Moberly, *Prophecy*, p. 186.
38 For further considerations of some of these themes, see the chapter in this volume by
    Andi Smith.
39 For more on this, see Tom Greggs' chapter in this volume, 'Beyond the Binary'.
40 In 1:5, 4:15, 8:2 and 9:12, more than in any other book of the New Testament.
41 For more on improvisation as a metaphor for Christian faithfulness, see S. Wells,
    Improvisation: The Drama of Christian Ethics, Grand Rapids, MI: Brazos Press, 2004.

Select bibliography

Coakley, S., 'Why Gift? Gift, Gender and Trinitarian Relations in Milbank and Tanner',
    Scottish Journal of Theology, 2008, vol. 61, 224–35.
Mauss, M., *The Gift: Forms and Functions of Exchange in Archaic Societies*, London:
    Routledge, 1990.
Webb, S., *The Gifting God: A Trinitarian Ethics of Excess*, Oxford: Oxford University Press,
    1996.

Chapter 11

Beyond the binary

Forming evangelical eschatology

Tom Greggs

Evangelical identity has its origins in strongly particularist senses of Christian self-identity, and has tended to form its own social culture over and against that of the world around (as witnessed to in its Puritan and Pietist past). While evangelicalism has been happy to assimilate itself to certain cultural phenomena, especially around economic market forces, its desire to be 'in the world but not of the world' determines that many evangelical impulses arise from a form of separationism which relies on straightforward binary descriptors of insider–outsider, saved–damned, elect–reject. Strong particularism gives rise to strong separationism, and underpinning this separationism is often a degree of eschatological self-certainty which seeks such utter self-assurance as to push to the outside anyone who seems vaguely other or an outsider to the central issues perceived to be definitive for inclusion in the Kingdom of God. For this reason, we evangelicals often engage in seeking ever-narrower circles of acceptability – from the Reformation to Puritanism to Pietism to card-carrying evangelicalism of various kinds.[1] Even within the latter, there are often issues which become 'fundamental' to being seen to be insiders, whether that be certain attitudes to the manner in which the Spirit inspires Scripture, timetables of the *eschaton*, or scholastic arguments about the minutiae of dogma which become defining issues for salvation. What is most pernicious is that often these issues that determine insider 'soundness' arise not from articulations of what we stand for, but of what we stand against. Assurance of our place within the Kingdom comes to be governed by what it is we are able to stand against in order to stand on the Lord's side, and the other's otherness to us all too easily becomes the other's otherness to God: perceptions about the present become predictions about the future and judgements upon a person or a group.

Even when, as evangelicals, we seek to be more charitable, our conversation frequently revolves around where we place that binary dividing line. In more charitable moments, evangelicals may ponder about the pious Muslim, or those who have never heard the gospel, or those who do not have the capacity to proclaim faith in Christ, or those who die in infancy.[2] However, the question is still commonly who is on the inside and who is on the outside, and shows a worrying preparedness to make eschatological judgements about people today. While we may wish to shout that the judgement in the end is God's, the language of our own theology so often suggests that we are party to the knowledge of who will fall on each side of the divide: to say that God in the end will decide but simultaneously to ponder about the fate of different groups of those outside of the empirical church (and sometimes outside of the soundly empirical evangelical churches) is to make judgements that do not belong to now but properly to the *eschaton*, and do not belong to us but properly to God.[3] In that way, this form of strong separationism is simply the flip-side of poor forms of dogmatic universalism – depreciating God's sovereignty and inevitably making judgements about individuals.[4]

No more can this form of binary line-drawing form the basis of our eschatological doctrinal reflection; our binary judgement-making as human beings must be moved beyond the sense that we are able to determine what is meant by *extra ecclesia nulla salus*. The desire to move beyond binaries may be difficult to justify given that the separationist tenor of Scripture sounds so clear.[5] However, dogmatic separationist accounts of Christian eschatology often fail to attend to the alarming complexity of Scripture and the scandalous particularism which undermines the binary categorization of people in what seems to be a most clear meta-narrative of salvation for the insider and destruction for the outsider. As Barclay puts it, 'a brighter hope can flicker around those dark expectations, often vaguely expressed or seemingly in contradiction to the prediction of utter destruction'.[6] There can be no doubt of the urgency of choosing to be on the Lord's side arising from the call of Scripture, but this should not in turn lead to antagonistic and pernicious self-definitions targeted at the dehumanizing condemnation of the other as if we were God, or as if the image of God in Scripture is of a God who dehumanizes and condemns.

This chapter seeks to address these issues by pointing to the reality that the categorizing of people into two binary opposed camps does not sit easily with either our tradition or the complexities of Scripture. The need to move beyond simple binaries in our eschatological speech is considered by pointing to the centrality of grace in salvation (which places the seeming insider beside the seeming outsider). This is followed by a consideration of who the outsiders are in the New Testament, and a discussion of the non-absolute nature of individual human beings (which determines the need to look to our own acts which are judged by God). It is hoped that in doing this, evangelical eschatologies will be enabled to be properly refocused on God and the present historical and worldly temporality in which God has placed us, with implications for social, political and economic structures and involvement.

Salvation by grace as the beginnings of evangelical eschatology

Although variously described, evangelicalism must have as its basis the grace of God as displayed in the life, death and resurrection of Jesus Christ.[7] One might say that it is the *sola gratia* which stands as the basis of each of the other great *solas*: only because of God's graciousness does God reveal himself in Scripture; only because of God's graciousness does God elect to be God in Jesus Christ; only because of God's graciousness does God grant us the gift of faith. It is only in living in response to the graciousness of God that evangelicals can understand their piety: the desire to follow Christ, to grow in faith, to engage in works of goodness is enabled uniquely as a response to God's undeserved and absolute free loving kindness. That God calls us to himself, however God may do that, determines that the relationship with God for humanity is one which results from God's graciousness and not from human work or deserving. Faith is created within the believer *ex nihilo* from outside of the believer by the Holy Spirit. Undeserving of salvation and of God's fellowship, the believer is granted both of these things by God in God's gracious election of humanity. A belief in the absolute depravity of humanity underscores this point firmly. No believer deserves God, 'since all have sinned and fall short of the glory of God'.[8]

The centrality of grace determines that conversion should never be understood as a work. Conversion is, instead, a response to God's graciousness, which recognizes that grace as undeserved – that is, as gracious. The initiator of our conversion is not the self but the God who makes himself known by the power of his Holy Spirit. A convert's response to God is only ever a response which is at best abductive,[9] moving towards or turning towards the God who, in his movement to us, attracts us to himself. Conversion is not a work which conditions God into salvation, but a response to God to whom salvation properly belongs: 'Salvation belongs to our God who is seated on the throne, and to the Lamb!'[10] Frequently, there exists a confusion of the subjective realization of God's graciousness in conversion and the life of faith with the objective reality of God's saving work on the cross; this in turn can begin to undermine the centrality of grace as the determining feature of the evangelical, as one who pertains to the good news. This does not remove the urgency of response to God's grace, or the call to proclaim God's grace and seek people to follow his will. However, it does determine that we do not understand the act of conversion as a work which brings about salvation. In turn, this determines that we do not equate conversion with God's grace, as if our conversion lulls God into being gracious. Moreover, it determines that we do not place limits on the higher and broader category of God's grace by identifying it only with the response to that grace in salvation. Put otherwise, grace both precedes and brings about conversion, but grace is not simply conversion and should not be empirically equated with conversion.

Recognizing the priority of grace begins to unpick the dangerous binary tendencies of evangelical eschatologies that engage in identifying insiders and outsiders based on judgements about the empirical (evangelical) church. The undermining that focusing on God's grace brings to eschatological reflection can be seen at this juncture in two principal ways.

The first implication that the prioritizing of grace brings for evangelical eschatologies is the recognition of the fallenness and depravity of *all* humanity – even those who have converted. The continued presence of sin in the life of the believer as *simul iustus et peccator* must bring with it the realization that believers stand side by side with unbelievers as those who have brought and continue to bring sin into the world. Salvation *sola gratia* relies on the knowledge of the undeserved nature of salvation by God. The universality of human sinfulness is such that, far from feeling aggrandized or special (and certainly far from feeling an insider), the believer is continually confronted with her wilful disobedience, even in the face of her conversion and turning to God. Applied to the contemporary church, Paul's language about the universality of sin not only places the convert in the same boat as the unbeliever, but in a far more precarious position within that boat. Paul asks the question 'Are we any better off?', to which the reply is not simply 'No', but 'No, not at all':[11] given that we who have turned to God know what we should be doing and fail to do it, we surely have no grounds to point to any supposed superior position before God in comparison to those who fail to obey God's will without knowing it. For our purposes, we may put it thus: realizing the grace of God as the source of salvation means that we realize that we stand together with all of fallen humanity – not in one binary category as insiders over and against another as outsiders. With characteristic wisdom, Bonhoeffer states this:

> On the one hand, the concept of the church, as Christ's presence in the world which calls for a decision, necessarily demands the dual outcome. The recognition that the gift of God's boundless love has been received without any merit would, on the other hand, make it seem just as impossible to exclude others from this gift and this love. The strongest reason for accepting the idea of *apocatastasis* would seem to be that all Christians must be aware of having brought sin into the world, and thus aware of being bound together with the whole of humanity in sin, aware of having the sins of humanity on their conscience.[12]

Finding ourselves undeservedly seeming to be on the inside brings with it a realization of the undeserved nature of being on the inside, and a co-identity with those who seem to be on the outside.[13] This is no denial of God's holiness (which is often pitted against those who hope for a wider hope) in favour of a monochromatic dull version of love, but is instead a wider hope that arises out of realizing God's holiness and our undeserving sinfulness: the more holy we understand God to be, the more our own sin comes into sharp focus and our unity with those we may be tempted to see as outsiders is realized. To recognize this, in turn, means that the evangelical must question the sharp eschatological dividing line she may be inclined to place between herself and other converts on one side, and those many others on the other side who are no less deserving of God's love than she is.[14]

It is this blurring of the lines which leads to the second implication that salvation by grace alone brings to bear on evangelical eschatology. This is that we have no right (especially in our precarious position before God) in positing a limitation on the grace of God or to the friendliness of Jesus Christ. Indeed, rather than introduce grace as a principle, or almost a new version of the law which is assented to through conversion,[15] it is necessary to understand grace as an outworking of the love and friendliness of the person of Jesus. Knowledge of Christ's love towards humanity, even to fallen sinners as ourselves, should guard us from rushing to place boundaries around where Christ's love and grace can be felt. Much wisdom is to be gained from Karl Barth's own expressed fears concerning those who rejoice in just such a limiting of God's friendliness by jumping anxiously away from the possibilities of a wider salvific hope:

> It would be well, in view of the 'danger' with which the expression is ever and again seen to be encompassed, to ask for a moment, whether on the whole the 'danger' from those theologians who are forever sceptically critical, who are again and again suspiciously questioning, because they are always fundamentally legalistic, and who are therefore in essentials sullen and dismal, is not in the meantime always more threatening amongst us than that of an unsuitably cheerful indifferentism or even antinomianism, to which one could in fact yield oneself on one definite understanding of that conception. One thing is sure, that there is no theological justification for setting any limits on our side to the friendliness of God towards man which appeared in Jesus Christ ...[16]

While we may not wish to move from a dogmatic form of separationism to a dogmatic form of universalism,[17] to have a wider hope grounded in the graciousness of God we may wish to point to the tension that exists in understanding our conversion as a response to God's undeserved free-loving kindness – a tension which sees the insider on the inside undeservedly and united to the outsider in shared sinfulness, and which thus makes us undogmatic about where the friendliness of God in Jesus Christ may be found because we are so dogmatic that the friendliness of God in Jesus Christ has found us.[18]

This tension must lead us to an uneasiness with binary approaches to eschatology: not divided from the outsider but united to her, the evangelical must become cautious of making eschatological predictions regarding the other. Such an emphasis on grace as is appropriate to evangelical theology begins to break down this self-definition in terms of an eschatological otherness to one perceived to be an outsider. However, even if evangelical conversionism and crucicentrism leads to this, it is my contention that biblicism leads us to go further. Taking seriously all of Scripture and Scripture's ability to address the church today, the evangelical is directed to ask the question: 'Could it possibly be that we are the outsiders?' It is this to which it is necessary now to turn.

Beyond the insider and outsider: where are we?

To speak of grace as the defining characteristic of evangelical theology, and to address some of the implications of that, does not go far enough. For grace is not an abstract principle that relates to God, but is a second-order description of the nature of God as revealed in the person of Jesus Christ. God's personhood determines that theology should never seek to establish propositional principles as if they are able to bind God's person in a prison of our own dogmatic making. The narrative of Scripture testifies to God's personhood and his activity with his people. Thus, rather than establishing principles that flow from the abstracted theological idea of God's grace, we do better to attend to the person of Jesus Christ to seek hints for our theological speech and our ethical and ecclesial behaviour. Grace is a mere descriptor of the person of Jesus, a person who must be attended to in his particularity.[19] In this particularity, we may well perceive something of the complexity of the tension pointed to above. Jesus' attitude to those who might be perceived to be religious outsiders to the Kingdom of God (sinners, tax collectors, Samaritans and gentiles) presents a situation which is far from easy to summarize in binary terms.[20] Rather, his relationships with those who seem to be outsiders arises from his person-to-person relationships.[21]

Furthermore, while there is no doubt that Jesus speaks at times in clearly separationist tones, it is not always so clear as one might automatically think as to which side of the binary separation we belong – a point which surely complexifies the matter. As one speaking to the religious people and institutions of his own age (different from our own), we do well to consider who it is that Jesus speaks against in our own times. If God's word continues to speak to us, surely we cannot simply associate the words of Jesus that are directed at the institutional insiders of his own day (the priests and the Pharisees, for example) as simply historical statements about one particular and singular instance of religiosity in his own cultural context.[22] If God continues to speak to us by the power of his Holy Spirit through his word, we must ask the question, when faced with Jesus' assertions about judgement: where are we in this text as God addresses his speech to us? What is perhaps most uncomfortable is that, as the religious (even if many of us may be uncomfortable with that descriptor) of our own generation, we may be wise to see ourselves as those in Scripture who presume we are the furthest inside, for whom the reality may well be that we are on the outside (read here the Pharisees). Are we correct to assume that we are the insiders always, or should we see ourselves as those who presume and perceive themselves to be the insiders while simultaneously excluding others and playing God in thinking we are able to make eschatological judgements about other humans?

Throughout the gospels, we are able to see this undermining of the insider–outsider binary, with those who perceive themselves as insiders finding their self-perceived confidence in their position before God. Jesus is the one who is not only treated as an outsider, but who proclaims the Kingdom of God to be for those we might perceive as outsiders: it is the prostitutes and tax collectors (the perceived outsiders) who will enter the Kingdom of God before those who are perceived to be and perceive themselves to be the insiders (Mt. 21:31). And we must be wary of simply ignoring the judgements pronounced on the Scribes and Pharisees as if they were directed only to these historical groups. The living nature of Scripture means that these judgements must be understood afresh and anew now, by us, who might also be judged under the harsh words of Jesus:

> Woe to you. ... For you lock people out of the kingdom of heaven. For you do not go in yourselves, and when others are going in, you stop them. ... For you

cross sea and land to make a single convert, and you make the new convert twice as much a child of hell as yourselves.[23]

It seems that for the religious of Jesus' time and for ourselves, this saying is sure: judgement begins in the house of God.[24]

Lest we think that these charges apply only to historical figures in New Testament times and to see them as otherwise is to engage in flights of hermeneutical fancy, Jesus not only presents us with a discussion which points backwards in history, but which points forwards to the apocalypse. In this, we can see at a future point (and not simply a past one) a level of surprise and shock by those who presume themselves to be insiders in some of Jesus' most disturbing binary language: as those who live before the *eschaton*, these warnings surely apply equally as strongly to us as to Jesus' contemporaries. In short, in Jesus' pointing to the future judgement, we are even historically here in the text. In some of the seemingly clearest indicators of Jesus' binary approaches to eschatology, we read about both the sheep and the goats saying: 'Lord, when was it that we saw you hungry or thirsty or a stranger or naked or sick or in prison, and did not take care of you?'[25] Evidently, the eschatological determination of the individual is not simply based on any empirical visibility as to which section of humanity we belong to prior to the judgement, but on the way in which we treat the least of Jesus' brothers and sisters. This appears to lead to surprise and questioning of Jesus' judgement: those who expect to be sheep find themselves as goats, and those who expect to be goats find themselves as sheep. Clearly, there is no easy equating of those who in history are seen to be on the inside or outside with those who at the end find themselves on the inside or outside respectively. Matters are a little more complex than that.

The danger in pointing to such verses for our tradition is that all too easily we can slip into a movement away from grace back again towards a works-based approach to salvation.[26] However, evangelical 'activism' is an activism which flows from faith and is enabled by faith. Indeed, the context of Jesus' words here might seem to point in that direction: the sheep inherit the kingdom which was prepared for them from the foundation of the world (Mt. 25:34), and thus at a deeper level not one which simply becomes theirs by virtue of their actions. How best to understand these acts is thus not a straightforward issue to consider; this is no simple works-based soteriology. But it is equally not a soteriology which confuses the correct belief about justification by faith alone with the grace that justifies through faith.

One might do well, however, to attend to the reality that, as human beings, we are determined by our acts: none of us is an absolute being, but we are all the results of the actions we undertake within the contingencies of our human histories. This is a problem for eschatology. Not only are we confronted with a situation of often seeking to describe the absolute judgements made over non-absolute beings, but we are also confronted with issues regarding justice, such as what we consider comprises a person, and whether the whole of a person is the person at the moment of death, and whether a person who dies at an earlier age should be judged in the same way as a person who lives to their dotage.[27] Do we consider potential or only actuality in terms of the way we seek to understand an individual's eschatology? If we understand a person to be made up of the acts in which that person engages (that is, if what a person does is constitutive of who a person is), then we may begin to be able to move beyond such binary articulations of eschatology which give rise to these issues. If the act of a person is here determinative of the person's place among either the sheep or the goats, rather than who the person understands or perceives herself to be, we must consider what this means for eschatological reflection. It is the acts of a person which are judged here with regard to those for whom the kingdom was prepared before the foundation of the earth. In seeking to emphasize this, but not dangerously morphing it into a works-based salvation, we may say that these actions themselves arise from God's grace towards us: in his grace, he enables us to engage in following after him with acts of grace which make our being correspond with that of his, which he self-determines through his own acts of grace.[28] Thus, as human beings we are human becomings, whose acts begin to transform our lives to correspond to the will and grace of God. It is these acts which are judged.

But still there remains the issue of how to deal with these acts in terms of non-absolute beings – indeed, beings who are always becomings by virtue of on-going history and temporality. What constitutes a person who progresses towards her end? Is the end of a person's life the fullest or even the only point at which a person truly is who she is? Is a person the same person today as she was ten years ago, etc.? As historical creatures from the perspective of history, none of us is singularly a saint, and none singularly a sinner: for all, there are acts which are sinful and acts which are gracious.[29] Once again (as in the previous section of this chapter with regard to Christian sinfulness), the binary divide in terms of categories of people does not sit easily. Even the most heinous of sinners will have brought about joy and grace throughout their life (even if only as a child to their mothers); and even the most holy of saints is still a justified sinner. A strong belief in the absolute depravity of humanity, however, must surely determine that no good can be produced apart from God.[30] When faced with these issues and the difficulties of knowing to which side we ourselves belong at the great judgement, we may well be wise to say only that God judges those acts which arise from his grace to be in correspondence with his will, and those which do not to be contrary to him. The surprise of those on the side of the sheep may well indicate that there are some (perhaps many) whose actions of grace arise from God's graciousness without an overt recognition of this: 'Lord, when was it that we saw you ...?' This may seem strange to our conversionist impulses, but it is surely a reminder that faith is never simply cognition: that is only ever the path to *gnosticism*. Faith is life lived in correspondence to God; in short, faith is innately actualistic. Such realizations help us to understand more deeply the meaning of judgement. Often wrongly confused with condemnation (*katakrinein*), the Greek word for judgement (*krinein*) bespeaks 'separation'. Judgement should not be considered as an act of destruction, but one in which there is separation. And while this may be absolute, it need not necessarily apply to categories of humans as if each were comprised of absolute beings. Paul writes, for example:

the work of each builder has become visible, for the Day will disclose it, because it will be revealed with fire, and the fire will test what sort of work each has done. ... If the work is burned, the builder will suffer loss; the builder will be saved but only as through fire.[31]

There is clearly, for Paul, a further reward for the builder whose foundation survives (v.14): there are clear future eschatological (as well as present existential) benefits to a life converted to faithful activism. But there is not an absolute judgement made over the non-absolute human, whose acts are judged. Moltmann speaks of this as 'God's creative justice' and advocates:

The image of the End-time 'fire' is an image of the consuming love of God. Everything which is, and has been, in contradiction to God will be burnt away, so that the person who is loved by God is saved, and everything which is, and has been, in accord with God in that person's life is saved.[32]

Again, this is not to lead us from dogmatic separationism to dogmatic universalism, but to open our theology up to a generous particularism which recognizes the complexities of Scripture and of human life. In this way, our emphasis on conversion does not fall into the trap of becoming tainted by post-Enlightenment notions of knowledge as abstract bodies of information: no doctrinal statement (even one about the infallibility of Scripture or substitutionary atonement) can ever save us. Our understanding of conversion must be to a life of following after Christ in faith – engaging not in acts that save us (as only God in his grace can do that) but in acts that correspond to God's grace. This does not lessen the urgency of mission or of conversion: to live a life without Christ is an unthinkable possibility for the person of faith, and it is to live a life within (existentially and eschatologically) the possibilities of death and hell. However, in this, it is necessary to realize that any acts that correspond to God's grace must flow from God's grace (even if at best met abductively by ourselves through conversion), and it is necessary to find something of the grace of God in the good acts of each builder since it is God who alone brings about goodness within the depravity of humanity.

If the previous section demonstrated the co-sinfulness of all, this section seeks to understand how to describe the goodness of those who appear to be on the outside while making us aware of the acts we engage in as those who perceive ourselves to be on the inside, a perception which may actually place us on the wrong side of our own binary divide. In both, it is necessary to move beyond simple binary language in eschatology.

Attending to the now and attending to God

What does this mean for our emphasis on conversion? Are we depreciated in our place before God? It may be no bad thing for us to be humbled for a while on this score: conversion is only ever a response to grace and never grounds for self-aggrandizement over and against the rest of humanity. However, there is no real reason for such a recognition of the complexities of these eschatological matters to undermine the importance of conversion or to dampen evangelistic zeal. Clearly, a life lived in correspondence to the will of God is the life desired by God and by his church. Lives which result in people determined by their acts of faith in response to God's grace are not only lives which will receive great eschatological reward (we do well here to remember the language of Jesus about treasures stored in heaven), but they are also lives which will be filled with the Holy Spirit and the fruits that the Spirit brings. A peace in the present regarding eschatological issues in the future is no small matter, and one which has sizeable pastoral implications. It determines that our eschatological reflection does not merely fulfil the function of preaching 'the gospel at gun point',[33] but offers a possibility of finding peace in the present. Eschatology is not reflection on the teaching of the church about on-going and continued egoism for all eternity – an egoism grounded in a belief that *I* will go on. Eschatology is, instead, about both life (eternal life) and life more abundantly (full and deep life).[34] Eschatology is not simply about the future; it is about attitudes regarding the present.

Having advocated the need to move beyond simple binary articulations of eschatology given the complexity of the biblical witness, it may now seem odd to advocate the assurance that turning to Christ can bring for the convert. However, herein lies the difference between insurance and assurance. Faith is no contractual insurance policy, but is about following after Jesus in a full hope that in the end is God.[35] When as converts we focus on the true and ultimate *eschaton* for all creation – God – then our other concerns, worries and preoccupations are relativized.[36] Here, one may see the clear and full reason for faithfulness: we are saved from the hell of unbelief, and made truly human in the life of faith as we are enabled by acts in correspondence to God's will to become the human beings we have been destined to be from and to all eternity. This is no limitation of justification by faith, but a recognition of its right and proper place – not as if the doctrine were a means of salvation, but instead seeing it as a second-order reflection on the means of the assurance of salvation brought by the realization that before us ultimately is God, the same God whose being we already know is self-determined by the acts of his grace. The life for those without this assurance is a life without its blessings and its peace. This is surely as strong a story and as positive an impulse for the spreading of the *Good* News as there can be. The urgency of conversion is an urgency for transformation of individuals in the present, and through them a transformation of the world.

This has radical political, social and economic implications.[37] However, these political implications are far from those normally associated with evangelical eschatologies – those of building up power in the world and engaging in a binary divisive clash of civilizations: such eschatologies pertain more to Babylon than to the New Jerusalem.[38] When faced with the reality that before us stretches an eternity in which is God, the matters of this life begin to be seen for what they are. This is not in a way that should result in an otherworldly focus, but a clear focus on this world. Not divorced from the world as heavenly insiders to worldly outsiders, we are judged by the acts which we do that will determine the beings we are in our becomings. Those beings we are becoming are not determined by the strength and power we gain in this world or by the perceptions of those who understand themselves to be insiders in worldly terms. Instead, present worries about ourselves are put into context by a God who will judge our acts based on the way in which we treat the least of Christ's brothers and sisters. The eschatological call to evangelicals is a call to activism in the present, but this must be an activism which arises out of self-sacrifice rather than self-righteousness. If we are to take Scripture seriously on eschatological matters, it is time to stop seeing the specks in our brothers' and sisters' eyes (placing them on the wrong side of the binary divide), and begin to address our own attitudes to money, status and power. When much of the world has little if anything to eat and no fresh water, lacks basic medical provision and finds itself suffering oppression, evangelicals must ask ourselves what our response will be to Jesus' saying:

> I was hungry and you gave me food, I was thirsty and you gave me something to drink, I was a stranger and you welcomed me, I was naked and you gave me clothing, I was sick and you took care of me, I was in prison and you visited me.[39]

Responding to God's grace through conversion determines a following after God's ways throughout life. This is the way of learning to separate (to judge) what is passing from what is eternal through the acts of our lives which determine our being in correspondence to the grace of God, and which display the fruits of the Spirit that arise from that correspondence.

To end where this chapter began, evangelical self-identity often seeks to maintain itself by being counter-cultural to the world. This is no innately bad thing. The questions to be asked concern more to whom and to what it is we seek to be counter-cultural. To be counter-cultural by seeing ourselves as the righteous insiders destined to be eternally on the Lord's side brings with it the folly of a self-perceived insider status that fails to recognize the grace of God to sinners (even sinners like ourselves) and the grace of God in acts of human graciousness. It fails to recognize that in the end is God, and not our own self or our categorization of people. Our challenge in our activism is to be properly and eschatologically counter-cultural. The call upon evangelical theology is to be counter-cultural to a culture dominated by the ego (even in eschatological discourse).[40] It is a call to be counter to those very aspects of society to which we have assimilated – market forces and consumerism, in which worth and value is confused with monetary cost.[41] These so-called values (unlike our actions towards the weak, powerless and poor) will only ever pass away – things to be consumed by the purging fire of God.

Eschatology is about trusting the end to God, for he is the ultimate.[42] And for us now, it is about building up treasure in heaven, and attending to the places where we find Christ now rather than simply waiting to see him face to face, while realizing the connection between these two moments: it is about tending to the starving, helping the oppressed, visiting the prisoner, aiding the sick and welcoming the stranger. For in these acts are our eternal determinations. We must move beyond a simple binary, so often understood through vaguely *gnostic* or Enlightenment understandings of knowledge; lives of faith governed by the cross, Scripture, conversion and activism are far more than this. Lives lived in response to God's gracious salvation must begin to be lives transformed into grace. In Wesley's words, they shall be lives:

> Changed from glory into glory
> 'Til in heaven we take our place,
> 'Til we cast our crowns before thee,
> Lost in wonder, love and praise.[43]

This transformation does not belong only to the future, but begins now as we become children of God, and as our gracious acts correspond to the grace of our Father in heaven.

Notes

1 For a brief history of this, see S. J. Grenz, *Revisioning Evangelical Theology: A Fresh Agenda for the 21st Century*, Downers Grove, IL: IVP, 1993, pp. 22–7.

2 One can see this sort of enterprise in N. M. de S. Cameron, 'Universalism and the Logic of Revelation', in J. I. Packer (ed.), *The Best in Theology*, vol. 3, Carol Stream, IL: Christianity Today, Inc., 1989.

3 To suggest that these dividing lines are necessary in order to know who it is one should try to convert and who it is one should welcome into the church relies on far too substantialized a doctrine of the church. The church is present where the Holy Spirit calls it into being, and its existence is never simply for the sake of itself but for the sake of the other. The church exists, therefore, for those outside of the church: to that end, serving the other (in a manner which recognizes that pastoral work is missionary activity and vice versa) is what is of paramount importance – a point which relativizes the needs to draw such binary dividing lines for ecclesial purposes.

4 In dogmatic universalism, saying all are saved logically determines that each individual is saved and thereby also includes judgements over individuals.

5 D. Fergusson, 'Eschatology', in C. E. Gunton (ed.), *The Cambridge Companion to Christian Doctrine*, Cambridge: Cambridge University Press, 1997, p. 241.

6 J. M. G. Barclay, 'Universalism and Particularism: Twin Components of Both Judaism and Early Christianity', in M. Bockmuehl and M. B. Thompson (eds), *A Vision for the Church: Studies in Early Christian Eschatology in Honour of J. P. M. Swete*, Edinburgh: T&T Clark, 1997, p. 216.

7 This is implied in both the 'Bebbington quadrilateral' and the 'Larsen pentagon'. Larsen, furthermore, very helpfully differentiates between the (objective) reconciliation with God through Christ's atoning death and the (subjective) work of the Holy Spirit in bringing about conversion and the life of Christian faith. See T. Larsen, 'Defining and Locating Evangelicalism', in T. Larsen, *The Cambridge Companion to Evangelical Theology*, Cambridge: Cambridge University Press, 2007, pp. 1, 9–12; and D. W. Bebbington, *Evangelicalism in Modern Britain: A History from the 1730s to the 1980s*, London: Unwin Hyman, 1989, pp. 2–17.

8 Rom. 3:10.

9 On the formal nature of abductive logic, see P. Ochs, *Pierce, Pragmatism and the Logic of Scripture*, Cambridge, Cambridge University Press, 2004, pp. 28–30, 235–40. As applied to Christian theology, see P. Ochs, *Another Reformation: Postliberal Christianity and the Jews*, Grand Rapids, MI: Brazos Press, 2009.

10 Rev. 7:10.

11 Rom. 3:9. Clearly in the context of Romans, this is directed at the Jewish believers, but can equally well be applied to the Christian church in our own position before God.

12 D. Bonhoeffer, *Sanctorum Communio: A Theological Study of the Sociology of the Church, Dietrich Bonhoeffer Works*, vol. 1, Minneapolis, MN: Fortress Press, 1998, pp. 286–7.

13 One can see these kinds of thought processes in Barth's considerations of the atheist thought of Max Bense: K. Barth, *Fragments Grave and Gay*, London and Glasgow: Collins Fortress, 1971, pp. 45–6.

14 The doctrine of sanctification does not invalidate my point here: sanctification is not tantamount to salvation.

15 Here is not the place to consider the third use of the law.

16 K. Barth, *God, Grace and Gospel*, Edinburgh: Oliver & Boyd, 1959, pp. 49–50.

17 'As propositions, they can only contradict each other. As pictures, they can both be held up, either alternatively or, occasionally, together, as pointers to the God whose grace and judgment both resist capture in a system, or in a single picture.' M. E. Boring, 'The Language of Universal Salvation in Paul', *Journal of Biblical Literature*, 1986, vol. 105, 292.

18 '... this very talk of *apocatastasis* may never be more than the sigh of theology wherever it has to speak of faith and unfaith, election and rejection.' D. Bonhoeffer, *Act and Being: Transcendental Philosophy and Ontology in Systematic Theology, Dietrich Bonhoeffer Works*, vol. 2, Minneapolis, MN: Fortress Press, 1996, pp. 160–1.

19 These are themes I have discussed elsewhere in relation to Barth. See T. Greggs, '"Jesus is Victor": Passing the Impasse of Barth on Universalism', *Scottish Journal of Theology*, 2007, vol. 60.

20 Although this book is expressed more in terms of a theology of the religions, for some of this complexity, see G. O'Collins, *Salvation for All: God's Other Peoples*, Oxford: Oxford University Press, 2008.

21 We should think, for example, of the likes of the Samaritan woman at the well, the Roman centurion whose faith Jesus commends and the Syro-Phoenecian woman.

22 Such singularly historical readings have not only avoided having to address the convicting nature of these passages in the New Testament, they have also led to dangerous anti-Semitic readings of New Testament texts.

23 Mt. 23:16.

24 This language is picked up from 2 Pet. 4:17.

25 Mt. 25:44, cf. 25:37–9. I must acknowledge here the insights of C. Rowland, 'The Lamb and the Beast, the Sheep and the Goats: "The Mystery of Salvation" in Revelation', in Bockmeuhl and Thompson (eds), *A Vision for the Church*. Rowland advocates that Matthew's eschatological teaching must be read in the context of the whole narrative. When one does this:

> the Gospel leaves readers uncertain whether they can have the assurance that they are among the 'sheep' rather than the 'goats'. ... Indeed, there is a surprise at the identity of the children of God when the Last Assize takes place.
>
> (p. 188)

Rowland asserts a similar hermeneutical key for Revelation.

26 Clearly, there would be dangers in building an eschatology from any one text singularly. The *sensus plenior* of Scripture is what should be desired and sought. A focus on Mt. 25

alone might well lead one along dangerous lines away from justification by faith alone. However, this text is drawn on in order to recognize the warning voice of Scripture against an all too self-assured sense of the Christian ability to judge and too great a willingness to systematize the mysteries of salvation into simple dogmatic statement. This chapter does not want to undermine justification by faith alone, but to recognize its benefits and challenges in a different way from that often assumed – through the life of discipleship and the assurance of salvation. As Bonhoeffer puts it: 'Because we are justified by faith, faith and obedience have to be distinguished. But their division must never destroy their unity, which lies in the reality that faith exists only in obedience, is never without obedience.' D. Bonhoeffer, *Discipleship*, *Dietrich Bonhoeffer Works*, vol. 4, Minneapolis, MN: Fortress Press, 2001, p. 64.

27 Cf. J. E. Sanders, 'Is Belief in Christ Necessary for Salvation?', *Evangelical Quarterly*, 1988, vol. 60, 249.

28 'In so far as God not only is love, but loves, in the act of love which determines His whole being God elects.' K. Barth, *Church Dogmatics*, II/2, London: T&T Clark, 1957, p. 76. For more on the self-determining nature of God's act, see E. Jüngel, *God's Being Is in Becoming: The Trinitarian Being of God in the Theology of Karl Barth. A Paraphrase*, Edinburgh: T&T Clark, 2001. The reader is also directed to chs 3 and 4 in this volume, by Paul Nimmo and Paul Jones respectively.

29 The saint is clearly only ever *simul iustus, simul peccator*.

30 Indeed, a belief in the *creatio ex nihilo* must also determine that that which is good can only come from God.

31 1 Cor. 3:13, 15.

32 J. Moltmann, *In the End – the Beginning*, London: SCM, 2004, p. 143. Cf. J. Moltmann, *The Coming of God: Christian Eschatology*, London: SCM, 1996. In this, Moltmann sees judgement not as an end, but as a beginning (pp. 250–2).

33 This is the charge Barth cited against Billy Graham. See Eberhard Busch, *Karl Barth: His Life from Letters and Autobiographical Texts*, London: SCM, 1976, p. 446.

34 See Jn 10:10.

35 For all that members of the evangelical community may be uncomfortable with J. A. T. Robinson, in the title of his book at least he was right. See J. A. T. Robinson, *In the End God*, London: Collins, 1968.

36 This point puts quibbling discussions about pre- or post-millennialism into sharp relief.

37 For a solid introduction to eschatology and politics, see R. Jenson, 'Eschatology', in P. Scott and W. T. Cavanaugh (eds), *The Blackwell Companion to Political Theology*, Oxford: Blackwell, 2007.

38 We do well to remember the power dynamics of the early church which present situations in which they *as the weak and powerless* have true power not in this world, but by virtue of eschatological justice. The New Testament church is as far from a Christian super-power as is possible, and any direct deductions for present nation-state politics cannot be made on the basis of the small and oppressed early Christian church's eschatology: present nations (even Christian ones) are not the historical concern, but the place of the eschatological rewards of the faithful in a situation of oppression and injustice.

39 Mt. 25:35–6.

40 For more on this theme, see ch. 8 in this volume, by Elizabeth Kent.

41 One could point here to a range of ways in which evangelicalism could be called to be counter-cultural. However, the reason for choosing principally financial issues is because this is an aspect of society into which evangelicalism has integrated, despite all of the difficult biblical passages about use of money. The focus on this one aspect is not meant to be exhaustive but indicative: issues to do with finance are pointed towards as they are so often ignored, and as they themselves comprise issues at the heart of human sociality.

42 On ultimate and penultimate things, see D. Bonhoeffer, *Ethics*, *Dietrich Bonhoeffer Works*, vol. 6, Minneapolis, MN: Fortress, 2005, pp. 146–70.
43 *Hymns and Psalms*, Peterborough: MPH, no. 267.

Select bibliography

Barth, K., *Fragments Grave and Gay*, London and Glasgow: Collins Fortress, 1971.
Barth, K., *God, Grace and Gospel*, Edinburgh: Oliver & Boyd, 1959.
Bonhoeffer, D., *Sanctorum Communio: A Theological Study of the Sociology of the Church*, *Dietrich Bonhoeffer Works*, vol. 1, Minneapolis, MN: Fortress Press, 1998.
Moltmann, J., *In the End – the Beginning*, London: SCM, 2004.
O'Collins, G., *Salvation for All: God's Other Peoples*, Oxford: Oxford University Press, 2008.
Rowland, C., 'The Lamb and the Beast, the Sheep and the Goats: "The Mystery of Salvation" in Revelation', in M. Bockmuehl and M. B. Thompson (eds), *A Vision for the Church: Studies in Early Christian Eschatology in Honour of J. P. M. Swete*, Edinburgh: T&T Clark, 1997.

Chapter 12

Evangelicalism and the political

Recovering the truth within

Andi Smith

Throughout modernity an emphasis on piety and reason has distorted an evangelical understanding of the political. The tradition has subsequently become orientated away from its rightful emphasis on truth as evidenced in the church's particularity towards an apologetic obsession with the universal good.[1] This chapter outlines how evangelicals might begin to orientate the central themes/practices of the tradition towards a more truthful recovery of the political.[2] I aim to engage with the lived practices and passions of the evangelical tradition as those of a people seeking for their witness to be ordered by the authority of God's revelation in Christ as 'good news'. Too much scholarly debate concerning our understandings of the political is dominated by crude and unhelpful characterizations of the church which fail to take seriously the lived witness of faithful servants. It is my hope that by asserting a form of reorientation which cherishes the central tenets of the tradition, others might be encouraged to discern the detailed performing of their faith in this more particular and constructive manner without giving up on evangelicalism.

That some evangelicals fail to recognize the church as political, or tend in some cases to abuse its power, is testimony to the grip of the Enlightenment upon the evangelical imagination, further exemplified in evangelicalism's modernist trajectory of divisions between mind and practice, self and community, practice and theory, tradition and knowledge.[3] There will of course be those who wish to argue that the entire problem with evangelicals, particularly in the US, is that they are far too political. In this chapter, I hope to enable the reader to begin to discern how such a position is reliant upon an understanding of the political that has been distorted by unquestioned Constantinianism and wholly divorced from the practices of the church as the primary polity of the Christian community. Politics is concerned with the ordering of life,[4] and my argument encompasses the authority of Scripture, the locating of the self, and the holiness of the church as fragments of truthfulness which remain central to an evangelical ordering of its common life.

Recovering the authority of Scripture: embracing a politics of narrative

Within contemporary debate on the nature and character of the political there is a sense that the protagonists are deeply unsure as to the locatedness of their voice. Our defence and articulation of a particular position appear without a context which could make our claims either intelligible or substantive.[5] A truthful politics is subsequently identified by its being the most applicable to the ordering of all reasonable persons. Hauerwas describes this distortion as Scripture's 'being translated into a *more general* theological medium'.[6] While it might be construed otherwise, an alternative attentiveness to the particularly of Christ is neither sectarian nor bigoted, for it marks our continual beginning and end from which there are an immeasurable number and variety of rich sharings. The politics which I recognize in much of evangelical witness exists as an overflow from the particular towards the universal, which demands attentiveness to the particularity of the tradition yet liberates beyond that tradition to speak truthfully amidst many other voices.[7] Hauerwas writes that 'the universality of the church is based on the particularity of Jesus' story and on the fact that his story trains us to see one another as God's people'.[8] He later writes:

> I am not suggesting that in the absence of God people lack the resources to live morally. I am raising a more profound question, whether in the absence of God people can find the resources, socially and personally, to form and sustain the virtues necessary for the recognition and fulfillment of our historical nature.[9]

In a peculiar combination of contrast and symmetry evangelicalism continues its appeal to Scripture as God's divine and authoritative revelation while concurrently projecting the claims of Scripture to be universally intelligible.[10] As such, the tradition then appears fearful that the only alternative to its current understanding of Scripture is the adoption of either relativism or the abandonment of Scripture, neither of which it is prepared to accept.[11]

Both inside and outside of the church the understandings of the church's role have become increasingly divorced from the practices of that *narrative*. Here narrative means those practices, people and places which constitute the story of the church as being formed through its living in light of God's revelation in Christ, in whom its claims are both intelligible and normative. The good news of the evangelical tradition has too often – in the desire to save the world – been reduced to a universal assertion of particular texts concerned predominantly with our inner/ spiritual transformation, a mechanistic approach concentrating upon an ironically subjective area of the church's life.[12] Theologians such as Hauerwas, Lindbeck, Milbank, Wells, Cavnagh *et al.*, have drawn attention to the dominance of enlightened reason over the ability of the church to understand the virtues of its particular community as grounded in the narrative and language of its particular faithfulness to the person of Christ: a particularity evidenced in the normative practices of its being. It is that narrative which we both evidence and participate in through the reading of Scripture not as linguistic text but as the locating of ourselves within that story by which our lives have been so utterly captivated.

To emphasize the good news of the gospel as the lived narrative of the church is to recognize that the politics of the church is concerned with the witness of a people orientated towards that good news. Scripture is the revelation of God's presence guiding particular groups of people, by particular means, towards an affirmation of his sovereignty. The narrative of such a people has a core which is of God's gracious revelation and it tells of the politics of the church as grounded in the continued retelling of these people and their attentiveness to central acts of revelation. That these acts in their active and repetitive remembering order the life of the people and thus the narrative of the church is inescapably theo-political. Yoder writes:

> That story [of Abraham, Moses, Jeremiah and Jesus] is about a people, a civil reordering in their very existence, not only potentially or by implication. No bridge or translation is needed to make the Bible a book about politics. The new order, or new humanity does not destroy the old, but that does not make the new order apolitical. Its very existence is subversive at the points where the old order is repressive and creative where the old is without vision. The effect of the Bible in society is to order and re-order because that is its theme. What it recounts is what it does.[13]

Yoder reminds the church that the good news of the gospel 'impinges upon the fate of the community' because it marks not only our orientation in the present but is the foretelling of our destiny.[14] Scripture demands participation while altering the very direction of our ontology as it illuminates how *the church is politics* by locating it in a narrative ordered by the cross. Our understanding of the political is defective if it must articulate either a universal response to, for example, the needs of the poor, or equally the assertion of an ideal for the poor. For the good news reminds the tradition that it understands the poor, not in light of economic reform or political ideology, but as located within that narrative by which God has reconciled all of history and therefore as witness to an alternative *polis*.[15] The *polis* of the narrative does not thus declare ideological assertions but rather forms a community to live faithfully in this world.

Employing Scripture in support of a particular idea reduces the narrative of an entire community to a particular textual interpretation frequently denoted by the prior epistemological assertions of the age.[16] It is not accidental that we currently obsess over churches' attitudes towards sexual relations, nor that such obsessing most frequently occurs exempt from our primary understanding of God's faithfulness to his people. Ironically, evangelical objections to abortion, civil partnerships or the supposed erosion of family values are examples of how the political understanding of the evangelical tradition has negated its politics as the formation of a particular people constituted by participation in particular practices, located within the scriptural narrative.[17] Such assertions say nothing of a community whose narrative welcomes sinners as a sign of God's hope, who model relationships in light of Christ's faithfulness and who consider their primary belonging to that community baptized and formed in faithfulness to Christ. The tradition is therefore unable to speak of Scripture as fundamentally changing the world, if by this we limit the scope of Scripture to a series of mere ideological assertions without the realization of a lived community.[18] In this place the evangelical appeal to Scripture's authority risks being detached from the cross as the central act of God's narrative and fails to observe the politics of the church as the ordering of its common life to the Lordship of Christ. Yoder reminds the church that 'Jesus' acceptance of the cross ... was dictated by a different vision of where God is taking the world (eschatological) ... dictated by a truer vision of what the world really is (ontological)'.[19]

The objectification of Scripture as authoritative text fails to recognize that, to both Jewish and early Christian, the reading of Scripture 'was as his or her own story' and it spoke of their place in the universe.[20] In their desire to articulate their politics by an appeal to universal reason and the absolute rule of God, evangelicals risk diminishing the very truthfulness which their tradition otherwise seeks to maintain. By reducing the ontology of the church to a series of well *reasoned* (a creative use of modern epistemological theory) ideas, the evangelical *use* of Scripture has consistently failed to recognize the church as that community of narrative by which the truthfulness of our discipleship *is* the appropriation of an alternative politics. In desperation to qualify our legitimacy within the construct of secular politics the evangelical tradition has surrendered an understanding of its central practices as the primary polity by which our life is formed as a response to God's revelation made real in the particularity of the church.[21]

The politics of the evangelical tradition has so frequently negated the practices of its central narrative in pursuit of a more universal politics that its methodology has rendered the evangelical use of Scripture ineffectual. In this context the politics by which evangelicals are alternatively known as a community faithful to the authority of Scripture will speak less of what we are opposed to and more of the kind of people we are by our participation in that narrative. The politics of Scripture offers participation in the narrative of the cross, shaping a community to understand truthfully a world in which Christ is Lord of all history, rather than causing a knee-jerk reaction to the emerging needs of that world. There ought not to exist any sense of separation between the narrative to which the church attends and the character of its witness.[22] The dissolving of this separation occurs in the very reading, hearing and reflecting upon Scripture as *authoritative and historical acts* located in the reality of God's covenanted people. At the heart of evangelical attentiveness to the authority of Scripture there remains a deep and profound acknowledgement of this approach. For within the evangelical tradition one can observe the truthfulness of those whose struggle and witness is testified to by the way they locate and participate in the struggle within the narrative of the church.

Genuine evangelical attentiveness to the authority of Scripture exposes the temporal nature of all other authorities, for the politics of the church are a penultimate sign of God's eternal kingdom. The claims of the church are not the ideological assertions of a particular system; rather, they are assertions of what we 'believe' in their describing a body formed in the likeness of Christ through participation in the central acts of its narrative.[23] The church speaks of itself as a community of the cross, and thus its truthfulness is witnessed in its capacity for suffering and its being formed through attentiveness to one who is the Prince of Peace.[24] The political narrative of the church thus differs from its secular counterpart in that the intelligibility of its speech is not based upon the anthropological, or the autonomy of human experience, but rather the theological, as it locates the truthfulness of its witness in Christ. The politics of the evangelical tradition is evidenced much less (even if this goes mostly unrecognized) in its quiet, repeated attentiveness to the hearing of Scripture than in the orientating of its life towards an authority wholly alien to that of the secular state.

The politics of narrative cannot be rejected as merely unrealistic, for in attending to Scripture as authoritative we are called to recognize that Christ is the Lord of all history. The attentiveness and submission of the evangelical tradition is the habitual questioning of that which is termed to be 'real'. The formation of the church is not, then, the instantaneous response (conversion) to a new idea, however radical that idea might be, but rather a surrender to participation in that community in whom God is most fully revealed; it is surrender to a new politics which exposes the folly of the old, for to live truthfully requires the continued participation in the becoming of a new creation.[25] In failing to recognize our politics as the continued narrative of the church requiring a participation in a lived witness, evangelicals negate the authority of Scripture as that narrative in which all of creation is orientated towards the cross of Christ. To reduce Scripture to the rhetoric of ideological assertions reduces its authority to the image of ourselves, and such abstraction might justify endlessly differing political ends, while concurrently rendering the church weak and incapable of recognizing the political complexities of the world in which it participates. In attending faithfully to the authority of that narrative, evangelicals participate in the hearing and seeing of the other, for it is here that they 'remember God's care for Israel'.[26] The authority of Scripture should orientate the church and in so doing witness to the appropriation of God's authority. The narrative of Scripture is the politics of the church speaking truthfully by locating the present within God's time; the narrative to which we belong is as such a 'particular pattern of presence in the world'.[27] We must learn to sit much more comfortably with the alleged limitations of such a place, for these are not limitations but rather reminders of God's grace.

In taking seriously the genuine authority of Scripture the evangelical understanding of the political ought, therefore, to be evidenced in those communities that participate in such practices as friendship with the stranger, love of the weak and vulnerable, patience in suffering, as exemplified nowhere more clearly than in our continued celebration of Christ's death and resurrection.[28] From this place, any subsequent articulation of broader political issues might be considered intelligible in its making sense of the world through the exemplification of a given community. The truthfulness of the church is then discerned in its ability to tell of a people formed in the loving service of Christ, for this is the story of the church in which

Scripture maintains the authority of the church's particularity. Understanding our locatedness within the narrative of Scripture as the central politics of the church is an open narrative in which the universality of its vision derives from confidence in the particularity of its practices. The church is able to affirm the cry of the oppressed not because of any universally intelligible account of rights but rather because, through repeated participation in its most central practices, one is formed in welcoming the other as a gift to be nurtured and cherished. It is through our submission to the God who orders all history and liberates all people from their oppression that such a mode of being is both intelligible and possible. In song, prayer and feasting such things move from being either simple ideas or grand imperatives to being the appropriation of God's reality. In the beauty and truthfulness of its being, the church does not point to an ideal beyond itself but rather is the truth of God's kingdom coming. This is no small sectarian gesture to set us over and against society, but rather participation in the ordering of our history. There is to be no domination here, but in humility and obedience, we are to state, 'This is all I know'; utterances other than this surely rob the world of our being God's continued giving, a robbery aspirations to universal grandeur can hardly justify.

Evangelicals must be aware that we do not make Scripture intelligible, but that our witness is made intelligible by its being located within the fullness of the scriptural narrative. The truthfulness of Scripture claims and narrates the politics of the church, not *vice versa*, and the church joyfully and humbly participates in the fullness of God's revelation. Such locatedness requires of the church our participation in the practices of that narrative as the continued telling of God's love for the world. Such participation will require that evangelicals relearn to be political in a manner utterly alien to the politics of the world.

Political autonomy and the body of the church

The story of the evangelical revival is a narrative which has been devastatingly distorted in the service of external political goods, not least those autonomous interests of the Enlightenment which have been identified as central to the project of industrial capitalism. It is in the brutality of capitalist modernity that one witnesses the cruelty of a political system which perpetuates the autonomy of the individual,[29] a cruelty which the evangelical emphasis on the self, when reduced to notions of individual piety, has all too easily perpetuated. This distortion clearly evidences how evangelical scholars commonly narrate the subject of the evangelical revival to be that of the individual 'self' and the 'self's emancipation' before God. The language of individual autonomy and personal piety, exemplified through appeal to personal experience and private conversion as the verification of our reason, has a crippling dominance within a tradition in which considerations of the political are often subsequently dismissed as 'private'.[30]

Evangelicalism ought to require the rejection of such individuality, instead recognizing the truthfulness of its account of that collective (the church) whose unity is the appropriation of our worshipping the triune God. The evangelical revival is the story of those persons who, having been made autonomous by the emerging trends of liberal and industrial Enlightenment, recovered truthfulness in their eccle-siology. In their participation in the body one might identify what they did and were together as neighbours and friends in the face of that oppression. It is the story of a people captivated by truth and formed in their unity with one another as the appropriation of God's character.[31]

Within the evangelical tradition great emphasis is traditionally given to the need for individual conversion, inner holiness and a personal experience of the Holy Spirit, by which evangelical piety has repeatedly and tragically denoted the self in individualist and autonomous terms: 'my conversion, my discipleship, my faith, my God'. The practice and political assertions of the evangelical tradition have come to be dominated by those articulations best fitted to the pietistic service of individual ends all too reminiscent of the emerging capitalist economy.[32] It is sug-gested that the experience of the individual is distinct from, and superior to, those of others in its being recognized as a symbol of our personal piety, using language familiar within a free market economy. We determine the language of Christian faith as the projection of self in difference and opposition to the other, central tenets of an economic state based on competition and autonomy. We choose to adopt the language and assertions of the church in parallel to the political construct of free market consumer choice. Common rhetoric suggests that 'I may speak authorita-tively of that which I have experienced to be true'. The language of conversion is not concerned with the revelation of God's new creation but the mere differentiat-ing of individual preferences and opinions which label my holiness as distinct from another's sinfulness.[33]

In sharp contrast to this picture of individual autonomy, attentiveness to the pol-itics of the church as narrative suggests that there are fragments of hope within the evangelical tradition which reflect a picture of the church as a collective unity, through which the self might most truthfully be known. The evangelical revival, through its attentiveness to the personal as the subject of God's love and mercy, enabled and encouraged a recovery of the self before God as self.[34] What we must continue to resist is the notion that 'personal' equates to 'private'; few understand-ings could be further from that truth we call trinity. It is in our being before Christ, through participation in the Christian narrative, that the self paradoxically recog-nizes absolute dependence on the other as our glorification of the triune God. Yoder writes:

> Jesus doesn't know anything about radical personalism. The personhood which he proclaims as a healing, forgiving call to all is integrated into the social novelty of the healing community. ... The idea of Jesus as an individual-ist or a teacher of radical personalism could arise only in the context that it did, that is in a context which, if not intentionally anti-Semitic, was at least sweep-ingly a stranger to the Jewish Jesus.[35]

In contrast to the distortions outlined above, the polity of the evangelical revival spoke profoundly of the self as being of ultimate value and thus capable of participation in the establishing of an alternative politics as our humble response to the revelation of God's grace. The significance of such a reinterpretation and its recovery of the self before God is easily lost for those who no longer work under the tyranny of early industrialization commonly experienced by many subjects of the evangelical revival. The evangelical attentiveness to the individual is, in its most truthful form, an appropriation of God's love as always personal but never as private. It is the participation of the self with the other in the giving of glory to God which constitutes the church as the body of Christ in its being the image of the triune God. It is in the locating of the self in communion with the other that the church as the body of Christ constitutes an alternative politics and thus bears a visible witness to the presence of Christ.

Such a reconfiguration of the self in the evangelical tradition will be opposed by those who suggest that the origins of evangelicalism did little but perpetuate the individualistic and autonomous nature of the Enlightenment. It is argued that the language of blessings and salvation were reduced to notions of autonomous rights and individual liberty. These shifts should be identified as a negation of the truthfulness of the tradition in the midst of which one evidences a worshipping body as the ultimate appropriation of the self.[36]

The nervousness which surrounds our understanding of the self is central to the political vision of the evangelical tradition and a reminder that the *polis* of the church stands in contrast to those individualist and autonomous assertions which dominated the liberal political thought of the Enlightenment. It is right that an evangelical understanding of the self stands within and bears witness to the body of Christ as the politics of the church. It is a symbol of our truthfulness that those who in their collective worship experience an account of the self before God also experience a profound disparity between such an account and the modern assertions of individual autonomy. The loss of such disparity is a mark of the evangelical tragedy and a denial of Christ's authority; it is this which an evangelical recovery of the political must overcome.

Overcoming such distortion is possible if the evangelical tradition recovers an understanding of its body politic as the performing of faith. That is to say that the truthfulness of its unity as the image of one who reveals God's self as trinity *is* our participation in the practices of that tradition. The body politic of the church witnesses to the truthfulness of the Christian narrative when in singing, praying, gathering and feasting, the tradition locates the self in the fullness and particularity of God's time. This is the appropriation of an alternative politics.[37] The distortions of evangelicalism which I refute gain their energy by reducing an evangelical understanding of the self to a series of ideas or epistemological assertions regarding a person's autonomy; what attentiveness to the lived narrative of the church reveals is that the truthfulness of the tradition requires acknowledgement of its practices, for it is in these practices that the common life of the church is ordered.[38] The self of autonomous desire is not found at the heart of evangelical revivals but rather in the politics of the state. Here, it stands in contrast to the self made whole in worship of the triune God, for the modern self relies upon a negation of the other as obstructive to the interests of the self. The nature of Christian discipleship is distinctly unsettling, for it speaks of the personal in terms unintelligible to those whose politics is based on a denial of God's reality, which in turn requires a distortion of the self as something other than the image of God. It is here that the politics of the evangelical tradition is good news.

What is required of evangelicals, if we are to recover the truthfulness of the self, is participation in those acts which constitute the collective retelling of that narrative which both recognizes and requires the primacy of the church as the collective image of Christ's body.[39] This retelling necessarily involves the church's continued re-orientating of itself in light of the cross, and is thus the witness to an alternative politics which rejects violence and embraces the other even unto the point of suffering and death. Such a polity recognizes an appropriation of that self in its most truthful form. We are most fully who God created us to be when our actions are an appropriation of God's reality; this is not a place which denies the self but rather speaks most truthfully of the self. Those acts which evidence the continued character of the church as essentially dependent upon one's capacity for the other hold the appropriation of the self in God's narrative as a gift before that modern politics in which the self is always autonomous. It is in the unity of the church that the character of its *polis* reflects the dependency of one upon the other – the one might revel in the fullness of that other. Such practices ought not be concerned with individual taste but with our participating in the narrative of the church enriched by others throughout generations. It is here that the body politic of the church bears witness to the truthfulness of Christ in light of a secular politics concerned with reducing ethics to the level of preferential taste.

The *polis* of the church does not perceive or experience the other as a problem to be overcome, but rather as a very sign of God's hope and presence. A genuine politics of the self is that of an open church grounded in the hospitality and friendship of its common practices. Evangelicals have been strong in their articulation of Christ's salvation as personal; where the personal has become private the tradition has failed to reflect the glory of God revealed in the trinity and must be resigned to the limitations of a secular politics alien to the body of Christ. This is not the narrative of the church but a Christianization of a secular politics. Such an experience will unquestionably be unnerving for the confident arrogance of personal piety which guards us from that vulnerability necessary for a more truthful account of the self. Yet the nervousness which evangelicals experience in their recovery of the body politic is a gift of God, for it guards them from a desire to lose the self, either within the fictitious mass of society or in the abundance of ego, which has for too long crippled its political imagination.

Political ends and the pursuit of that which is holy

I now turn to our understanding of the tradition's orientation towards the holiness of God. I appeal to a consideration of church as that community of the cross which seeks the intelligibility of its witness in the suffering of its saviour. It is in the cross of Christ that one observes the perfection of God's kingship and the establishment of an alternative politics to that of violence. In appealing to the cross of Christ as the central act of all history, in which every act of the church seeks its truthfulness, we assert something other than 'philosophical curiosity', for it is 'a necessary expression of the conviction that God has worked in past history and has promised to continue thus to be active among us'.[40] The politics of those who confess the holiness of Christ is the politics of Christ's revelation as the naming, moving and describing of all history.[41] It is that event in which all history has its meaning. The discipleship of the church is an attempt to live in the fullness of that meaning. A politics orientated towards that which is holy marks not only the inspiration of the church but also its obedience in sharing in Christ's destiny. It is in this manner that the politics of the church embraces the suffering of the cross as its ultimate and immediate reality.[42]

The polity of the church, experienced within the evangelical tradition's emphasizing of Christ's holiness and the church's need for sanctification, recognizes the character of its discipleship as that which is formed not in the pursuit of reason but in faithfulness to Christ who is holy. The evangelical tradition maintains strong emphasis on the centrality of the church as both a gathered and a worshipping community, for in its worship the church names its being in the body of Christ, which is the assertion and the description of our reorientation towards the cross of Christ.[43] Such an affirmation requires our continuous confessing of the sinfulness of the tradition, for it describes not only the direction of the church, but also the very character of the journey which makes such claims intelligible. The gathered confession of our sinfulness seeks confidence, forgiveness and healing in our confessing the holiness of Christ.[44] It is precisely because the church confesses faith in Christ that it bears witness to the forgiveness of sin through which one might begin to speak of that sin in intelligible terms; for to say that evangelicals recognize the character of their polity as dependent on Christ in this manner is to recognize that the fullness of our being comes only as gift of Christ's revelation. That such character is marred by its sinfulness is recognition of our dependency upon Christ, who comes to the world not as reformer of our ideas but as saviour. Such a suggestion may appear to be little more than a description of the obvious for the direction of the church, as the character of its community is surely in service of Christ. Yet the evidence of the church's recent history appears to suggest that, in terms of our understanding the church as political, it is precisely the obvious which has become lost or confused, for to state that the practices of the church as political are an appropriation of Christ's truthfulness is to say something particular about both Christ and the church.

Christ does not exist as the enhancement of those political goods which might be known without reference to him. Rather, we receive by grace the revelation of Christ's truthfulness as the absolute political reality of the universe. It is Christ who both judges and redeems all history. It is this sense of particularity that the evangelical tradition has consistently aimed to recover in its articulation of the church as that community the character of whose witness is bound up in its striving for holiness. Holiness is not, then, the pietistic self-interest of certain individuals in their attaining of increasingly middle-class norms; it is rather the capacity of the church to live peaceably because its very truthfulness comes only through its being in one who died on a cross. For the life of the church to be ordered by its pursuit of that which is holy stands in contrast to a politics of reason and rationality in which coercion inevitably merits violence. For to be ordered by Christ's holiness is to recognize the truthfulness of the cross as exposing the deceit of violence; or the truthfulness of our concern for the welfare of the neighbour or the nation as exposing the folly of capitalist reform; or the sacrifice of patient suffering as exposing the limits of medicine; or the truthfulness of poverty as exposing the depravity of wealth. These are not disciplines which one discerns as the only remaining option for the church, but are rather virtues of that character formed through its being in the first and the last servant of Christ.

Simplicity, charity or patience do have merit in themselves and ought to be nurtured in society at large, but each comes to the church in its being ordered only by the cross. We speak of these things in their being signs evidenced in the beauty of the church which is but foolishness to the Greeks:

> What matters about such a deed is not the changes it immediately brings about in the social order, nor the people who it pushed into a different position than they wanted to hold, but what it signifies. ... Sometimes there is a word that needs to be said, in the confidence that it is our Lord and his Holy Spirit and not we and our eloquence who will make of our sign a message.[45]

The church born in service of Christ thus seeks the character of its witness not in matters of survival or even in the attainment of 'best results', for these are but a hindrance to the imagination of our faithfulness, but rather in its ability faithfully to speak of and act like the one in whom its service is truth.[46] It is this particularity which holds the church in sharp contrast to secular notions of the political for the ends of liberal modernity, such as the pursuit of freedom and justice without reference to their necessary communities of practice. This is the continuous alluding to that which cannot possibly be fully known, for it negates the substance of a given particularity necessary for the intelligibility of its claims. In contrast the signs of the church offer a full account of our reality before God, for we are free from the political oppression which is modernity. Our very participation in the witness of the church reminds us that Christ, not the church, is saviour of the world; to perform within that salvation is but a reminder of God's grace.[47]

The evangelical tradition has all too often come to the service of the state, largely as the misguided result of its own insecurity and vulnerability. In doing so the tradition ceases to recognize the primacy of Christ, as the actualization of an alternative politics, and the cross of Christ, as the truthfulness of its discipleship, in which church practices gain their intelligibility. It is perceived as insufficient to reject the means of violence as a people ordered by the exemplification of one who overcame violence in the suffering of the cross; instead one is encouraged to take a more realistic account of the political. Realism functions as an elaborate disguise for the church's lack of faithfulness. In contrast, I suggest that the realistic politics of the church ordered by the particularity and authority of Christ's revelation liberates the church to become communities of peace-making, patient care, abundant joy and passionate faithfulness – practices constituted by their locating the church as living in God's time and towards God's self always as the holy other. This is not causal: Christians do not witness to that which is holy in order that they might secure this world, but because they are people formed in their appropriation of Christ's death and resurrection.[48] The dominance and pessimism of that which is considered 'real' fails to recognize Christ-like discipleship as the political reality of the church in which our very character is ordered by the most real moment in history. Secular distortions of the political thus continue in their coercing of the church toward a good other than that of its saviour, in whom the very breath of the church is intelligible.

While secular political theorists will argue at length over complex political theory, all of which seeks to establish an understanding of the political from within the present political structures, the evangelical tradition must ensure that the political character of its witness continues in its appropriation of that which is holy. This means that, above all else, the tradition must cease regarding the holiness of God's revelation as an ideal, as the cross of Christ ought, in the life of the church, to be normative.[49] The claims of the present *polis* ought to be discerned as alien and unintelligible to the church's witness. An understanding of such holiness requires that the language and actions of the church are formed through its worship of God as that time and place in which the church realizes the fullness of that for which it has been created. The evangelical tradition will thus speak of hope in suffering and life for the dead because this is that to which it witnesses in the life of Christ and thus in the life of the church. Such claims are not to be understood as distinct from the life of the church. They require recognition of the central practices of the church as the appropriation of an alternative politics in which the Christian life is so formed to be holy. For those within the evangelical tradition I suggest that such recognition might first involve a vulnerable recognizing of the extent to which we have neglected our attending to the central practices of the church as the primary polity through which the truthfulness of Christian discipleship is formed.

Notes

1 Yoder considers it the central tragedy of Constantinianism that Christians understand the political only first by their 'assuming it is our business to make history come out right'. J. H. Yoder, *For the Nations: Essay Public and Evangelical*, Grand Rapids, MI: Eerdmans, 1997, p. 122.

2 I am reminded of Karl Barth, who, writing in the shadow of war, remained convinced that 'we are entitled and compelled to regard the existence of the Christian community as of ultimate and supremely political significance'. My purpose is to expound precisely how this might be so. See Karl Barth, 'The Christian Community and the Civil Community', in *Against the Stream*, London, SCM Press, 1954, p. 19.

3 Such trajectories are compounded by our consistent willingness to accept and embrace our Constantinian heritage as of benefit to the church's 'ultimate' purpose. For those

who question the relevance of earmarking our Constantinian heritage in a largely post-Christian environment, I draw attention to the continued role of the church in the armed forces and the highest levels of parliamentary life.

4   Note that 'politics' derives from the Greek word *polis*, meaning city, denoting the ordering of life within that city. Hauerwas perceives this ordering as 'a community's internal conversation with itself concerning the various possibilities of understanding and extending its life'. To this end he determines tradition to be crucial in 'providing the means for a community to discover the goods it holds in common'. S. Hauerwas, *A Community of Character*, Notre Dame, IN: University of Notre Dame Press, 1981, p. 61.

5   Yoder argues that the substantiation of the church as *polis* rests on the 'person of Christ', 'neighbor, teacher and servant, a person who in every act we must either confessor disavow; a person from whose full humanity must be tested every effort to state Christian ethical guidance in terms of norms and principles'. Yoder, *For the Nations*, p. 109. See also Hauerwas, *A Community of Character*, pp. 53ff.

6   Ibid., p. 55.

7   Forrester writes: 'Christians are not obsessed with the need to follow a detailed regime meticulously and well, they are passionate enough to take risks, break free, trust and above all, love.' D. Forrester, *Truthful Action: Explorations in Practical Theology*, Edinburgh: T&T Clarke, 2000, p. 17.

8   Hauerwas, *A Community of Character*, p. 51.

9   Ibid., p. 128.

10   One ought not to give up on the authority of Scripture but this authority also requires attentiveness to the narrative which constitutes the church community. See ibid., p. 60.

11   Yoder describes this as a failure to recognize that 'the unique alternative of the church is the functioning of the congregation under the spirit'. Yoder, *For the Nations*, p. 94.

12   Hauerwas denotes a need to move beyond the 'using' of Scripture. Hauerwas, *A Community of Character*, p. 55. The spiritualization of the church and thus of the political, is, according to Yoder, the Enlightenment's betrayal of the church 'denying that the newness of the gospel can take on flesh'. Yoder, *For the Nations*, p. 82.

13   Ibid., p. 84.

14   Ibid., p. 167.

15   'All politics should be judged by the character of the people it produces. The depth and variety of character which a polity sustains is a correlative of the narrative that provides its identity and purpose.' Hauerwas, *A Community of Character*, p. 51.

16   Hauerwas writes of this context that:

> Scripture is mined for concepts and images, which are claimed to be biblically warranted but have the effect of legitimizing the loss of any continuing engagement of a community with the biblical narratives. ... No image of God, no matter how rich, can substitute for the 'life giving power' which arises from a community's capacity to sustain the prophetic activity of remembering and reinterpreting the traditions of Yahweh.

> (Ibid., p. 59)

17   Commenting specifically on the distorted prioritizing of the nuclear family in contrast to the call of the disciples, Yoder writes:

> What matters is the quality of life to which the disciple is called. ... This lifestyle is different, not because of arbitrary rules separating the believer's behaviour from that of 'normal people', but because of the exceptionally normal quality of humanness to which the community is committed. The distinctness is not cultic, but rather a non-conformed quality of involvement in the life of the world. It thereby

continues an unavoidable challenge to the powers that be and the beginning of a
new set of social alternatives.

(J. H. Yoder, *The Politics of Jesus*, Carlisle, Paternoster Press, 1994, p. 37)

Hauerwas notes of the prohibition on adultery that it 'stems from the profoundest commitment of the community concerning the form of sexual life necessary to sustain their
understanding of marriage and family'. Hauerwas, *A Community of Character*, p. 70,
cf. pp. 196–229.

18 Ibid., p. 55.
19 Yoder, *The Politics of Jesus*, p. 210.
20 Ibid., p. 76ff.
21 I frequently engage with evangelicals who consider voting or lobbying an important
political act but regard their participation in the Eucharist, singing God's praise, praying
with thankfulness and confession or even being part of a church community as optional.
This is a devastating illustration of this argument.
22 Yoder, *For the Nations*, p. 41.
23 This idolatrous use of Scripture leaves Hauerwas cautious about some aspects of
liberation theology. See Hauerwas, *A Community of Character*, p. 53.
24 Yoder notes that the new society of the church is marked by its capacity for suffering,
caring, forgiveness, servanthood, sharing and drawing upon one another. It is this capacity for suffering which rejects the modern articulation of the political in terms of 'dilemmas and directions': it seeks not the illusory end of all suffering but 'God's suffering
servanthood with men in their suffering'. See Yoder, *For the Nations*, pp. 176, 101, 111.
25 In the revelation of God in the otherness of the world, Yoder identifies the ability of those
who do not locate themselves within the Christian community (particularly Tolstoy and
Gandhi's influence on Martin Luther King) to speak truthfully of Christ. Expounding the
unhelpfulness of our Constantinian assumptions, Yoder urges the church to recognize its
presence 'in the midst of the followers of non-Christian and post-Christian faiths' as a
constructive aid to this awakening. Ibid., pp. 88, 93, 151; cf. Yoder, *The Politics of Jesus*,
p. 240.
26 Hauerwas, *A Community of Character*, p. 53.
27 Yoder, *For the Nations*, p. 93.
28 Wells and Cavanaugh have made good progress in expounding such an understanding in
light of Hauerwas' and Yoder's early reflections. I suspect the place of many evangelicals is to make sense of such faithfulness outside of the academy. S. Wells, *God's
Companions: Reimagining Christian Ethics*, Malden, MA: Wiley-Blackwell, 2006;
W. T. Cavanaugh, *Torture and Eucharist*, Malden, MA: Blackwell, 1998.
29 See Elizabeth Kent, ch. 8, this volume.
30 Yoder recognizes those ecclesial movements which participate in the narrowing of
Scripture from the civic to the internal and individual as 'potentially, if not necessarily a
betrayal'. Yoder, *For the Nations*, p. 35.
31 Yoder argues that the 'integrity with which Christian ethics is concerned is not the perfection or the innocence of the individual Christian but the welfare of the neighbor. The concern ... is for rigorously refusing to be the cause of the neighbor's suffering.' Ibid., p. 110.
32 Some of these themes are explored in terms of eschatology by Greggs in this volume, ch.
11, 'Beyond the Binary'.
33 Central to Yoder's recovery of an evangelical witness is his rejection of such individual
autonomy which he observes as endemic to modernity and thus as distorting both the
scriptural narrative and the truthfulness of the church as a peoplehood. Yoder, *For the
Nations*, pp. 39, 92.
34 Yoder is right to assert that such a recognition of the self risks 'slipping over and taking
confidence in the adequacy of her or his interpretation'. Yet it is through our willingness

humbly to engage in such risks that the church remains mindful of God's Lordship over all things exemplified in the church. Ibid., p. 180; cf. p. 185.

35 Yoder, *The Politics of Jesus*, p. 108.
36 Yoder writes:

> Whereas other social groupings are by definition established around a shared self interest, so that their very structure causes them to be more self-seeking, the church is the one society in which the terms of membership make people less rather than more selfish. *By no means is this to say that the church is exempt from temptation, especially to the sins of pride and self-satisfaction. This is however not because of the confession of commitment to Jesus Christ but in spite of it.*
>
> (Yoder, *For the Nations*, p. 115, emphasis added)

37 Ibid., p. 57.
38 The great fear of tyranny is not in opposing ideas but in the performing of an alternative reality.
39 On the essential collectivity of the church recognized in the terms, 'royal priesthood', 'holy nation', 'chosen race' and 'God's own people'. See Yoder, *For the Nations*, p. 40.
40 Yoder, *The Politics of Jesus*, p. 232.
41 Ibid., p. 233.
42 Ibid., p. 124.
43 Yoder argues that even in his affirmation of the church's servanthood what is required is but a re-orientating towards the cross as the re-orientating of power. Ibid., p. 154.
44 Hauerwas argues that it is precisely this capacity for such virtues as forgiveness which name the authority of Scripture as that of a learned people capable of forgiving. It is this formation which marks the politics of the church as distinct from the politics of the world, for the latter functions 'under the illusion that power and violence rule history, assuming it has no need to be forgiven'. Hauerwas, *A Community of Character*, p. 69.
45 Yoder, *For the Nations*, pp. 122–3. The continued witness of the evangelical tradition pioneers acts which it knows to be intelligible only in their being signs of that which is more fully exemplified in their liturgical being of church. From an end to child labour in the nineteenth century to the disarming of gangs in the twentieth century, the acts of the church in the formation of unions or the emergence of street pastors comes as an extension of that which is appropriated in our remembrance of the Eucharist.
46 It is to this end that Barth's understanding of the relationship between the Christian community and the civil community argues in part that: 'As disciples of Christ, the members of his church do not rule: they serve. ... The church can only regard all ruling that is not a form of service, as diseased and never as a normal condition.' Barth, 'The Christian Community', p. 40.
47 Yoder, *The Politics of Jesus*, p. 18.
48 Ibid., p. 232.
49 That the social ethic of Jesus is normative for the church is a central feature of Yoder's task. See ibid., pp. 11, 97.

Select bibliography

Barth, K., *Against the Stream*, London: SCM Press, 1954.
Hauerwas, S., *A Community of Character: Towards a Constructive Social Ethic*, Notre Dame, IN: University of Notre Dame Press, 1981.
Hauerwas, S., *The Peaceable Kingdom: A Primer in Christian Ethics*, Notre Dame, IN: University of Notre Dame Press, 1983.

Yoder, J. H., *The Priestly Kingdom: Social Ethics*, Notre Dame, IN: University of Notre Dame Press, 1984.

Yoder, J. H., *Body Politics: Five Practices of the Christian Community Before the Watching World*, Waterloo, ON: Herald Press, 1992.

Yoder, J. H., *The Politics of Jesus*, Carlisle: Paternoster Press, 1994.

Yoder, J. H., *For the Nations: Essays Public and Evangelical*, Grand Rapids, MI: Eerdmans, 1997.

Chapter 13

A word about the Word

Building scriptural bridges with the Muslim community

Sarah Snyder

The Qur'an respectfully describes Christians and Jews as 'People of the Book' because of their commitment to Scripture: 'O People of the Book! You have no ground to stand upon unless you stand fast by the Law, the Gospel, and all the revelation that has come to you from your Lord' (Q5:68).[1] Most Christians share this commitment to Scripture, despite a quite different understanding of the nature and content of scriptural revelation. Evangelical prioritizing of the biblical text offers an important, often unrecognized, bridge in Muslim–Christian dialogue, and one in which the evangelical community could play a more substantial role.

According to the Qur'an, the Muslim community was encouraged to engage respectfully in discussion over Scripture with Jews and Christians. God commanded Muhammad: 'If you were in doubt as to what We have revealed to you, then ask those who have been reading the Book from your Lord (*rabbika*)' (Q10:94).[2] The qur'anic and biblical revelations are thought by Muslims to derive from a single heavenly book called the *Umm al-Kitāb*, meaning 'Mother of the Book'.[3] In particular, the Qur'an names the torah (*tawrāt*) revealed to Moses,[4] the psalms (*zabūr*) given to David,[5] and the gospel (*Injīl*) revealed to Jesus,[6] and describes these earlier revelations as 'the Word of God', 'the Book of God', 'Guidance and Light', 'the Criterion (between right and wrong)' and 'the testimony of God.'[7] The Qur'an, it seems, recognizes divine revelation as a recurring, rather than a once-for-all, means of divine communication,[8] declaring: 'It is He Who sent down to you (step by step), in truth, the Book, confirming what went before it; and He sent down the Law (of Moses) and the Gospel (of Jesus) before this, as a guide to mankind' (Q3:3a).

This chapter explores differences in Christian and Muslim understanding of the Word of God and its relationship to Scripture. It hopes to prompt conversation, over Scripture, between Christian and Muslim, through shared testimony and deeper exploration of the relevance of God's Word in today's fractured world. Relationship with an 'other' lessens misunderstanding and fear, and, surprisingly, may even enable us to see ourselves and our relationship to God in new and exciting ways. Questions from those who read the biblical text for the first time can challenge and enrich our faith, and help us articulate deeply held beliefs in a fresh and accessible manner. Evangelicals have, perhaps rightly, been criticized for their lack of engagement with the Muslim community, yet without a relational foundation how can the church realistically hope to share the gospel with its Muslim neighbours? Many evangelicals are unaware of the extremely high Muslim view of scriptural authority. The challenge to read Scripture with each other – that is, to read Bible and Qur'an – is beyond the comfort zone of most Christians and Muslims, but is a vital bridge towards effective communication between the two communities.

Jews, Christians and Muslims share the view that the Creator God[9] speaks to his creatures, and that his utterances are in some way recorded in writing for our benefit. Revelation in this instance is verbal, involving words, spoken and written, communicated from the divine to the human realm. While members of all three monotheistic faiths recognize other ways in which God communicates – by his supernatural acts, in particular by creation, for example – Scripture is unique in being the locus of revealed words. There is a relationship, though variously understood, between God's eternal Word and the words of Scripture, giving Scripture an authority that other books do not share.

What is 'Scripture'?

The concept of 'Scripture' is not, however, universally understood. Christians and Muslims risk misunderstanding one another when they try to fit the 'other' into their own categories. While many in the West understand Scripture (Latin, *scriptura*, meaning 'a writing') as synonymous with Bible, the Greek *ta biblia* is a translation of the Hebrew *ha-s'farim*, meaning 'the books' – the name given to the Jewish sacred writings as early as the second century BC.[10] Indeed, as late as the second century AD, the 'Bible' of the Christian church *was* the Jewish Scriptures. The Scriptures were heard, not read, by the majority – only a privileged few possessed the necessary skills to read them. Centuries of emphasis in the West on Scripture as written word has lost sight of the primarily oral foundations of divine revelation.

Many believing Christians and Muslims do not draw such a distinction between that which is 'fixed' as text and the dynamic vitality of the spoken word of God. Rather they desire to hear God speak through the written word. The author of Hebrews declares that: 'the word of God is living and active, sharper than any two-edged sword, piercing until it divides soul from spirit, joints from marrow; it is able to judge the thoughts and intentions of the heart' (Heb. 4:12). At a very early stage in Islamic history, Muhammad b. Idrīs al-Shāfi'ī (*d.* 820 CE) described how the Qur'an concerns everything and contains, explicitly or implicitly, solutions to all the problems of human life at present and in the future.[11] Thus, Muslims and Christians, on the whole, share the view that God's speaking, as recorded in Scripture, is not a once-upon-a-time historic event, but a continuous, timeless speaking just as 'present' today as it was in the past. There is, in other words, some correlation between the divine, eternal Word of God, and the written words of Scripture. The exact nature of this correlation is differently understood by each community, but most evangelicals agree that what Scripture says, God says. The biblical reader or listener is hearing God speak, not merely the words of the human authors. This is possible because of the action of God's Holy Spirit, working not only within the original authors to ally their perspective with the divine, but also subsequently in the hearts and minds of readers and listeners, opening their eyes and ears to that which is beyond mere human understanding. The fact that the Bible contains 66 books, temporally and spatially diverse, with countless authors, scribes and editors, is subsumed by belief in its overall unity – one Scripture, one author, one Word.

The New Testament authors understood the words of the Hebrew Scriptures to be synonymous with the words of God.[12] The author of Romans, for example, states clearly that the Jews 'were entrusted with the oracles of God' (Romans 3:2), no doubt a responsibility as much as a privilege. The Old Testament (Hebrew Scriptures) is also replete with references to 'the Word of God (or the Lord)' as a category within which individual writings are subsumed. Psalm 119 uses the word *dabhar* or *imra* (God's word, singular) 42 times when referring to a wide range of biblical material, from *torah* (law) to testimonies and commandments.[13] The Bible, in other words, refers to itself as a single entity with a divine source, not as a collection of human documents.

Many evangelicals affirm the Bible not just as a book containing the words of God, but as the Word of God, understanding it word-for-word as the speech of God, recorded by humans. Evangelical use of the term 'dictation' has been misunderstood in the past, for it does not concern a mechanical conveyance of words from God to man, and bears little similarity to Muslim understanding of this process. Rather, it speaks of an assurance that the words of human authors were written under divine guidance such that they fully and accurately represent the words of God. Jesus himself inspires confidence in such a view when he declares that 'it is easier for heaven and earth to pass away, than for one stroke of a letter in the law to be dropped' (Lk. 16:17).[14] In his mind, it seems, as in the minds of the New Testament authors, every word of the Hebrew Law was synonymous with the Word of God.

Such a concept is deeply challenging and mysterious and, from a human perspective, seemingly impossible. How could the eternal Word of the almighty God in any way be 'captured' or confined by human language? The potential for misrepresentation in translation between human languages is immense, let alone the possibilities for misunderstanding divine-to-human communication. Yet while Christian understanding recognizes some human element within this communication, the Muslim understanding does not. The Qur'an, for Muslims, literally is the very speech of God. No human hand played any part in altering the words first revealed in Arabic to the Prophet Muhammad. Still today, the only true language of qur'anic revelation is classical Arabic. Even those who no longer understand it are encouraged to recite the Arabic Qur'an, preferably by memory. Its rhythmic beauty has a powerful impact on those who listen, and this, Muslims believe, is a miraculous feature of the Qur'an.

Christians, by contrast, believe that it is only by the action of God's Holy Spirit that humans can begin to grasp the meaning of Scripture. The languages in which the words were originally recorded are less important than the ability to understand them, and reformers such as Wycliffe risked their lives to communicate the biblical message in the vernacular. Hence, we discover the evangelical motivation for continuous translation of the Bible, not only to the mother tongue of each community, but to the most up-to-date use of those languages so that the Bible is accessible to all.[15]

Scripture's relationship to the eternal Word of God

Questions about the relationship between the eternal Word of God and the human language of Scripture have challenged generations of thinkers. During the early years of Islam, a controversy raged between those who declared that the words contained in the Qur'an could not be the very words of God, for they are created – spoken and written down in the human realm – and those who maintained that every word is divine. During the reign of the ninth-century caliph Al Ma'mun, the chief justice, Ibn Abu Du'ad, was from the Mu'tazila school which claimed that the Qur'an was not the actual, eternal, words of God (i.e. uncreated), but rather created by God. The prevailing view at the time, championed by Ahmad Ibn Hanbal, was that the Qur'an was indeed uncreated, and the very essence of God's word. The Mu'tazilites believed such a claim compromised the unity of God – for God is one with no other besides him.[16] Their opposition claimed that any suggestion that the Qur'an was created puts it in the human rather than the divine realm, thus divesting it of all authority. During the resulting 'inquisition of the creation of the Qur'an' (*mihnat khalq al-Qur'ān*) the Mu'tazilites were defeated. Still today, the prevailing Muslim view is that the Arabic Qur'an is the very Word of God. Its text is eternal and does not change according to differing contexts. The Muslim American Society records:

> The Qur'anic words should be attached to their meanings forever if they are to be eternal. Otherwise, they would be dated human conventions that become obsolete as soon as their meanings shift in the flux of time and space. Rather than conveying something eternal, they would then point to something that once was and is no more.[17]

Challenges to this view have re-appeared in modern times, and one qur'anic verse is often at the centre of such discussions, translated as follows:

> It is not fitting for a man that Allah should speak to him except by inspiration, or from behind a veil, or by the sending of a Messenger to reveal, with Allah's permission, what Allah wills: for He is Most High, Most Wise.
>
> (Q42:51)

This verse describes the manner in which the revelations passed from the divine to the human realm as *wahy*, a form of non-verbal communication often translated as 'inspiration'. Abu Zayd, a reforming Muslim scholar whose ideas are not accepted by the majority, interprets this verse as identifying not just one, but three ways in which God communicates with man: by inspiration, *or* from behind a veil *or* by sending a messenger. The first channel, inspiration, is a general form of non-verbal communication. The second channel, from behind a veil, is the mysterious way in which God spoke directly to Moses out of the bush and on the mountain.[18] The third channel, Abu Zayd argues, is the manner in which the Qur'an was revealed, whereby a mediator, the angel Gabriel, communicated God's speech, *kalām Allāh*, to Muhammad by *wahy*, non-verbal communication. In this instance *wahy* is not, therefore, synonymous with God's actual speech (*kalām*).

Abu Zayd pointed out that the previous Scriptures of Jews and Christians were also revealed by *wahy*: it is not a means that is unique to quranic revelation, but the way in which God generally reveals his Word to humans.[19] The qur'anic message was given to Muhammad in 'clear Arabic', claims Abu Zayd, because God wants to communicate clearly with his creatures in the language of those to whom he sends a messenger. The Qur'an records God's words on the subject: 'We did not send a Messenger except (to teach) in the language of his (own) people, in order to make (things) clear to them' (Q14:4). Hence the biblical Scriptures were also given in their own languages. According to this logic, while fully accepting the Qur'an as the Word of God, Abu Zayd denies that 'the Qur'an presents *literally* and *exclusively* the Word of God'.[20] He goes on to argue that it is through recitation that the Qur'an represents a domain of communication where both God and humans meet. Initially this was through the Prophet Muhammad, whose voice conveyed the Word of God in human form. Through ritual recitation the language of the Qur'an has subsequently infiltrated everyday language, for example in greetings and in prayer.[21]

Fazlur Rahman, another reforming Muslim scholar, also differentiated between the Word of God and the human language in which his Word is expressed. Like Abu Zayd, he argued that the Qur'an was revealed by God in response to the particular needs and circumstances of its recipients. Revelation, he proposed, was determined by the socio-historical context in which Muhammad lived. While its source lay in the transcendent realm, the actual utterances were influenced by the Prophet himself.[22] While this view is, in itself, revolutionary in mainstream Islamic thinking, the notion that the contexts of revelation aid in understanding the meaning of the Qur'an is not disputed. Knowledge of *asbāb al nuzūl* (the occasions of revelation) has always played a role in qur'anic interpretation. While the first revelations to Muhammad were totally unexpected, the remainder were revealed in response to circumstances in Mecca and Medina. Knowledge of these circumstances is all the more important because the revelations recorded in the Qur'an are not given in the order in which the Prophet received them. According to tradition, their order was directed by Muhammad under the guidance of the angel Gabriel. One area where the chronology of revelation becomes important is the theory of abrogation. This states that a later qur'anic verse can supersede an earlier one, which has important legal implications.[23] The occasion of each revelation is also considered when applying legal principles to modern contexts, and to aid in understanding the meaning of individual verses. It cannot, however, be compared to the historical-critical methods of biblical scholarship so prevalent in the West since the Enlightenment. While, in practice, faithful readers of the Bible and Qur'an share the hermeneutical challenge of bridging the gap between the original context of revelation, and their own, the ways in which they approach it are very different. Christian acknowledgement of the human element in authoring the Bible permits greater freedom in exploring the historical context of its authors. Muslim belief in the divine dictation of the Qur'an prevents such analysis.

Qur'anic revelation

Muslims view the Qur'an as the verbatim words of God, spoken through the lips of the Prophet Muhammad (God's messenger, *rasūl*) yet unaffected in any way by Muhammad himself. Christians often misunderstand this concept, suggesting that Muhammad was the qur'anic author. In fact, Muslims believe, every word of the Qur'an was revealed to the Prophet via the angel Gabriel (Jibrīl) from when he was 40 years of age (609 CE) until his death in 632 CE. Tradition reinforces the view that this illiterate prophet was a passive recipient of revelation, in which the Word of God was literally placed in his mouth to enable communication to a human audience. The thirteenth-century mystic Jalāl al-Dīn al-Rūmī, described it thus: 'Men have fashioned ... birds of stone, and out of their mouths the water comes and pours into the pool. All possessed of reason know that the water does not issue out of the mouth of a stone bird, it issues out of another place.'[24] Likewise, Rūmī confirmed: 'It was [the Prophet's] tongue that spoke; but he was not there at all, and the speaker in reality was God.'[25] Tradition records the way in which the Prophet first received these revelations, narrated by 'Aisha, one of his wives. He was meditating in a cave when the angel appeared unexpectedly and asked him to read. Being illiterate, he replied, "I do not know how to read."' The Prophet added:

> The angel caught me (forcefully) and pressed me so hard that I could not bear it anymore. He then released me and again asked me to read, and I replied, 'I do not know how to read,' whereupon he caught me again and pressed me a second time till I could not bear it anymore. He then released me and asked me again to read, but again I replied, 'I do not know how to read (or, what shall I read?).' Thereupon he caught me for the third time and pressed me and then released me and said, 'Read: In the Name of your Lord, Who has created (all that exists).'[26]

On the face of it, similarities can be noted with the reaction of some biblical prophets as they first heard the Word of God. God told Jeremiah, for example:

> 'I appointed you [as] a prophet to the nations.' Then I [Jeremiah] said 'Ah, Lord God! Truly I do not know how to speak, for I am only a boy.' But the Lord

said to me, 'Do not say, "I am only a boy"; for you shall go to all to whom I send you, and you shall speak whatever I command you.'

(Jer. 1:5b–7)

Deuteronomy 18 records God's words through Moses, concerning the manner in which he will speak through future prophets:

I will put my words in the mouth of the prophet, who shall speak to them every-thing that I command. Anyone who does not heed the words that the prophet shall speak in my name, I myself will hold accountable.

(Dt. 18:18–19)

A crucial difference in Muslim and Christian understanding of prophecy, however, is the latter's acknowledgement of the human contribution. The author of 2 Peter offers powerful affirmation of this dual divine/human role: 'no prophecy of Scripture is a matter of one's *own* interpretation, because no prophecy ever came by human will, but men and women moved by the Holy Spirit spoke from God' (2 Peter 1:21). The Bible attests to the way in which God acts concursively with and through his creatures. Contrary to Western logic, human freedom to act or speak is not denied or compromised by God's freedom to do the same. The biblical authors were members of faithful, confessing communities for whom God's presence and direction was a daily reality. Thus, the spoken and written Word of God have a divine and a human source working in tandem, made possible by the action of God's Holy Spirit.

Muslims do not share this concept of dual authorship, though prophets are attributed a unique status as God's messengers by living lives entirely free of sin.[27] Muhammad is understood to be the last of the prophets, and the Qur'an records God reminding him of his biblical predecessors, who likewise suffered persecution and rejection for communicating the words of God. Episodes from the lives of the biblical prophets are recounted in the Qur'an, and bear close resemblance to the biblical narratives, though their inclusion is to remind and to teach (a lesson) rather than as a historic record. Few Muslims see the need to read the Bible, and yet the fuller biblical narratives of the prophetic stories in the Qur'an offer helpful context, and were freely referenced by the earliest Muslim exegetes.[28] One of the greatest Muslim scholars, Al-Tabarī (839–923 CE), drew on biblical knowledge in his qur'anic commentary and his extensive history. He explored, for example, the identity of Abraham's supposed faults, suggesting three times in which Abraham lied.[29] The first two instances are given in the Qur'an (Sura 37:89 when he feigned illness in order not to worship idols, and Sura 21:63 when he denied destroying the idols), but the third, Tabarī takes from Genesis 12:13 when Abraham told Sarai to say she was his sister, not his wife.

The Qur'an continually affirms that it brings the same message preached by the previous (biblical) prophets.[30] Sura 42:13 declares:

The same Religion He has established for you as that which He enjoined on Noah – that which We have sent by inspiration to you – and that which We enjoined on Abraham, Moses, and Jesus: namely, that you should remain steadfast in Religion.

Interestingly, Sura 3:67 reminds us that 'Abraham was not a Jew nor yet a Christian; but he was true in Faith'. Muslims believe that all the biblical prophets were Muslim because they 'submitted to God'. Sura 2:112 supports this universal emphasis: 'whoever submits his whole self to Allah and is a doer of good he will get his reward with his Lord; on such shall be no fear nor shall they grieve.' The term 'Islam' means submission to God, and in this way Muslims understand the biblical prophets to have been followers of Islam, rather than uniquely Jewish (or Christian). The Qur'an therefore encourages Jews and Christians to accept its message: 'Oh you People of the Book! Believe in what We have (now) revealed, confirming what was (already) with you' (Q4:47).

Biblical revelation

Evangelicals traditionally hold a high view of the divine element in biblical authorship, maintaining that all Scripture is *theopneustos* (expired by God).[31] Christian understanding of this difficult term varies widely, but most evangelicals agree that God, in working through human authors, is not hampered by their sinful outlook or limited perception. Many express confidence that the words of Scripture are without human error or distortion, reflecting his perfect intention,[32] and eternal relevance.[33] Commenting on 2 Timothy 3:16, Calvin wrote: 'the Law and the Prophets are not teachings handed down at the whim of men or produced by human minds, but are dictated by the Holy Spirit', and concerning subsequent readers, he noted that 'only those who have been enlightened by the Holy Spirit have eyes to see what should have been obvious to all'.[34]

The subtle, but important, distinction between Muslim and Christian understanding of scriptural revelation is that the Qur'an contains the very words of God, while the Bible contains human words written under divine guidance. This is the cause of much misunderstanding between Muslims and Christians discussing Scripture. Even Muslims with a high regard for the Bible are suspicious of the human element in biblical authorship, arguing that distortions and errors inevitably crept in as humans tried to record the words of God.

The conviction that the words of Scripture are both fully divine, and yet fully human, also flies in the face of western logic. The New Testament writers, however, seemed less troubled by the distinction, referring to the Hebrew Scriptures sometimes as texts in which God is speaking, and other times to their human authors. Excerpts from the Psalms in the Book of Acts, for example, are attributed both to David (Acts 1:16) and directly to God (Acts 4:25). Is it possible that human authors wrote freely within their human capacity and understanding, and yet they wrote entirely that which God intended? Or is there inevitably some form of compromise in the suggestion that God's words are also human words?

Prevailing Greek theories of a higher and a human intellect influenced the Christian view of inspiration in which the human intellect is overtaken by the divine, such that it is God who speaks. Martin Luther declared:

> It is cursed unbelief and odious flesh which will not permit us to see and know that God speaks to us in Scripture and that it is God's Word, but tells us that it is the word merely of Isaiah, Paul or some other man who has not created heaven and earth.[35]

John Calvin stated:

> [The Apostles] were sure and genuine penmen of the Holy Spirit, and their writings are therefore to be considered oracles of God: and the sole office of others is to teach what is provided and sealed in the Holy Scripture.[36]

Were he referring to the Qur'an, many Muslims would be quite comfortable with his description.

In the post-Enlightenment period, when textual variants of biblical manuscripts were compared, the role of the human authors and recipients took priority, as witnessed by the growing importance of the historical-critical method. The notion that God might use sinful men to write his Word, opened the Bible to accusations of error.[37] A common response to this problem was the suggestion that God communicates truth through the overall message of Scripture,[38] not through the specific wording. Logically, humans are finite and cannot fully comprehend the divine, so God must communicate in terms that they are capable of understanding, especially through stories. Appealing as it appears, this view confines God's communicative potential to that of his creatures, and denies the role of his Holy Spirit in equipping humanity to see and hear beyond that which is humanly possible. While few would argue that humans can fully understand the mind of God, the idea that the Bible is a human shell in which the divine message is contained, implies that some biblical words carry greater authority than others. The Bible clearly contains many genres of writing, some of which appear to offer little in the way of spiritual nourishment, yet evangelicals insist that every word reflects the will and intention of God and is therefore included for a purpose.

The qur'anic view of the Bible

By contrast, the Qur'an does not consider the 'Scriptures' now in the hands of Jews and Christians to be a faithful representation of the revelations given to previous prophets. Rather, they have been subject to alteration (*tahrīf*) and change (*tabdīl*). A Western scholar of Islam explains:

> While it is stated [in the Qur'an] that Jesus received from God a Scripture called the Gospel (or Evangel – *Injīl*), there is nothing to suggest that this was

any more like our actual gospels in the New Testament than the *tawrāt* received by Moses was like the actual Pentateuch. Indeed Muslims usually deny that our actual gospels are the book received by Jesus, since that consisted entirely of revelations from God and not of historical statements about Jesus.[39]

Christians, of course, are in full agreement that the biblical gospels were not a 'revelation' to Jesus. It is Jesus himself who is the revelation, and the gospels declare the truth about him.[40] The Qur'an, however, is clear that the biblical Scriptures have been distorted by human hands, and contain errors over which the Qur'an stands as judge and corrector: 'Some of [the people of the Book] conceal the truth which they themselves know' (Q2:146); they 'conceal Allah's revelations in the Book' (Q2:174) and 'the transgressors among them changed the word from that which had been given them' (Q7:162).

While the Qur'an contains, *verbatim*, the very words of God, the previous Scriptures, in their altered (*muharrat*) forms, no longer possess this quality, but reflect instead the hearts and minds of their human scribes. In its favour, Muslims argue, the Qur'an was revealed to one man, the Prophet Muhammad, in one language, Arabic, in a tiny geographical location (Mecca and Medina), during a short period of time (23 years). It was written down and compiled in book form very soon afterwards, such that the oral revelations were recorded, it is claimed, exactly as given. Muslims believe this to be God's final revelation, superseding, yet in some ways also confirming, the previous revelations.

Word inlibrate[41] and incarnate

It has not gone unnoticed that Muslim understanding of the Qur'an as the written Word of God bears some resemblance to Christian understanding of Jesus Christ, the Word incarnate. Muhammad al-Ghazzālī (*d.* 1111 CE), a highly respected Muslim theologian, challenged Christian interpretation of the opening of John's gospel. He argued that the 'Word' mentioned in verses 1 to 4 refers not to Jesus but to God, or rather to his eternal attributes of knowledge and speech, while 'the Word ... made flesh' of verse 14 requires allegorical interpretation:

> at the beginning of the passage the expression 'the Word' is applied to the knower as dissociated from corporeality in fact, that is, to God; while at the end of the passage the same term is also applied to the knower or the speaker as possessing the attribute of corporeality in fact, that is to say, to God's Messenger [i.e. Jesus].[42]

The Qur'an describes Jesus as 'Word', but differences of opinion between Christians and Muslims over the meaning of this title are apparent as early as the eighth century. John of Damascus attacked Muslims for not believing that Jesus, the Word of God, is fully divine. His argument is, perhaps, reminiscent of Muslim discussions over the created or uncreated status of the Qur'an (see above):

Since you say that Christ is Word of God and Spirit, how is it that you revile us [Christians] as *Hetairiastai* [Associates, i.e. those who put another alongside God]? For the Word and the Spirit are not separated from the one in whom they are by nature. If therefore His Word is in God, it is evident that the Word is also God. But if the Word is outside of God, then according to you God is without reason and without life. And so, fearing to provide an Associate for God, you have mutilated Him.[43]

Only Jesus, and no other prophet, is entitled 'Word' in the Qur'an.[44] The angels tell Zachariah: 'Allah gives you the glad tidings of John, witnessing the truth of a Word from Allah ...' (Q3:39) and subsequently the angels inform Mary: 'Allah gives you glad tidings of a Word from Him: his name will be Christ Jesus' (Q3:45). Sura 4 explains: 'Christ Jesus the son of Mary was a Messenger of Allah, and His Word, which He bestowed on Mary, and a Spirit proceeding from Him ...' (Q4:171). The Arabic in this last verse signifies a particular 'Word' – God's – rather than just any word, while in the previous two verses, the term (*kalimatin*) is indefinite and follows the preposition 'from' (*min*) – 'a word from God' – thus, potentially, maintaining a distinction between Jesus and God. Western scholars of Islam have pointed out the strong echo with the Christian notion of *logos*,[45] but this is quite different from Muslim understanding of 'Word'. The opening of John's gospel refers to the eternal, creative Word that was present at the creation of the world and became incarnate in the person of Jesus. The gospel writer must have been aware of prevailing Greek ideas about *logos*. In Greek philosophy, it is the unifying principle between the perfect world of divine existence, and the imperfect physical world in which humans and all physical matter exist. The Jewish philosopher, Philo of Alexandria, whose ideas influenced later Christian theology, taught that the *logos* was the intermediary between God and the cosmos, in other words, between Creator and created. Seen in this context, the gospel writer appears to present Jesus as the creative link between God and humanity. Colossians 1:19–23 also records:

For in [Jesus] all the fullness of God was pleased to dwell, and through him God was pleased to reconcile to himself all things, whether on earth or in heaven, by making peace through the blood of his cross. And you who were once estranged and hostile in mind, doing evil deeds, he has now reconciled in his fleshly body through death, so as to present you holy and blameless and irreproachable before him – provided that you continue securely established and steadfast in the faith, without shifting from the hope promised by the gospel that you heard, which has been proclaimed to every creature under heaven.

In contrast to Muslim belief that the Qur'an is entirely divine, without any human essence, Christians view Jesus as both human and divine, bridging the divide between Creator and created.[46] This is important to Christian understandings of the purpose of Jesus – that he was revealed to rescue sinful humans from the consequences of their sin, which required that he was both human and divine. Muslims do not share the view of humanity's inherent sinfulness, rather they emphasize humanity's forgetfulness and lack of knowledge about how to respond to the Creator. The Qur'an is perceived as a guide, revealing God's will for mankind and showing his creatures how to submit to his sovereignty.[47]

Mainstream Islamic commentary understands Jesus' title of 'a Word from God' as a reference to the miraculous birth of Jesus – that he was brought into existence by God's creative word. Sura 3:47 explains that in response to Mary's question, 'how shall I have a son when no man has touched me?' the angel answered, 'Allah creates what He wills: when He has decreed a Plan, He but says to it, "Be!", and it is!' Mahmūd b. 'Umar al-Zamakhshari (d. 1143 CE) commented on Sura 3:39, saying : 'Jesus is designated as "the word of God" and as "a word of His" because he alone originated through the word and command of God rather than through a father and a sperm.'[48]

This is not the only interpretation of Jesus' title however. Different terms (amr and qawl) are used elsewhere in the Qur'an to describe the creative command of God,[49] prompting further exploration of the meaning of Jesus as 'Word'. Tabarī, for example, acknowledged the interpretation that Jesus was created by God's commandment 'be' (kun) and he became (fa-yakūn), but prefers to interpret 'Word' (kalima) as 'announcement' (bishara).[50] An announcement is, by definition, news of something previously unknown to its recipient. Usage of the verb 'to announce' (bashshara) in the Qur'an is for either good or bad news, but mainly refers to the announcement of the birth of a child (for example, to Abraham and Zachariah) and of the day of judgment, bringing reward for believers and punishment for others – in both cases announcing a future event.[51] The noun 'announcement' (bushrā) is always given in the context of good tidings, for example the winds God sends to bring rain, or the reward for believers at judgment day.[52] It is also used as a reference to the whole qur'anic revelation. Sura 27:1–2, for example, describes the Qur'an as 'Glad Tidings (bushrā) for the Believers'[53] and Sura 16:89 declares: 'We have sent down to you the Book explaining all things, a Guide, a Mercy, and Glad Tidings to Muslims (muslimin).' (Note that the Arabic for 'Muslims' here means those who submit to God, rather than the narrower definition we use today.) Such a title is not so far away from Christian understanding of Scripture, for 'Good tidings' is a translation of the Greek euangelion (Latin evangelium).

The point of tidings, be they good or bad, it seems, is not so much the announcement itself, but the response of those who hear it. It is only 'good tidings' for those who hear and believe, not for those who turn their backs. The question, of course, is whether the qur'anic tidings extend to Jews and Christians, or uniquely to Muslims.[54]

Tabarī's reference to Jesus' title as an announcement seems to be a description of the glad tidings about his birth given to Mary by the angel.[55] Another qur'anic commentator, Fakhr al-Din al-Rāzī (d. 1209 CE), says Jesus was called 'a word' because he was the *fulfilment* of the word spoken to the prophets.[56] Certainly, the qur'anic Jesus holds a unique place among God's messengers, and is one of the very few to whom God 'spoke'.[57] He could perform miracles, 'create' and 'give life'. Sura 3:49 records Jesus saying:

> I make [from the verb *akhluqu*, meaning 'create'] for you out of clay, as it were, the figure of a bird, and breathe into it, and it becomes a bird by Allah's leave: and I heal those born blind, and the lepers, and I quicken the dead, by Allah's leave; and I declare to you what you eat, and what you store in your houses. Surely therein is a Sign for you if you did believe.

While most of God's messengers were bearers of God's word, Jesus, it might be argued, actually spoke God's word. This implies a level of intimacy that few, if any, others had – that, at the very least, Jesus' purpose was to bring about the word, or will, of God on earth. The gospels also show Jesus speaking the word of God, especially as he performed miracles.[58] At his word, for example, the man with leprosy was healed (Mk 1:40–45); the sins of the paralysed man were forgiven (Mk 2:1–12); the storm stilled (Mk 4:35–41); and the hungry crowd of 5,000 had more food than they could eat (Mk 6:39–44).

Father Henri Lammens, a Belgian Jesuit and scholar of Islam, concluded that by speaking God's word, Jesus became an instrument of his revelation: 'Without doubt [Muhammad] simply wanted to suggest that the Messiah served as an instrument, an intermediary of divine revelation: this interpretation fits realistically with his understanding of prophecy.'[59] Colin Chapman, another Christian scholar of Islam, takes this further as he considers how Jesus' disciples might have responded to his words and actions: 'If Jesus spoke the words of God in performing these miracles, was not Jesus himself the Word of God? And if he is the Word of God, can he be separate from God Himself?'[60]

Nearly thirteen centuries earlier, John of Damascus articulated the view that God and his Word are of one essence, not two:

> For there never was a time when God was not Word: but He ever possesses His own Word, begotten of Himself, not, as our word is, without a subsistence and dissolving into air, but having a subsistence in Him and life and perfection, not proceeding out of Himself but ever existing within Himself. For where could it be, if it were to go outside Him? For inasmuch as our [human] nature is perishable and easily dissolved, our word is also without subsistence.[61]

Jesus' divinity is strongly refuted in the Qur'an, and by Muslims, who are keen to preserve the absolute unity of God and who misunderstand Christian talk of three 'persons'. Indeed Muslim and Christian claims about the status of Jesus lie at the heart of misunderstanding between the two communities. Most Muslims are convinced that Christians commit *shirk* (worshipping others besides God) in their adoration of Jesus, appalled at the suggestion that God himself begat a son.[62]

Equally, most Christians are unaware of the extreme reverence with which Muslims refer to Jesus, and the qur'anic acknowledgement of Jesus as God's Word, his spirit (Q4:171) and a mercy (Q19:21); of his miraculous birth and sinless life (Q19:19), in which he performed miracles (Q3:49) and healed the sick (Q5:110); of his ascension to heaven (Q4:158) and the promise that he will return again (Q43:61).

It is hoped that this chapter will stimulate further interest in exploring misunderstanding between Muslims and Christians. Faithful Christians and Muslims share, at least, the challenge of thinking and acting biblically/qur'anically in a world that rejects a God-centred outlook. Deeply held differences between the two communities need not prevent possibilities for discussion and friendship built around the shared reading of Scripture. The Qur'an encourages such engagement (Q10:94; 29:46), but is the church willing to respond?

Notes

1 See also, for example, Q5:47. All qur'anic citations are from the translation by A. Y. Ali, *The Qur'an: Translation*, New York: Tahrike Tarsile Qur'an, 2007. The more contemporary English translation by M. A. S. Abdel Haleem may be easier for the first-time reader, and also translates 'Allah', meaning *the God*, as 'God'.
2 See also the more challenging Sura 29:46.
3 Muslims doubt, however, the accuracy of parts of the Bible in use today; see below.
4 Q2:87 and 3.3.
5 Q4:163.
6 For example, Q3:3. This gospel, Muslims believe, was revealed to Jesus, and is therefore different to the four biblical gospels.
7 Examples can be found in Q2:53; 3:3; 5:44, 46; 6:91; 21:48; 28:43; 40:53.
8 W. Graham, 'Qur'an as Spoken Word', in R. Martin (ed.), *Approaches to Islam in Religious Studies*, Tucson: University of Arizona Press, 1985, p. 29.
9 While acknowledging the view that Muslims and Christians do not worship the same, trinitarian God, this article does not find this a helpful starting point in Muslim–Christian conversation. Muslims misunderstand Christian talk of the three 'persons' of the trinity, assuming Christians compromise the unity of the one God and thereby commit idolatry. However, shared reading of Scripture is a helpful way to focus discussions about the nature of God, and an opportunity to overcome such deep misunderstandings. The central role of Jesus Christ as the primary locus of revelation is discussed below.
10 Graham, 'Qur'an as Spoken Word', p. 24.
11 Al-Shāfiʿī, *Al-Imām al-Shafiʿī wa Taʾsīs al-Aydyūlūjiyya al-Wasatiyya*, Cairo, 1996, p. 66.
12 Cf. B. B. Warfield, *The Inspiration and Authority of the Bible*, London: Marshall, Morgan & Scott, 1951, pp. 299f.
13 J. I. Packer, *Fundamentalism and the Word of God*, Leicester: Inter-Varsity Press, 1996, p. 85, n. 3.
14 See also Jn 10:35.
15 The vision of the Wycliffe Bible Translators, for example, is 'to see the Bible accessible to all people in the language they understand best'. Available at: www.wycliffe.org (accessed 5 January 2009).
16 Muslim arguments against the divinity of Jesus bear many similarities. See discussion below.
17 Website of the Muslim American Society. Available at: www.masnet.org/news.asp?id =242 (accessed 5 January 2009).
18 The manner in which he did this is not known, for Islamic tradition prevents any

anthropomorphic description of God: when he turns his 'back', it is not a physical back as we have; when he speaks, it is not with a mouth as we do.

19 Abu Zayd lecture, 'God and Man in Communication', Leiden University, 2000, p. 6. Available at: www.openaccess.leidenuniv.nl/bitstream/1887/5337/1/OR134.pdf (accessed 5 January 2009).

20 Ibid., p. 7, emphasis added.

21 Ibid., p. 18.

22 F. Rahman, *Islam*, London: Weidenfeld & Nicolson, 1966, p. 33.

23 While three separate verses (Q2:219; 4:43 and 5:90) discuss the drinking of alcohol, for example, only the latest, chronologically, bans its consumption and this is the basis for Islamic prohibition.

24 Rūmī, *Discourses of Rumi*, London: J. Murray, 1961, p. 52.

25 Ibid., p. 51

26 *The Translation of the Meanings of Sahih al-Bukhari*, vol. IX, Lahore: Kazi Publications, 1979, pp. 91–2.

27 It is interesting, therefore, to explore the qur'anic narratives of prophets like Solomon or David, whose biblical record is less impeccable.

28 Subsequently, Muslim authors wrote their own fuller 'tales of the prophets', expanding on the details given in the Qur'an.

29 *The History of al-Tabari*, vol. 2, Albany: State University of New York Press, 1987, p. 63.

30 C. Chapman, *Cross and Crescent*, Leicester: Inter-Varsity Press, 2007, p. 98.

31 2 Tim. 3:16. In fact, the author of 2 Tim. would have had the Hebrew Scriptures in mind here. See also Mt. 5:18.

32 For example, Tit. 1:2.

33 For example, 1 Pet. 1:23–25; Ps. 119:89.

34 J. Calvin, *1 and 2 Timothy and Titus*, Nottingham: Crossway Books, 1998, p. 155.

35 Luther, cited in T. Engelder, *Scripture Cannot Be Broken*, St Louis, MO: Concordia Publishing House, 1944, p. 51.

36 J. Calvin, *Institutes of the Christian Religion*, bk 4, ch. 8 in *The Library of Christian Classics*, vol. XXI, ed. J. McNeill, tr. F. L. Battles, London: SCM Press, 1961, p. 1157.

37 Packer, *Fundamentalism*, p. 79.

38 For example, see C. H. Dodd, *The Authority of The Bible*, London: Collins, 1960, p. 42.

39 W. M. Watt, *Muslim–Christian Encounters: Perceptions and Misperceptions*, London: Routledge, 1991, p. 24.

40 The gospels, viewed in this light, bear some resemblance to the Muslim *hadith*, the highly esteemed records of the life and sayings of the Prophet.

41 Cf. H. Wolfson, *The Philosophy of the Kalam*, Cambridge, MA: Harvard University Press, 1976, pp. 244–62.

42 Ghazali, cited in F. E. Peters, *Judaism, Christianity, and Islam*, Princeton, NJ: Princeton University Press, 1990, vol. 1, p. 162.

43 'The Apology of John of Damascus', trans. J. Voorhis, *Muslim World*, vol. 24, 1934, pp. 394–5.

44 Other titles of Jesus given in the Qur'an include Apostle, Prophet, Messenger, Servant, Example, Spirit, Pre-eminent One, Sinless One, Miracle Worker, Sign, a Mercy and a Witness.

45 For example, H. Lammens, *L'Islam, croyances et institutions*, Beyrouth: Imprimerie Catholique, 1926, p. 58.

46 Debates around these issues raged in early Muslim circles, for example the Mu'tazilite challenge in the eighth century, and in Christian circles, for example at the Council of Nicaea. See further discussion of this in W. M. Watt, *Islamic Revelation in the Modern World*, Edinburgh: University Press, 1969, p. 104.

47 For example, Q27:2 and 2:2.
48 Zamakhshari's commentary on Q3:39 from *Al-kashshaf an haqa'iq ghawami al-tanzil* (The Unveiler of the Realities of the Secrets of the Revelation), cited in Peters, *Judaism, Christianty, and Islam*, vol. 2, p. 350.
49 R. Crollius, *The Word in the Experience of Revelation in Qur'an and Hindu Scriptures*, Rome: Universita Gregoriana, 1976, p. 54.
50 Al- Tabarī, *Jami' al-bayan 'an ta'wil ay al-Qur'an*, Beirut: Dar al-Fikr, 2001, vol. 3 (Q3:45), p. 330, and vol. 4 (Q4:171), p. 42.
51 All references in the later revelations, during the Prophet's time in Medina, concern the day of judgment.
52 Crollius, *The Word in the Experience of Revelation*, p. 33.
53 Other verses include Q2:97; 16:89, 102; 46:12.
54 Sura 2:97, for example, infers the 'good tidings' are confirmation of the previous Scriptures.
55 Al- Tabarī, *Jami'*, vol. 4 (Q4:171), p. 42.
56 Al-Rāzī, *Al-Tafsir al-kabir (Mafatih al-ghayb)*, Misr: al-Matba'ah al-Bahiyah al-Misriyah, 1938, vol. 7 (Q3:39), p. 36, emphasis added.
57 Moses being another – in Muslim tradition his title is *kalīm Allah*, the one 'to whom God spoke directly'.
58 Chapman, *Cross and Crescent*, pp. 364–5.
59 Lammens, *L'Islam*, p. 58, my translation.
60 Chapman, *Cross and Crescent*, p. 365.
61 John of Damascus, 'An Exact Exposition of the Orthodox Faith', in P. Schaff (ed.), *Nicene and Post-Nicene Fathers*, series 2, vol. 9, Massachusetts: Hendrickson, 1994, bk 1, ch. 6.
62 See, for example, Q4:171.

Select bibliography

Abdel Haleem, M. A. S., *The Qur'an: A New Translation*, Oxford: Oxford University Press, 2004.

Chapman, C., *Cross and Crescent*, Leicester: Inter-Varsity Press, 2007.

Packer, J. I., *Fundamentalism and the Word of God*, Leicester: Inter-Varsity Press, 1996.

Yusuf Ali, A., *The Qur'an: Translation*, Elmhurst, NY: Tahrike Tarsile Qur'an, Inc., 2007.

Chapter 14

The theological and political ramifications of a theology of Israel

Glenn Chestnutt

One of the central issues facing evangelical theology at the beginning of the twenty-first century is the recognition of the persistent call to the church to question itself about its relationship to the people of Israel. Chris Boesel is correct to challenge evangelical theology by asking: 'is the Christian Gospel of Jesus Christ as Good News for the world necessarily bad news for the Jewish neighbour?'[1]

Stephen Haynes contends that from the time of Augustine onwards a classical Christian understanding of Jews was that, though considered guilty of deicide, the Jews were to be preserved by Christians as witnesses to divine judgment and love. Their punishment for rejecting Christ was homelessness and dispersion, yet they remained God's people and if preached to in love by members of the 'true Israel' (the church) they would one day acknowledge their sinfulness, convert to Christianity and attain salvation.[2] Haynes argues that this theological interpretation and representation of Jews and Judaism is based strictly on Christian categories and resources, to the exclusion of Jewish self-understanding. He argues that Christian ambivalence towards Jews has occurred through the centuries because Christians are incapable of regarding the Jewish people otherwise than 'through the lens of Christian faith'.[3] As Boesel states:

> The true meaning and value – indeed, the very identity and reality – of Jews and Judaism are assumed to be grounded in the categories of Christian faith and theology. Hence the meaning of, value, identity, and reality of Jews and Judaism are imposed upon Jews from a region outside of and foreign to Jewish self-understanding. Jews are thereby reduced to a silenced object within the discourse of Christian faith. And the native resources of Jewish identity and reality are pressed into the service of a foreign interest; they help to inform and clarify a Christian understanding of the Gospel of Jesus Christ as Good News to and for the world.[4]

This way of understanding contemporary Judaism has made it difficult for people raised in the evangelical Christian tradition to view Jews as real human beings and to view Judaism as meaningful in its own right. Haynes highlights this difficulty when he states: 'when Christians are confronted with the word-sign "Jew", they are more likely to conjure theological types and antitypes, not to mention cultural and literary stereotypes than to think of real individuals with the same hopes, failures, and foibles as non-Jews.'[5] Boesel's argument therefore challenges evangelical theology to recognize the meaning, value, identity and reality of contemporary Jews and Judaism so as to attempt to convey the Gospel in a way that is not deemed anti-Judaistic or supersessionistic. Consequently, any contemporary evangelical theology of Israel must take these aspirations into account.

But this begs the question: does evangelical theology and the reformed tradition, with such a legacy of anti-Judaism and supersessionism, have inherent resources for such a task? This chapter contends that the theology of the Reformed theologian Karl Barth has within it such resources to counter anti-Judaism and supersessionism.

To many Barth might seem an unlikely interlocutor in attempting to build a contemporary evangelical theology of Judaism. It is a fact that he has often been overlooked with respect to any type of inter-religious encounter. Barth himself never really deals with the issue. Robin Boyd argues that this is partly why Barth has also been blamed for the 'virtual moratorium on inter-faith encounter between the publication of Hendrich Kraemer's *The Christian Message in a Non-Christian World* (1938) and the beginning of Vatican II in 1962'.[6] In tandem with this perception of Barth, pluralist theologians, such as John Hick and Paul Knitter, argue that fruitful inter-faith encounter necessitates a revision of traditional christology, and in particular a departure from Christian claims that salvation comes through Christ alone.[7]

Certainly, Barth in concert with many others from an evangelical understanding of Christianity, would have to reject most 'pluralist theologies' because, 'by definition, they posit other sources and norms of revelation outside or alongside Jesus Christ'.[8] Barth explicitly states that '[a]s there can be no other sons of God, so there can be no other lords nor witnesses to the truth apart from or side by side with Jesus Christ'.[9] On the one hand, this christocentric exclusivism has led to the oft-heard complaints from pluralists about Barth's view of other religions: that his is an extreme version of the claim that there is no salvation outwith the church.[10] On the other hand, some within evangelical Christianity have long opposed Barth's christology not only for its refusal to make a distinction between the ontic realization of reconciliation and its noetic appropriation,[11] but also because it appears to lead him down the road to universalism.[12]

Added to these concerns are those of scholars who depict Barth's view of Israel as ambiguous if not even anti-semitic. Klaus Scholder contends that Barth's theology effectively glosses over the significance of the so called *Jewish Question* and hence overlooks the crisis of the Jews during the 1930s and 1940s.[13] This was due to a lack of interest in the topic on Barth's part,[14] while his christocentrism prevented him from seeing the Jews as living humans, but rather as God's chosen people who are finally rejected by him.[15] Indeed Peter Ochs believes that, on first appearances, Barth's 'uncompromising' christocentrism may not be 'a source for Christian non-supersessionism' – a definite prerequisite for any significant contemporary Christian theology of Judaism.[16]

However Ochs concedes that: 'Barth has proved to be the single most significant contributor to ... Christianity's reaffirmation of Israel's enduring Covenant.'[17] This chapter argues, therefore, that a critical appreciation of Barth's theology of Israel demonstrates that, unfortunate phraseology notwithstanding, Barth's theological understanding of Israel lacks the hostility for which some scholars have castigated it. This chapter will make the case that Barth's position is not supersessionist in any classical sense of the word. Rather, in Barth's opinion, the election of Israel qua Israel is confirmed by God. Israel is not abandoned for the church. Rather, its continued existence is integral to the life of the church. Both should be seen together as the one people of God. Nevertheless, one place where Barth's view of Israel can be correctly criticized is in his attitude towards post-biblical or rabbinic Judaism. Barth develops his view of rabbinic Judaism in obedience to the authority of Scripture where both Christians and Jews are members of the one covenantal community. But, as has already been mentioned, for evangelical Christians to enter into any meaningful Jewish–Christian theological debate today, they have to take into account the fact that contemporary Judaism is categorically different from biblical Judaism. With this difference recognized, a dialogue with latter-day Judaism (and not simply second temple Judaism as a theological construct) can contribute much to the theological and political life of the church. This will help evangelical theology acknowledge that contemporary Jews are 'a people who continue to live in covenant partnership with God'.[18] Jews and Christians should thus be regarded by evangelical Christians as 'the one people of God' but with the understanding that evangelical Christians must recognize that 'Judaism has its own integrity, distinctive practices and theological traditions' which should be respected.[19]

This chapter therefore proposes that the Barthian corpus, and specifically Barth's account of extra-ecclesial truth in his Doctrine of Reconciliation, and in particular his discussion in §69.2 entitled 'The Light of Life' has resources within it which can contribute to a contemporary evangelical theology of Israel, which in turn has clear ramifications for the theology and politics of the church.

A critical appreciation of Barth's theology of Israel

David Fergusson is correct to describe Barth's discussion of Israel as 'rich, complex and ambivalent'.[20] Barth himself once confessed to Friedrich-Wilhelm Marquardt that he was 'decidedly not a philosemite'.[21] In any personal encounters he had with 'living Jews (even Jewish Christians)', Barth recounts that he had to 'suppress a totally irrational aversion' towards them, explaining this to Marquardt as a sort of 'allergic reaction'.[22] Yet Mark R. Lindsay also makes the salient point that Barth had:

> significant relationships with individual Jews through whom he also became acquainted with contemporary Jewish thought. If, in the early 1920s, he kept these acquaintances at a respectable scholarly distance, the Nazi years ... saw him adopt a far more positive perspective, from which he was able to stand in

both theological and humanitarian solidarity with the persecuted kinfolk of Jesus.[23]

A glimpse of Barth's increasing awareness of rabbinic Judaism comes in his book *Ad Limina Apostolorum* (1967). Here Barth devotes himself to serious study of the sixteen Latin texts of Vatican II, especially those concerning Israel and non-Christian religions. For Barth 'later and contemporary Judaism (believing or unbelieving)' is the sole natural proof of God.[24] Instead of regarding Jews as separated brethren to Christians, Barth posits:

> Would it not be more appropriate, in view of the anti-Semitism of the ancient, the medieval, and to a large degree the modern church, to set forth an explicit confession of guilt here, rather than in respect to the separated brethren?[25]

However, the oft quoted 'ambivalence'[26] of Barth's theology of Israel has fuelled the accusation that he is a supersessionist, a term that 'is tainted by the implication of anti-Semitism and its terrible consequences'.[27] R. Kendall Soulen, for example, suggests that Barth's view of election remains 'profoundly supersessionistic', for Barth understands Israel as 'that part of the one community of Jesus Christ that is elected in order to be rejected and to pass away'.[28]

Supersessionism, as defined by George Hunsinger, is:

> the idea that Israel has been replaced as God's people by the church. By rejecting Jesus as the Messiah, Israel allegedly forfeited its divine election. Along with certain corollaries (e.g., that the old covenant is nullified by the new), this notion has played a tragic role in the church's historic persecution of Jews.[29]

By this definition, it can be argued that Barth is not supersessionist in any classical sense. Barth himself states categorically that 'Israel's mission' is not 'superseded'. He notes that 'through everything the Old Testament again and again insists that God's election holds and will hold to all eternity'.[30] Eberhard Busch contends that: 'this is Barth's basic thesis. *This* is the issue for him, and not that the covenant with Israel is *replaced* by a different one.'[31] Instead, through Christ the covenant with Israel has become a truly 'perfect covenant', perfect in that it is now God's covenant not only with Israel but with humanity in general.[32]

For Barth, the community of the church that accepts Jesus as the Messiah does not 'supersede' the Jewish community that does not accept Jesus as the Messiah. What the church does do, however, is to offer the proper human response to the ultimate fulfilment of the covenant as divinely appointed in Jesus. The community that fails to accept Jesus as the Messiah does not lose its election (as in 'supersessionism'), but by definition excludes itself – albeit provisionally.[33] Barth's biblically based position[34] holds, therefore, that Christians and Jews stand in 'indissoluble unity';[35] they are the 'one community of God';[36] 'the bow of the one covenant' of grace.[37] Hunsinger is correct to suggest that '[t]o this complex eschatological situation, a term like "supersessionism" is irrelevant'.[38]

A stronger critique of Barth is triggered by his description of the synagogue as part of 'that dark and monstrous side of Israel's history', which is disobedient and idolatrous towards God.[39] He portrays the synagogue as the enemy of God which practises Jewish obstinacy to the Gospel. It is 'the personification of a half-venerable, half-gruesome relic, of a miraculously preserved antique, of human whimsicality' unwilling to take up the message '"He [Christ] is Risen!"'.[40] This leads Katherine Sonderegger to contrast a portrait of Barth as a political supporter of Israel with a portrait of him as an anti-Jewish theologian attached to his anti-Jewish presuppositions. She argues that while Barth has a deep interest in Jews, he has almost no interest in Judaism.[41] She writes:

> The solidarity between Christians and Jews that Barth so vigorously advocates is based upon the quiet assumption that Judaism does not exist. Jews exist, the people Israel exist, even the synagogue exists in error, but Judaism – an independent religious system and institution – does not.[42]

Sonderegger contends that, while Barth retains a place for Israel in the economy of salvation, the synagogue is portrayed as the negative counterpoint to the church. The Jewish people exist because the promises of God are irrevocable and the Jews remain elect in spite of their blindness. Barth's theology therefore, while being non-supersessionist, incorporates anti-Judiastic tropes. Sonderegger rightly claims that Paul's letter to the Romans, and in particular chapters 9–11, provide the background for Barth's controversial remarks about Judaism.[43] In speaking of Paul's analogy of the potter (Romans 9:20–21), Barth identifies Israel as 'vessels of dishonour' and the church as 'vessels of honour', with Israel's distinctive service being to 'witness to the divine judgment'.[44] Here, Barth's theology makes the classic Christian association that present-day Jews and Judaism are to be seen in the light cast by these biblical verses. But Sonderegger rightly cautions the reader not to make the same association between biblical and rabbinical Judaism as quickly or directly as Barth has done. Contemporary Judaism and Jewish practice are post-biblical and rabbinic: they are Judaism without 'temple worship'.[45]

Even with Barth's misplaced association between biblical and post-biblical Judaism, and his residual anti-Judaism, he sees the existence of Judaism today as a sign of hope for the salvation of all.[46] The fact is that for Barth, Israel and the church need each other. Nor only do they need each other, but they are also in union with one another – 'a unity which does not have to be established but is already there ontologically' because of their common foundation in grace.[47] Moreover, as Lindsay argues, Barth believes that: 'this unity is not merely a relic of the biblical age, but remains in force; the Jews ... remain loved and elect by God right up to the present day, *irrespective* of their attitude to Jesus.'[48] Lindsay is right to argue that, while Barth does not accord Judaism any 'lasting legitimacy as an independent religious system', the relationship between Christianity and Judaism is not as 'one-sided' as Sonderegger suggests.[49] He continues:

> If Judaism needs the witness of the Church, so too the Church needs the witness of the Synagogue as the indispensable root from which it has sprung and in which it must remain if it is to be complete.[50]

In this sense rabbinic Judaism 'testifies to divine grace in ways that are positive, salutary and capable of contributing constructively to the theological and ethical self-understanding of the church'.[51]

While there is negative stereotyping of Judaism in Barth's works, there are other resources available within the same corpus to overcome this difficulty and to recognize the aforementioned dependency. One such resource is provided by Barth's account of extra-ecclesial truth in his Doctrine of Reconciliation, in particular his discussion in §69.2 entitled 'The Light of Life'. While one must concede that Barth did not 'develop a specifically Israelite contour',[52] in this paragraph, in order to build a relationship between Judaism and Christianity, there are mechanisms which can help evangelical Christians recognize Jesus Christ in contemporary Judaism and not simply the Judaism of the first century. Here, Barth portrays two senses to truth *extra muros ecclesiae*, which have inherent theological and political ramifications for an evangelical theology of Judaism.

The first sense of §69.2 – 'The Word and the words': the theological ramifications of a theology of Judaism

There exists, in principle for Barth, the possibility of witness to the revelation of the Word of God occurring outside the confines of the church. In §69.2 he asks if there are 'true words' distinct from the one Word of God, Jesus Christ? In an attempt to answer this question he introduces the concept of 'parables of the kingdom'. Although the Kingdom of God is Jesus Christ, human words can, by God's grace, disclose the Kingdom. One set of parables is found in Scripture and the church's proclamation. The word of witness as Scripture is described as the 'direct witness', whereas the word of witness in the church is labelled the 'indirect witness', reflecting the relative proximity of each to the Word of Christ.[53]

If Scripture and church proclamation constitute an 'inner sphere' of a circle with Christ as the centre, then the secular world constitutes an 'outer sphere': true words can be found in both.[54] One can expect such words in the secular sphere, Barth asserts, on the basis of the universality of Christ's lordship and the objective and universal reconciliation effected in and through him. One need not, then, have recourse to a natural theology to claim that true words can be found outside of church walls. Secular parables can be grounded exclusively in revelation in Christ. They have their basis in Christ's lordship and atoning work, and not in some general revelation. They are 'true' insofar as they stand 'in the closest material and substantial conformity and agreement with the one Word of God'.[55] In fact, a true secular word 'will not lead its hearers away from Scripture, but more deeply into it'.[56] It will 'materially say what [Scripture] says, although from a different source and in another tongue'.[57] Secular words should also be compatible with the dogmas and confessions of the church. While secular parables should in general harmonize with these dogmas and confessions, in this sphere some newness is permissible. Secular parables can extend and fill in existing church dogmas, and might even provoke dogmatic revision.[58] But as useful as secular parables may be for the church, they cannot become norms, unlike the Bible, for 'they lack the unity and compactness and therefore the constancy and universality of His self-revelation as it takes place and is to be sought in Holy Scripture'.[59] For Barth, their use will always be provisional and done on an *ad hoc* basis.

Paul Louis Metzger is correct when he says that:

> It appears safe to assume that implicit in Barth's statements ... is the idea that witnesses may ... emerge from within the context of the non-Christian religions. Here then 'secular word' is taken to refer to the whole domain, which stands outside the parameters of the Bible and the church.[60]

Metzger's position is validated by Geoffrey Thompson, who in his unpublished PhD thesis, recounts a conversation he had with Hans Küng in 1992. During this conversation Küng stated that Barth had confided to him 'that although he [Barth] had not explicitly referred to them, he did have the other religions in mind when he was writing the account of extra-ecclesial truth'.[61]

Barth's concept of secular parables of the Kingdom, therefore, provides theological justification for a way of conceiving how the words (and actions) of non-Christian religions might be affirmed as 'signs' or 'parables' of the one Word of God, Jesus Christ. Bruce Marshall is correct to push this theological justification further when he states:

> Dialogue with the adherents of other views of the world can give the Christian community compelling reasons to change its own established beliefs, without requiring it to surrender its identity by epistemicly [sic] decentralizing the gospel narratives.[62]

Marshall continues:

> The degree to which the Christian community will find in the claims of other communities compelling reasons to change its own beliefs cannot be decided *a priori*, but can only be discovered on a case by case basis, by actual dialogue with those communities.[63]

Marshall is correct to advocate Christian dialogue 'with other religious communities in this *case by case fashion*' as any encounter and interaction between Christians and others might reveal commonalities between them; Christians may even have their own established beliefs challenged.[64] Marshall's 'case by case fashion' corresponds to Barth's '*ad hoc* and ephemeral'[65] situations.

It is precisely in this respect that Marshall believes the relation of Christianity to Judaism is unique.[66] The church shares with Israel a canonical text. There is no other community with which the church has this particular relationship, and indeed this allegiance of two different communities to the same normative text is without parallel among world religious traditions. By sharing a canonical text with Judaism, Christians 'should expect that dialogue with Jews will not only disclose a range of common beliefs and commitments already in place, but will consistently give Christians reasons to change their own beliefs'.[67]

It is Marshall's belief that Christians can learn from Jews how to read their own scriptures. They can learn how to interpret the text they share with Jews in ways which are more deeply formed by the details which cumulatively give the text its shape, and so be given 'reasons of the most forceful kind for modifying their own belief and practice'.[68]

Marshall's understanding of the unique relationship between Christianity and Judaism corresponds to Barth's views on who constitutes the community of those who are elected in Christ. Therefore it is acceptable to believe, in concert with Marshall, that:

> the fact that Jews and Christians share a canonical text, one which shapes and corrects the particular nexus of belief and practice which constitutes each community, is the chief condition for ... a dialogue in which Christians can learn from Jews about how to be Christians.[69]

Not only would an inter-religious encounter with Judaism serve the purpose of giving evangelical Christians a deeper understanding of Scripture; it could also function as a critique of evangelical dogma and practice. This understanding provides potential for evangelical preconceptions concerning the content of Scripture to be opened and challenged, thus bringing about new, fresh interpretations that are consistent with the Word of God and reformed tradition, while also allowing for the possibility of discerning God's presence in Judaism. It also provides an equally strong commitment from evangelical Christians to acknowledge openly that Judaism has it own integrity, distinctive practices and theological traditions.

The second sense of §69.2 – 'Creation and its "lights"': the political ramifications of a theology of Judaism

Most discussions concerning Karl Barth and truth *extra muros ecclesiae* focus on that part of §69.2 known as 'The Word and the words'.[70] Thompson is correct to believe that, for the purposes of inter-religious encounter, any discussion concerning Barth and truth *extra muros ecclesiae* should be extended to include what is commonly termed 'Creation and its "lights"'.[71] Here one finds a second and less commonly noticed aspect of Barth's understanding of truth *extra muros ecclesiae*, one which points to aspects of the created order and human creativity that relate indirectly to Jesus Christ.

Barth's basic claim here is that there are truths which belong to creation *qua* creation. In short, he posits various features of creation which, accessible through 'the application of ... common sense',[72] point to the order of creation itself as something 'lasting, persistent and constant'.[73] They are 'created lights which shine and may be seen ... in and with the being of the creaturely world'.[74] Such truths declare the 'orders', 'limits' and 'directions' in which human and all other creaturely life is lived.[75] As they point to the order and being of creation, they are reminders that creation is creation and not chaos: they 'shed a certain brightness in the darkness and resist the onslaught of gloom'.[76]

Under the heading of 'lights which illumine the cosmos', Barth includes scientific discovery, artistic intuition and creation, political revolution, moral reorientation and rearmament as examples.[77] In another list, under the heading of the 'essential constants of human existence',[78] he includes the 'state', 'work', 'trade', the 'different forms of human culture' and 'religion'.[79]

Even though Barth does not explicitly state that the lights of creation can become parables of the Kingdom of heaven, Thompson correctly believes that the argument in which they are set 'almost exactly parallels' that which is associated with Barth's application of the just state as a parable (analogy) of the Kingdom of God.[80] This is seen most clearly in Barth's essay 'The Christian Community and the Civil Community', which is his most concrete expression of the just state.[81]

For Barth the just state is a state which strives for justice, peace and the common good for all of its citizens, Christians and non-Christians alike. In striving for such justice, Barth believes that members of the church can make similar political decisions to 'non-Christians' because of their mutual dependency upon God. This is exemplified in a monograph he wrote in 1952, 'Political Decisions in the Unity of Faith'.[82] In their political decisions, Christians 'will look for a decision which is not arbitrary or just clever in a human sense, but which is made in the freedom of obedience to God's command'.[83] These decisions are placed on 'the extremely narrow frontier that divides the world from the Kingdom of God', and must aim at hitting the precise point 'where common sense speaks the language of the Holy Spirit and the Holy Spirit the language of common sense'.[84] Political decisions will always entail the willingness to take a confessional stance 'and to summon other Christians (and non-Christians!) at all costs to take the same decision (since God, known or unknown, is the God of them all)'.[85]

Barth's understanding of the mutual dependence of Christians and non-Christians upon God in this 1952 monograph parallels his understanding of the mutual dependency between Christians and Jews as the one community of God. There is no reason, therefore, to suggest that Barth's term 'non-Christians' should not be interpreted to include rabbinic Jews. Within Barth's paradigm then, Christians and Jews are able to make similar political decisions, albeit for different reasons.

As a parallel argument to 'Creation and its "lights"', Barth's model of the just state (as a parable of the Kingdom of God) promotes an understanding of democratic society which respects freedom and difference. It represents the desire for a political community 'which transcends racial, national, economic, and ideological interests'[86] in the quest for justice for all citizens. As Nigel Biggar suggests: 'it represents the hope for a [political] order ... in which the rights and liberties of its constitutive peoples [including Jews] are guaranteed.'[87] This is because 'each constitutive group and each of its members is assured of the freedom to live and grow and act, provided that they respect and co-operate with other such groups – whether linguistic, regional, social, or confessional – and their members'.[88] In this understanding then, evangelicals as representatives of the Christian community and rabbinic Jews are not only able to make similar political decisions, they should also be able to cooperate with each other and make common cause with each other for the betterment of society. This understanding challenges evangelical Christians to move beyond a sectarian view of the world and to engage fully with those who are different from them. In particular it challenges those theologies which use Israel as a theological trope for Christianity and which see Israel's re-establishment as necessary in order to bring about Christ's Kingdom. An evangelical theology of Israel should not espouse politics which are based on Israel as a theological trope. Rather, an evangelical theology of Israel should be founded on the notion that the church and Israel are the one people of God, and so they should work together for the common good of society. In this way, true acknowledgement of Jews as a living people can be celebrated, and true recognition of their theological and political hopes and desires can be fully explored in consultation with others such as Arab Christians and Muslims.

Conclusion: the particularity of an evangelical theology of Judaism

Barth's work is not a comprehensive 'theology of religions' or even a 'theology of religious traditions'. It is a theological resource for a particular type of inter-religious encounter. It is an explicitly Christian theological resource which inevitably constructs occurrences of extra-ecclesial truth on its own terms. As Thompson correctly observes:

> in general terms it is impossible not to work within the terms of a particular tradition, and some violation of [the other's] self-understanding is inevitable. Moreover ... attempts to adopt any tradition-free position are largely illusory.[89]

In the secularism, pluralism and diversity of the contemporary Western context, John Cobb is correct to consider 'whether there are any norms that transcend this diversity, norms that are appropriately applied to all'.[90] He is also correct to surmise that 'one such norm ... is the ability of a tradition in faithfulness to its past to be enriched and transformed in its interaction with the other traditions'.[91] An appropriation of Barth's work has the potential, in Cobb's words, to 'integrate the wisdom of alien traditions [Judaism] into one's Christian vision'.[92] Cobb is right when he suggests that '[t]his is not easy and there is no simple recipe'.[93] But this type of endeavour 'is faithful to Christ and precedented in our history'.[94]

Here lies the strength of using Barth's theology as a resource for a contemporary evangelical theology of Judaism: through the particularity of their faith, evangelical Christians can relate to contemporary Jews 'in the confidence that the grace of God made known in Jesus Christ is at work by the power of the Holy Spirit, even where it is not recognized'.[95] Such an affirmation requires that any encounter between evangelical Christians and Jews must be an open encounter which can only occur where there is genuine trust between them.[96] Fruitful encounter can only occur when each faith tradition also speaks with clarity and honesty out of 'the central logic of its faith'.[97] Evangelicals should speak and act in this encounter as committed and unashamed Christians; Jews should do likewise.[98] So, in encounter with Judaism, evangelical Christians should not attempt to hide or avoid their central doctrines, such as the trinity, even as Jews will assuredly refuse to hide or avoid theirs;[99] this despite Küng's fear that 'a conversation between Jews ... and Christians' would 'ultimately come to grief on the Christian doctrine of the Trinity'.[100]

Even where there are insuperable impasses on doctrinal matters, opportunities for cooperation at grassroots level on matters of common concern and commitment are possible.[101] These opportunities are more important than reaching doctrinal agreement or synthesis. This is an opinion which is fully reconciled to Barth's theology and one which Lesslie Newbigin describes as 'a real and already present fact of life' where '[p]eople of different ultimate commitments are in discussion with one another'.[102] Inter-religious encounter 'is not merely the formal dialogue of scholars' but is 'the more elementary matter of day-to-day conversation with our neighbours of other faiths'.[103] This is encounter which 'is very practical, concerned with the problems of ordinary life – the social, political, ecological, and, above all the ordinary and familiar'.[104]

This chapter has illustrated that Karl Barth's theology has the potential to contribute to a contemporary evangelical theology of Judaism. It has demonstrated how it is possible for evangelical theology to be open to the possibility of having an encounter between the church, from Barth's perspective, and rabbinic Judaism – an encounter which has the potential to make common political cause between evangelical Christians and Jews on issues and values that pertain to both faith groups. Judaism can also speak to evangelical Christianity about the church's own life, hence potentially enriching and transforming the church. The decisive conclusion then is that the church, in Barth's view, has the potential to 'be open to transformation by what it learns' from truth claims made by rabbinic Judaism.[105] But in response, evangelical Christians have to decide if they are ready to listen to God's grace as it comes through the voice of contemporary rabbinic Judaism.

Notes

1   C. Boesel, *Risking Proclamation, Respecting Difference: Christian Faith, Imperialistic Discourse, and Abraham*, Eugene, OR: Cascade Books, 2008, p. 5.
2   S. R. Haynes, *Jews and the Christian Imagination: Reluctant Witnesses*, Basingstoke:

Macmillan, 1995, pp. 28–63. For contemporary American developments of this ambivalent attitude to the Jews including evangelical Zionism see pp. 141–70.

3 Ibid., p. 125. See also p. 184.
4 Boesel, *Risking Proclamation, Respecting Difference*, p. 7.
5 Haynes, *Jews and the Christian Imagination*, p. 5.
6 R. Boyd, 'A Barthian Theology of Interfaith Dialogue', *Pacifica*, 1990, vol. 3, 291.
7 See for instance J. Hick and P. Knitter (eds), *The Myth of Christian Uniqueness: Toward a Pluralistic Theology of Religions*, Maryknoll, NY: Orbis Books and London: SCM, 1987.
8 G. Hunsinger, *How to Read Karl Barth: The Shape of His Theology*, New York and Oxford: Oxford University Press, 1991, p. 246.
9 *CD* IV/3, p. 93.
10 P. O. Ingram, 'The Christain Encounter with Non-Christian Religious Ways: A New Possibility', in F. O. Francis and R. P. Wallace (eds), *Tradition as Openness to the Future*, Lanham, MD: University Press of America, 1984, p. 107.
11 J. L. Mebust, 'Barth on Mission', *Dialog*, 1981, vol. 20, 19.
12 D. W. Dayton, 'Karl Barth and the Wider Ecumenism', in P. C. Phan (ed.), *Christianity and the Wider Ecumenism*, New York: Paragon House, 1990, p. 182.
13 K. Scholder, *Die Kirchen und das Dritte Reich*, vol. 1, Frankfurt: Propylaen, 1977, pp. 546–59, as cited in E. Busch, 'The Covenant of Grace fulfilled in Christ as the Foundation of the Indissoluble Solidarity of the Church with Israel: Barth's Position on the Jews during the Hitler Era', *Scottish Journal of Theology*, 1999, vol. 52, 477.
14 W. Gerlach, *Als die Zeugen schwiegen: Berkennende Kirche und die Juden*, Berlin, Institut Kirche und Judentum, 1987, p. 408, as cited in Busch, 'The Covenant of Grace fulfilled in Christ', p. 477.
15 F. W. Marquardt, *Die Entdeckung des Judentums für die christliche Theologie: Israel im Denken Karl Barths*, München, Kaiser Verlag: 1967, pp. 266ff., as cited in Busch, 'The Covenant of Grace fulfilled in Christ', p. 477.
16 P. Ochs, 'Judaism and Christian Theology', in David Ford with Rachel Muers (eds), *The Modern Theologians: An Introduction to Christian Theology since 1918*, 3rd edn, Oxford: Blackwell, 2005, p. 648.
17 Ibid.
18 D. A. S. Fergusson, 'Contemporary Christian Theological Reflection on Land and Covenant', in *Theology of Land and Covenant*, a report to the General Assembly of the Church of Scotland, May 2003, Edinburgh: The Church of Scotland Assembly Arrangements Committee, 2003, p. 17.
19 Ibid.
20 Ibid., p. 13.
21 K. Barth, *Letters 1961–1968*, Grand Rapids, MI: Eerdmans, 1981, p. 262.
22 Ibid.
23 M. R. Lindsay, *Barth, Israel and Jesus: Karl Barth's Theology of Israel*, Aldershot: Ashgate, 2007, p. 35.
24 K. Barth, *Ad Limina Apostolorum*, K. R. Crim (trans.), Edinburgh: St Andrews Press, 1969, p. 36.
25 Ibid., pp. 36–7.
26 K. Sonderegger, *That Jesus Christ was Born a Jew: Karl Barth's 'Doctrine of Israel'*, University Park: Pennsylvania State University Press, 1992, p. 6.
27 G. Hunsinger, 'Introduction', in G. Hunsinger (ed.), *For the Sake of the World: Karl Barth and the Future of Ecclesial Theology*, Grand Rapids, MI: Eerdmans, 2004, p. 3.
28 R. K. Soulen, 'YHWH the Triune God', *Modern Theology*, 1999, vol. 15, 40–1. See also R. K. Soulen, 'Karl Barth and the Future of the God of Israel', *Pro Ecclesia*, 1997, vol. 6, 413–28.

29 Hunsinger, 'Introduction', p. 3.
30 K. Barth, *Dogmatics in Outline*, London: SCM Press, 1949, p. 79.
31 E. Busch, *The Great Passion: An Introduction to Karl Barth's Theology*, Grand Rapids, MI: Eerdmans, 2004, p. 99.
32 *CD* IV/1, p. 33. The general, universal truth which embraces all humanity is that the God of the whole world is, by way of particularity, the 'God of Abraham, Isaac and Jacob'. See also Barth, *Dogmatics in Outline*, p. 74.
33 Hunsinger, 'Introduction', p. 5.
34 Ibid.
35 See E. Busch, 'Indissoluble Unity: Barth's Position on the Jews during the Hitler Era', in G. Hunsinger (ed.), *For the Sake of the World*, pp. 53–79.
36 *CD* II/2, p. 195.
37 Ibid., p. 200.
38 Hunsinger, 'Introduction', p. 5.
39 *CD* II/2, p. 287.
40 Ibid., p. 263.
41 Barth's understanding of Jews and Judaism is echoed in contemporary evangelical dispensational theologies and their understanding of Israel as a theological trope for Christianity. For instance, many evangelical Christians interpret the foundation of the modern state of Israel and its subsequent struggles as the fulfilment of biblical prophecy. This type of theological view clearly informs the political vision of many American evangelical Christian leaders:

> The return of Jews to the land of Israel is a fulfilment of biblical prophecy and foreshadows the end of the time of the Gentiles. It will be followed by the final events of world redemption including war, devastation, tribulation rapture and the thousand-year reign of Christ. In faithfulness to this Scriptural vision, support for the modern state of Israel is demanded. This entails *inter alia* support for settlements in the occupied territories, the rebuilding of the temple, the military security of Israel, and the assimilation of refugees into Arab countries. There is no support for Christian holy places – Jerusalem belongs to the Jews alone – while Catholic and Orthodox Christians are largely to be regarded as apostate. Islam is perceived as an evil, satanic religion.
>
> (see Fergusson, 'Contemporary Christian Theological Reflection on Land and Covenant', pp. 16–17)

42 Sonderegger, *That Jesus was Born a Jew*, p. 142.
43 K. Sonderegger, 'Response to Indissoluble Unity', in G. Hunsinger (ed.), *For the Sake of the World*, p. 82.
44 *CD* II/2, pp. 223–4.
45 Sonderegger, 'Response to Indissoluble Unity', p. 82. For Christians the destruction of the temple by the Romans brought the biblical period to a close. AD 70 marks the end of the Judaism of Jesus and Paul, the end of the priesthood and temple protocol and the end of Judaism as a religion that practised sacrifice.

> [R]abbinic Judaism ... began in the aftermath of this destruction, and ... is characterized by a new system of text and practice ... This is a different religious system than Second Temple Judaism, though it derives from it; a different religious system than Christianity, though it bears family resemblance.
>
> (see Sonderegger, 'Response to Indissoluble Unity', p. 84)

Sonderegger describes Christianity and Judaism as 'doublets' – 'two identities separate yet mirroring each other; each must 'retain their separate identities'. Inherent in these separate identities is criticism of the other. See Sonderegger, *That Jesus was Born a Jew*, pp. 178–9.

46 K. Barth, 'The Jewish Problem and the Christian Answer', in R. G. Smith (ed.), *Against the Stream: Shorter Post-War Writings 1946–1952*, London: SCM, 1949, p. 200.

47 *CD* IV/1, pp. 671.

48 Lindsay, *Barth, Israel and Jesus*, p. 109.

49 Ibid.

50 Ibid.

51 Fergusson, 'Contemporary Christian Theological Reflection on Land and Covenant', p. 13.

52 P. Chung, 'Karl Barth's Theology of Israel: An Impasse in Jewish–Christian Relations'. Available at: www.plts.edu/articles/articles.html (accessed 21 July 2006).

53 *CD* IV/3, p. 96.

54 Ibid., p. 97.

55 Ibid., p. 111.

56 Ibid., p. 126.

57 Ibid., p. 115.

58 Ibid., p. 127.

59 Ibid., p. 131.

60 P. L. Metzger, *The Word of Christ and the World of Culture: Sacred and Secular through the Theology of Karl Barth*, Grand Rapids, MI: Eerdmans, 2003, p. 127.

61 G. Thompson, '"As Open to the World as Any Theologian Could Be ..."? Karl Barth's Account of Extra-Ecclesial Truth and Its Value to Christianity's Encounter with Other Religious Traditions', PhD thesis, University of Cambridge ,1995, p. 3.

62 B. D. Marshall, 'Truth Claims and the Possibility of Jewish–Christian Dialogue', *Modern Theology*, 1992, vol. 8, 235.

63 Ibid., p. 236.

64 Ibid., emphasis added.

65 Metzger, *The Word of Christ and the World of Culture*, p. 127.

66 Marshall, 'Truth Claims and the Possibility of Jewish–Christian Dialogue', p. 236.

67 Ibid.

68 Ibid., p. 237.

69 Ibid., p. 238.

70 See, for example Hunsinger, *How to Read Karl Barth*; Metzger, *The Word of Christ and the World of Culture*; and D. Lochhead, *The Dialogical Imperative: A Christian Reflection on Interfaith Encounter*, London: SCM, 1988.

71 This view is also held by Welker, who believes that this section is crucial to any discussion of inter-religious encounter. He expressed this opinion to the author in a conversation in Heidelberg on 29 July 2006. (The headings 'The Word and words' and 'Creation and its "lights"' are borrowed from G. Thompson's article 'Religious Diversity, Christian Doctrine and Karl Barth', *International Journal of Systematic Theology*, 2006, vol. 8, 3–24.)

72 *CD* IV/3, p. 143.

73 Ibid., p. 142.

74 Ibid., p. 141.

75 Ibid., p. 157.

76 Ibid., p. 142.

77 Ibid., p. 501.

78 Ibid., p. 743.

79 Ibid.

80 See Thompson, '"As Open to the World as Any Theologian Could Be ..."?', p. 194.

81 K. Barth, 'The Christian Community and the Civil Community', in *Community, State and Church*, Garden City, NY: Doubleday Anchor, 1960, pp. 149–89.
82 K. Barth, 'Political Decisions in the Unity of the Faith', in *Against the Stream: Shorter Post-War Writings 1946–1952*, pp. 149–64.
83 Ibid.
84 Ibid., p. 160.
85 Ibid., p. 154. The necessity for taking a position, ethically, and summoning others to that position, is also expressed in Barth's doctrine of creation. Cf. *CD* III/4, pp. 8–9.
86 N. Biggar, *The Hastening That Awaits: Karl Barth's Ethics*, Oxford: Clarendon Press, 1993, p. 168.
87 Ibid.
88 Ibid.
89 Thompson, '"As Open to the World as Any Theologian Could Be ..."?', p. 173.
90 J. Cobb, 'Beyond Pluralism', in Gavin D'Costa (ed.), *Christian Uniqueness Reconsidered: The Myth of a Pluralistic Theology of Religions*, Maryknoll, NY: Orbis Books, 1990, p. 92.
91 Ibid.
92 Ibid., p. 91.
93 Ibid.
94 Ibid.
95 See D. Migliore, *The Power of God and the gods of Power*, Louisville, KY: Westminster John Knox, 2008, p. 132.
96 See T. Ramadan, *Western Muslims and the Future of Islam*, New York: Oxford University Press, 2004, p. 201.
97 See Migliore, *The Power of God and the gods of Power*, p. 132.
98 Ibid.
99 Ibid.
100 H. Küng, *Islam: Past Present and Future*, Oxford: Oneworld Publications, 2007, p. 503.
101 See Migliore, *The Power of God and the gods of Power*, p. 132.
102 L. Newbigin, as paraphrased and cited by G. R. Hunsberger, *Bearing the Witness of the Spirit: Lesslie Newbigin's Theology of Cultural Plurality*, Grand Rapids, MI: Eerdmans, 1998, p. 216.
103 Ibid.
104 World Council of Churches, 'Guidelines on Dialogue' (Kingston, 1979), in J. A. Scherer and S. B. Bevans (eds), *New Directions in Mission and Evangelization I: Basic Statements 1974–1991*, Maryknoll, NY: Orbis Books, 1992, p. 13.
105 Cobb, 'Beyond Pluralism', p. 93.

Select bibliography

Boesel, C., *Risking Proclamation, Respecting Difference: Christian Faith, Imperialistic Discourse, and Abraham*, Eugene, OR: Cascade Books, 2008.

Fergusson, D. A. S., 'Contemporary Christian Theological Reflection on Land and Covenant', in *Theology of Land and Covenant*, a report to the General Assembly of the Church of Scotland of May 2003, Edinburgh: Church of Scotland Assembly Arrangements Committee, 2003, pp. 11–17.

Haynes, S. R., *Jews and the Christian Imagination: Reluctant Witnesses*, Basingstoke: Macmillan, 1995.

Lindsay, M. R., *Barth, Israel and Jesus: Karl Barth's Theology of Israel*, Aldershot: Ashgate, 2007.

Marshall, B. D., 'Truth Claims and the Possibility of Jewish–Christian Dialogue', *Modern Theology*, 1993, vol. 8, 221–40.

Migliore, D., *The Power of God and the gods of Power*, Louisville, KY: Westminster John Knox, 2008.

Ochs, P., 'Judaism and Christian Theology', in David Ford with Rachel Muers (eds), *The Modern Theologians: An Introduction to Christian Theology since 1918*, 3rd edn, Oxford: Blackwell, 2005, pp. 645–62.

Thompson, G., 'Religious Diversity, Christian Doctrine and Karl Barth', *International Journal of Systematic Theology*, 2006, vol. 8, 3–24.

Postscript

Seeking a centred, generous orthodoxy

Richard B. Hays

The late Hans W. Frei was reluctant to give a label to his theological stance, loath to locate himself in one of the binary pigeonholes that dominate popular accounts of religious belief: 'conservative' vs. 'liberal'. In a short essay published just a year before his death, he advocated instead a theological approach that he described as 'generous orthodoxy'.[1]

While Frei's vision has been influential among the intrepid minority of theologians and pastors who are often characterized as 'postliberals', it has on the whole failed to elicit large-scale enthusiasm or even comprehension. At least in the United States, public theological discourse seems to gravitate towards the simplistic, slogan-shouting style of television talk shows. Reasoned, generous conversation is in short supply. And too often it seems that the only alternative to the hardline culture-warriors of both left and right is a warm and fuzzy, culturally accommodated piety that is broadly socially inclusive but innocent of any serious theological thought. In this dangerously thin theological atmosphere, the word 'evangelical' has sadly assumed the connotations – especially in the popular media – of 'intolerant', 'chauvinistic', 'anti-intellectual' and even 'warlike'.

It is therefore with a sense of anticipation and gratitude that I welcome the publication of *New Perspectives for Evangelical Theology.* This new book by a group of younger British and American scholars is a collaborative project that seeks to stimulate fresh reflection on the content and, just as importantly, the *character* of a theology that can rightly be called evangelical. The cultural and political setting in the UK is slightly different from that of evangelical thinkers in the United States, but many of the issues they face are similar. They are thoughtfully seeking a new way forward, a way that is sensitively responsive to Scripture itself and to all that is best in the broader Christian tradition. We might therefore hope that this manifesto – no, not a manifesto, but a probe – might shed some much-needed light on matters of common concern to the church throughout the English-speaking world.

The chapter by Tom Greggs, in seeking to rethink eschatology in a more deeply biblical way that transcends simplistic binary thinking, nicely articulates a goal that is programmatic for this volume as a whole: '*to open our theology up to a generous particularism which recognizes the complexities of Scripture and of human life.*'[2] Hans Frei, were he alive today, would stand and applaud.

Each of the key terms in Greggs's desideratum carries weight. The theology he hopes to pursue has a *particular* character: that is, it will be grounded in Scripture and the church's classic confessional tradition. It will be distinctively Christian in its identity. It will therefore not be a lowest-common-denominator theology that can appeal equally to everyone in a pluralistic culture. Yet, at the same time, it will be *generous* in its desire to converse patiently and sympathetically with those outside the community of faith, as well as with others who interpret Christian faith in different ways.

I am particularly heartened to see Greggs' emphasis on the *complexities* of Scripture and human life. One of the grave shortcomings of some popular evangelicalism is its too-easy assumption of the simple unitary character of the biblical witness, and of its application to our lives. A smug bumper sticker that I used to see in America cluelessly trumpets its own hermeneutical naïveté: 'The Bible said it, I believe it, that settles it.' By contrast, one of the encouraging features of the present volume is the authors' willingness to grapple with actual close readings of the biblical texts and to acknowledge the presence of tensions and perplexities that stimulate careful scholarly study and interpretation. To treat the Bible's complexity with this sort of alert respect is to grant it *more*, not less, authority than those interpreters who superimpose *a priori* propositional grids upon it. Likewise, the authors in this volume recognize that human experience poses genuine hermeneutical challenges that require patient and intellectually disciplined theological responses. To acknowledge such complexities in both world and Scripture is not to be less evangelical, but to insist that the good news with which we are entrusted must truthfully acknowledge our created and fallen human condition and the historically contingent manner in which God has chosen to reveal himself to us.

If we believe that the word of God is living and active, sharper than any two-edged sword (Heb. 4:12), we should expect our encounter with that living word to challenge and change us. To the extent that the authors in this volume have reclaimed this sort of vision as authentically evangelical, they have exemplified what Richard Briggs describes in chapter 2 as 'a theology and a spirituality centred joyfully around the living and active Word of God, bringing grace and truth in the *evangel*, God's good news for the human race and the whole of creation'.[3]

Briggs' verb 'centred' points to one more important aspect of the paradigm shift which this volume both advocates and models. In understanding human social relations, we may distinguish between *bounded* and *centred* groups.[4] The bounded group draws up clear lists of membership criteria and erects heavily guarded fences to protect itself, like a gated residential community. It closely monitors its members to ensure the purity and safety of those inside. The centred group, on the other hand, is much less concerned about outer boundaries, less worried about policing uniformity of thought. Instead, it understands group membership in terms of a common directional orientation towards a shared centre; it is therefore less like an exclusive residential community and more like a city with a vibrant cultural life that draws people to the downtown area for work and pleasure alike, and thereby generates a strong sense of civic identity. So one way of describing the present book is to read it as a proposal for the urban revitalization of evangelicalism, seeking to convert it from being a bounded group to being a centred group.

Of course, to apply this metaphor to the church and theology requires us to see that the centre towards which we are drawn is not some new form of church organization or theological programme, but God, God as revealed in Jesus Christ. Recognizing that truth, and believing that he is 'Lord of all' (Acts 10:36) will set us free from the fear that so often paralyses theological discourse: fear of saying the wrong thing, fear of relinquishing control, fear of straying off the narrow path. In short, it will free us to breathe, and to become more evangelical, inviting others to join us in a pilgrimage towards the centre while acknowledging that we ourselves have not yet arrived there (cf. Phil. 3:12–15).

It seems to me that the authors assembled in this symposium share, in one way or another, such a vision, and they are inviting the rest of us to join them on the way. I have not yet met them personally, but, judging from their chapters, they seem to me to be good company. They also appear to be headed in the right direction. Perhaps we should join them.

Notes

1 H. W. Frei, 'Response to "Narrative Theology: An Evangelical Appraisal"', *Trinity Journal*, 1987, vol. 8, 21–4. See also G. Hunsinger, 'Hans Frei as Theologian: The Quest for a Generous Orthodoxy', *Modern Theology*, 1992, vol. 8(2), 103–29.
2 See 'Beyond the Binary', ch. 11 in this volume, p. 161, italics added.
3 See ch. 2 by Briggs in this volume, p. 14.
4 The missionary anthropologist Paul G. Hiebert adapted these categories from mathematical set theory and applied them to the analysis of the church's engagement with non-western cultures (see P. G. Hiebert, *Anthropological Reflections on Missiological Issues*, Grand Rapids, MI: Baker, 1994, pp. 107–36). I am indebted to Mark D. Baker ('Bounded or Centered? The Book of Galatians', *In Touch*, Mennonite Brethren Biblical Seminary, Fall/Winter 2009, pp. 6–7) for introducing me to Hiebert's work and sketching its relevance for theology and biblical interpretation.

Index